A Pursued Justice

A Pursued Justice

Black Preaching from the Great Migration to Civil Rights

Kenyatta R. Gilbert

BAYLOR UNIVERSITY PRESS

Unless otherwise stated, Scripture quotations are from the New Revised Standard Version Bible, copyright 1989, Division of Christian Education of the National Council of the Churches of Christ in the United States of America. Used by permission. All rights reserved.

Cover Design by AJB Design, Inc.

Contemporary published and unpublished sermons included in this volume are reprinted with the permission of the authors and The Abyssinian Baptist Church, 132 Odell Clark Place, New York, NY 10030.

Library of Congress Cataloging-in-Publication Data

Names: Gilbert, Kenyatta R., author.
Title: A pursued justice : Black preaching from the great migration to Civil Rights / Kenyatta R. Gilbert.
Description: Waco : Baylor University Press, 2016. | Includes bibliographical references and index.
Identifiers: LCCN 2016003768 (print) | LCCN 2016015635 (ebook) | ISBN 9781481303989 (hardback : alk. paper) | ISBN 9781481304009 (ePub) | ISBN 9781481305402 (ebook-Mobi/Kindle) | ISBN 9781481305419 (web PDF)
Subjects: LCSH: African American preaching—History—20th century.
Classification: LCC BV4208.U6 G55 2016 (print) | LCC BV4208.U6 (ebook) | DDC 251.0089/96073—dc23
LC record available at https://lccn.loc.gov/2016003768

CONTENTS

Preface ix

Acknowledgments xiii

Introduction 1
The Migration of Hope

Part I

1 The Exodus 11
History and Voices of the Great Migration

2 The Promised Land 35
Social Crisis and the Importance of Black Preaching

Part II

3 Preaching as Exodus 53
Prophetic Imagination, Praxis, and Aesthetics

4 Exodus Preaching 71
Gospel and Migration

5 Exodus as Civil Rights 103
King and Beyond

Conclusion   131
Petitionary Truth Telling

Appendix A: Chapter 4 Sermons   137

Appendix B: Chapter 5 Sermons   155

Notes   169

Bibliography   193

Index   205

PREFACE

For nearly a decade, I have been chasing down answers to three formative questions posed and addressed in this volume: What does it mean to preach prophetically? Why is it important to discuss the nature and function of prophetic preaching in context-specific ways? And, What must be the scope of prophetic preaching in the postmodern context? A *Pursued Justice* explores the distinctive nature, function, and vital role prophetic preaching played in northern Black churches and communities during the Great Migration period of the first half of the twentieth century; it also explores how a distinctive form of African American prophetic preaching came to prominence.

This book continues lines of inquiry from my earlier research and first book *The Journey and Promise of African American Preaching*, where I set the stage for a holistic view of preaching and examined the interrelatedness and interplay of three distinctive accents of the African American pulpit: the *prophetic*, *priestly*, and *sagely* voices, what I term *trivocal preaching*. To summarize, the *prophetic* voice mediates God's activity to transform church and society in a present-future sense based on the principle of justice. The *priestly* voice attends to the Christian spiritual formation of hearers by encouraging them to contemplate their personal relationship with their Creator and enhance themselves morally and ethically. The *sagely* voice carries a sapient function and is distinguished by its focus on the preacher and congregation's wisdom, treasured past, and realistic hope for future generations. Based on the community-transforming details surrounding Jesus' inaugural vision recorded in Luke 4:16-21, I define *trivocally conscious preaching* as a ministry of Christian proclamation—a theo-rhetorical discourse about God's good will toward community with regard to divine intentionality, communal care, and the active practice of hope—that finds resources internal to Black life in the North American context.

When I published *The Journey and Promise* in 2011, I laid out a basic thesis that I believe continues to be valid and relevant today. I argued that *African American preaching absconds its character and charge to the church and the public unless it recovers its elemental prophetic, priestly, and sagely voice.* However, subsequent to testing my theoretical claims while conducting workshops and plenaries in a sundry of intercultural, intergenerational, and multiracial settings, and after having reflected on many rich postpublication conversations, I now recognize that my initial work could have more explicitly conveyed the inclusive vision that was always intended. While it is true that all Christian preaching, regardless of context, should cohere to Jesus' inaugural vision set in Luke 4, we do well to tell our own stories about what holistic preaching resembles when addressing human concerns from our different provinces of experience.

Acknowledged or not, all authors write from a local, culturally determined contextualized space. Often is the case, regrettably, that Black scholars reflecting on historically marginalized North American communities shoulder inequitable burdens as writers in a racialized society. Because the theological academy puts a premium on scholarly works modeled after centuries-old norms and dominant paradigms established by Europeans and Euro-American scholars, works that deviate from set norms are generally met with academic suspicion at best, and contempt or indifference at worst. Writing as an African American practical theologian, it is important for me to state that I recognize that readers will view this disclosure as a barrier, perhaps thinking that a book written by an African American is for African Americans exclusively. To think this way undermines the teleological goals of this study.

One implication of this study is that through the lens of America's Great Black Migration, the term "migration" might become a useful metaphor for examining and describing the relationship between identity construction, geographical movement, and hope across racial, ethnic, and class lines. The conversation in which I am interested seeks to enjoin any and all people into a constructive conversation that gives emphasis to how one's distinctive perspective on a subject might become useful pedagogy that widens another's field of perception. Our particular stories matter when our concern is the gospel, for they are our truest contribution to our world's grand narrative. To live in pursuit of a genuine and beloved community is to respect and value our own stories and the range of particular stories of others. Thus to paint with a broad brush some hermetically sealed interpretation of preaching to discover a grand metanarrative or seek to harmonize stories would be wrongheaded of me.

Contextual awareness in Christian preaching helps us to see that, in the preaching event, the unveiling of a sacramental dimension occurs, which reveals God and implores receptors of the preached word to reinterpret their life and activities both in light of Jesus' passion and in the sphere of their own particular passion stories. Because our stories matter, and since the clothes of culture always shape meaning in the task of preaching, naming our own historical reality increases the significance of preaching a prophetic Word; therefore, we are never permitted to say that we understand the meaning of prophetic preaching, or any preaching for that matter, without becoming part of the arrived-at meaning itself.

Our postmodern world has been shaped by a diversity of communal narratives—several mass migrations, both voluntary and involuntary. The Great Black Migration in the United States is not unlike current and recent movements such as the Hispanic Migration within and to the United States, the Black Caribbean Migration to Britain, African and Arab migrations to Europe, European migrations to the United States, and Chinese internal migration from rural to urban centers. Common among them all are context-specific accounts of political and economic provocations and consequent effects, spoken and unspoken concerns around renegotiating communal identity, and perspectives on the human quest for survival and hope. Indeed, our postmodern era has been shaped by several mass migrations, both voluntary and involuntary. The mass movements of people have always resulted in complexities and challenges, of one sort or another, for social and political systems bowing under the strain of accommodating newcomers. Given the various crises around the globe that trigger migrations and those complications that result from the movement of people over geopolitical and cultural boundaries, mass migrations invariably propel human effort toward the creation of universal community or beloved community comprised of and affirming the worth of all human beings. Prophetic preaching is one of the ways of urging persons toward universal community.

My investigation represents an important attempt to demonstrate the connection between social justice as an aspect of the human condition, contextual theology and identity construction, and the power of the prophetic Word to impact social change. Our realities are storied, particular, and divinely given to be discovered, reclaimed, shared, and appreciated for what they are, and this is the gift and challenge in the human quest to thwart moral and ethical evils and preserve the dignity and humanity of all humankind.

Whether first-, second-, or third-generation Irish, Italian, Korean, German, or Latin American, all must do the arduous work of naming their own storied reality, assessing their community's rhetorical situations, and addressing that community after hearing from God. If a particular community's concern emanates from the gospel, this can only mean that the community must bear the responsibility of uncovering its own particular identity as a journeying people in a strange land.

As you read this book, I hope you will gain a fuller appreciation for preaching, namely, what it means to preach in pursuit of justice in the world while practicing hope.

Kenyatta R. Gilbert
Howard University

ACKNOWLEDGMENTS

Fruit comes in its season and never ripens in the absence of patience, nurture, and nourishment. This work is the fruit of a great many conversations had with a varied and benevolent cast of individuals who joined me in my academic garden. First, I wish to thank my Princeton Seminary academic mentors, Drs. Sally A. Brown, Peter J. Paris, James F. Kay, Cleophus J. LaRue Jr., Brian K. Blount, and Patrick J. Miller Jr. I have benefited from their constructive counsel and earnest commitment to my scholarly growth and professional development. I would also wish to express my gratitude to three award-granting institutions, whose financial assistance met me at pivotal periods on this decades-old writing journey. The Fund for Theological Education granted me a substantial fellowship, which supplied the bones for this project; Louisville Institute's First Book Grant for Minority Scholars added flesh to this book's vision; and the Andrew Mellon Foundation's summer fellowship transfused the needed blood for me to reach the final stages of research.

I also wish to express my sincere appreciation for those special persons and staffs of the libraries holding significant collections of scholarly resources used in this study. The late Ms. Annetta Gomez-Jefferson of Wooster, Ohio, offered me unrestricted access to her personal collection of Ransom's published and unpublished materials; Giles Wright Jr. granted me the use of an unpublished transcript recording one migrant's journey north; Dr. Joe

William Trotter Jr. gave me invaluable assistance with the migration literature; Dr. Ida Jones shepherded me through the stacks and the Benjamin E. Mays and E. Franklin Frazier papers collections at Moorland-Spingarn. I also visited the following libraries: Princeton Theological Seminary, Princeton University, New Brunswick Theological Seminary, the Schomburg Center of the New York Public Library, Rutgers University, Moorland-Spingarn Research Center at Howard University, and Howard University School of Divinity's African American Heritage Collection.

I would like to express my deep gratitude to my Howard University deans, Drs. Alton B. Pollard III and Gay L. Byron, for granting me sabbatical leave support; my faculty colleagues, especially Dr. Frederick L. Ware, for his wise counsel and keen eye on early chapters; my bright and gifted graduate research assistants, Mr. Brandon Harris, Mr. Reggie White, and Mrs. Kinwana T. Rogers McGrigg; my Howard and Washington Theological consortium students from Virginia Theological Seminary, Catholic University, Wesley Seminary, and Lutheran Seminary; and Drs. Carey C. Newman and Gladys S. Lewis for their expert editorial guidance and coaching.

Finally, I extend my heartfelt appreciation to my loving and brilliant companion, Dr. Allison Blow Gilbert, and our precocious and wonderfully spirited triune blessing—Olivia Copeland, Ella Jane, and Ava Sage—immeasurable sacrifice, boundless affection, and remarkable patience have uprooted the weeds and stimulated my garden's growth. To you I owe the deepest debt.

INTRODUCTION

The Migration of Hope
From Prophetic Preaching to Civil Rights

But Moses said to the Lord, "O my Lord, I have never been eloquent, neither in
the past nor now . . . I am slow of speech and tongue." Then the Lord said to him,
"Who gives speech to mortals? Now go, and I will be with your mouth and teach
you what you are to speak."

—Exodus 4:10-11a, 12

Perhaps the most common misconception about African American prophetic preaching[1] is that it began or came into full flower with the
preaching of Dr. Martin Luther King Jr. and other preachers of civil
disobedience during the racial justice movements of the 1950s and 1960s.
But King's justice cries were offspring of earlier venerable prophetic Black
preaching that found expression in the wake of a failed Reconstruction
period, widespread agricultural depression, the rise of Jim Crow laws, and
America's entry into World War I. Aroused by the flood tide of southern
migrants to America's northern city centers during the interwar years, commonly labeled the Great Migration period,[2] Black clerics such as Baptist
pastor Reverend Adam Clayton Powell Sr., AME Bishop Reverdy Cassius
Ransom, and AME Zion pastor Florence Spearing Randolph rose up to
speak truth to power within their northern congregations and to the wider
public sphere. Even though the majority of Black preachers invoked con-
ventional interpretations of the Bible and utilized traditional preaching

methods as a solution to social problems, their prophetic preaching named the dehumanizing effects of substandard housing, racial and gender discrimination, and unstable employment as realities contrary to God's will.

These respected early twentieth-century clerics cultivated a prophetic consciousness in their preaching that King's generation and subsequent generations received as direct heirs. Their preaching criticized the dominant social forces afflicting Black life in the United States and, simultaneously, offered words of promise from Scripture. Among other themes of spiritual uplift, their prophetic words of a hopeful future that God would one day give essentially functioned to help migrants forge a vital link between their former southern lives and their new lives in the industrial North. Like King, these preachers were guided by both a vital hermeneutic of God's good intention for creation and the resolute conviction that listeners in their northern Black congregations needed a way to articulate their misery in order to be freed from America's forged cultures of silence. Perceptible in King's "I've Been to the Mountaintop" sermon and in representative sermons of others of his generation, and, though to a lesser extent, in preaching today, are certain characteristic features that demonstrate an organic connection with the distinctive mode of prophetic preaching that emerged out of the particular matrix of social and ecclesial factors in northern Black congregations during the Great Migration.

Between 1916 and 1918, an average of five hundred southern migrants a day departed the South as part of the core experience of the Great Migration, and more than 1.5 million relocated to northern communities between 1916 and 1940. A Pursued Justice principally appeals to the primary wave of 1916 and the unremitting secondary wave, following the same channels, that began in 1921 or in the fall of 1922 and that continued until the beginning of the Great Depression. Sensational propaganda created by labor agents and the Black press launched and sustained the momentum of the massive internal transfer of Black southerners, giving it a peculiar character. As W. E. B. Du Bois observed, the distinctive characteristics of the Great Migration and the role of clergy among its participants lay in the mass exodus being orderly and by and large leaderless. No Black Moses figure emerged leading southern Blacks to their so-called Canaan. Just as Black clerics generations prior had many times invoked the biblical Exodus narrative as the central motif mirroring their existential plight in America,

Great Migration preachers similarly drew on the scriptural record of Israel's Exodus saga.

The flight from Pharaoh's Egypt as a biblical master lens for Afro-Atlantic peoples was not a new phenomenon.[3] More than a century prior to the first major wave to America's northern cities, Reverend Absalom Jones, cofounder of the Free African Society with AME founding bishop, Reverend Richard Allen, used the Exodus narrative to interpret the plight and process of God's sovereign agenda to set enslaved Africans free from their White colonial oppressors. Jones' message, titled "A Thanksgiving Sermon" and based on Exodus 3:7-8, preached on January 1, 1808, celebrated the ending of the African slave trade. Jones linked the overturning of Israel's affliction in Egypt to the Black freedom struggle in colonial North America.[4] Cast as a nineteenth-century Moses, Absalom Jones urged his Black congregants to glimpse God's heedfulness to the cries of enslaved Africans and to see God at work in pricking the hearts of White legislators in Congress and Parliament to abolish the slave trade.

Jones entreated his hearers to see their liberation as tied to a larger salvific agenda. If God is impartial, then abolition in the context of the enduring misery of Blacks and their Christian witness must provide redemptive value beyond physical emancipation. What if part of the divine purpose, Jones reasoned, is that "the knowledge of the gospel might be acquired by some of their [White] descendants in order that they might become qualified to be messengers of it, to the land of their fathers."[5] The Exodus motif is an essential part of Black Christianity's socioreligious imagination. Through generations of African American Christian practice, the Exodus story has permitted Blacks to collapse the distance between the ancient worldview and theirs and, as a collective, to see points of congruence within the narrative world of the Israelites despite the obvious difference of circumstance.

But as church membership rolls swelled during the early twentieth-century exodus, Black religious voices in the northern cities on the resettlement side of the migration geography became particularly significant to successful transfer. The Black Joshuas and Calebs of the center city who observed the growth of ghettos saw the need for transforming the focus of Black congregational life from its preoccupation with church worship to more conspicuous involvement in the sociopolitical arena. The northern pulpit vanguard at the forefront transformed their worship space architecturally and established small group ministries such as the South Carolina,

Virginia, and Mississippi clubs upon resettlement; they became the essential bridge for Blacks to link the southern migrant's "Old World" sensibilities to newfound experiences in America's so-called Canaan Land. For Promised Land seekers, the out-of-Egypt or Joseph-to-Moses swath of the Exodus narrative only represented a symbolic starting point. But turn of events during the Exodus saga highlights important correlations in terms of relating the ancient story to the modern period. Although *A Pursued Justice* attends to migration happenings from the migrants' point of departure to their eventual settling in the North, prioritized attention is given to the prophetic proclamation that captured the listeners' imagination within northern churches after migrants had set down roots.

What then is the connection between the "Great Migration," as an African American watershed, and the "prophetic preaching" it necessitated in certain northern Black congregations? How did the northern Black congregational culture affect the ways in which listeners heard sermons in the period? What was it about the northern environment that fueled the passions of people on the move and kept them there? Black ministers in the South, acting at the behest of Whites who preached accommodation with the status quo, could not seize the sacred imaginations of those captive to migration fever. No sermon could dissuade Blacks who had made up their minds to exit. But the voices that called out from northern Black pulpits or were read about in the sermon editorial section of the *Chicago Defender* or *New York Amsterdam News*, which played up the advantages of relocating, compelled mass migration and became crucial to successful transplanting.

The prophetic vision and ecclesiastical inventiveness of Reverdy Ransom, Florence Randolph, Adam Powell Sr., and a few other daring clerics in the period, allowed newly transplanted exiles to see their lot squarely and pick up the pieces of their displaced lives in a strange new land. Their contextually informed view of scripture, creative rhetorical strategies, and empowerment language awakened hope for listeners within their urban Black congregations. Representatives of three of the six major historical African American denominations, the prophetic sermons of these urban Black ministers were deeply rooted in the spirit of the prophetic, covenantal Mosaic tradition, one traceable to the legacy of the ethno-culturally mixed multitude who followed Moses out of Egypt. Indeed, Israel's journey to freedom from no nationhood status as vassals freed from Egyptian persecution to their loose tribal confederation period under charismatic judges to their sense of national independence under the rule of a long succession of good and bad kings constitutes a distinct prophetic tradition peculiar to Israel. Yet the idea that God's word of prophecy continues to impinge upon history in particular circumstances and within specific communities, despite historical contrast, is crucial to understanding the distinctive nature of African American prophetic preaching in northern congregations during the Great Migration. At one with the speech of the biblical prophet figure, the prophetic sermons of Reverdy Ransom, Florence Randolph, and Adam Clayton Powell Sr. naturally arose out of specific situations.

In the same way that the biblical prophet's message revealed the divine plan in temporal space, a small cadre of Great Migration preachers felt similarly entrusted to act as God's instruments. Their rhetorical strategies broadcast an outlook of divine intentionality to numerous exigencies of the interwar period, and in poetic fashion preachers named their reality to transform it. To mediate change within their congregations and communities, these preachers took seriously the immediate sociohistorical situation of listeners in their theological reflections. Their critical awareness of the racial prejudice Absalom Jones and other Black Methodists experienced when barred from the first-floor benches they normally used in the worship service at St. George's Methodist Episcopal Church differed only by time and space. And when looking forward, the prophetic preaching tradition that flowered within northern Black congregations during the Great Migration must be seen as the fount from which Boston University clerics Martin Luther King Jr. and Samuel Dewitt Proctor imbibed.

The prophets of the Great Migration fostered in them a deep prophetic consciousness that King would take to the Dexter Avenue Baptist Church pulpit in Montgomery, Alabama, and Proctor both to his university appointments at North Carolina Central in Raleigh and Virginia Union in Richmond and to the Harlem Abyssinian Baptist pulpit as successor to Adam Powell Sr. and Jr. Based on Revelation 22:18-19, the legendary Gardner C. Taylor's parting words as pastor of Concord Baptist Church, Brooklyn, New York, on June 24, 1990, the week of South African president Nelson Mandela's visit, for example, epitomize the daring prophetic witness of the Great Migration preachers. Consistent with their message, Taylor cautioned his congregation to notice that while God's word does not need revision or update, human documents always require amendments. "The original Constitution of the United States that identified you and me as three-fifths of a citizen," Taylor proclaimed, "needed to be changed and the cost in blood and money and human anguish is still being paid."[6] Though the homiletic contexts differed, a singular fact remained fluid and constant from period to period: African American prophetic preaching comes into existence as a fitting response to rhetorical situations that need and invite it.[7]

As a particular dimension of African American preaching or *trivocal* preaching, prophetic Black preaching is a ministry of Christian proclamation—God-summoned discourse about God's good will toward community with respect to divine intentionality, which draws on resources internal to Black life in the North American context. As a biblically informed, contextually shaped mode of discourse, prophetic Black preaching (1) *unmasks systemic evils and deceptive human practices by means of moral suasion and subversive rhetoric*; (2) *remains interminably hopeful when confronted with human tragedy and communal despair*; (3) *connects the speech-act with just actions as concrete praxis to help people freely participate in naming their reality*; and (4) *carries an impulse for beauty in its use of language and culture.*

The common thread of all prophetic preaching traces from the recognition of injustice, and that the preacher will name injustice for what it is, and what justice should be. African American prophetic preaching is not fundamentally different from prophetic preaching in general, except to the extent that it is seen as God-summoned speech clothed in cultural particularity. African American prophetic preaching is fundamentally a rhetoric of humanization—a sacred discourse about divine intentionality. It is spoken Word that begins in prayer and attends to human tragedy to hear God's revelation, and it is a procedure for broadcasting what is received to the human audience for whom it is intended. Any examination into the nature and function of prophetic preaching lifts and values the mutually enriching relationship between biblical interpretation and sociocultural contexts. How context shaped these preachers and their sermons from this period is crucial to understanding how they captured the sacred imaginations of their hearers and turned the world upside down.

Few scholars have examined African American prophetic preaching. Even fewer have attempted to define its principal characteristics. The result: insufficient categories exist for proper analysis of African American prophetic preaching.[8] This being the case, this investigation seeks to demonstrate that a careful analysis of the biblical, theological, historical, and sociocultural elements appearing in prophetic preaching reveals that a basic description of African American prophetic preaching as a distinctive discourse is obtainable. Before discussing the continuing relevance of the prophetic mode as it is carried forward or abandoned in subsequent eras, the primary aim of this particular investigation is not to unveil some objective, all-purpose notion of prophetic Black preaching. Rather, it is fundamentally a deep analysis and cogent description of prophetic Black preaching as a distinctive speech form in a discrete period.

This study examines the vital role prophetic Black preaching played within African American churches and communities during a period of intense social upheaval: showing how a small cadre of notable clerics of early twentieth-century America cultivated a prophetic consciousness in their preaching that daringly challenged the dominant social forces afflicting Black life during the Great Migration period, offered words of divine expectation from scripture, and exposed the conspicuous collapse of American democracy for its Black citizens.

Chapter 1 attends to the social and ecclesial realities of the Great Migration, which underlie the attempt to define prophetic preaching within the boundaries of a discrete historical period. It then proposes the thesis that a distinct form of prophetic preaching concerned with divine intentionality emerged to offer a radical critique of the status quo and to empower listeners in northern Black congregations to maintain their dignity and humanity amid the dehumanizing forces of the Great Migration period.

Chapter 2 focuses on the overall social, ecclesial, and homiletic contexts in which the sermons of Bishop Reverdy Cassius Ransom, Reverend Florence Spearing Randolph, and Adam Clayton Powell Sr. were preached. An engagement takes place with the broader discussion of African American prophetic preaching: exploring key historical developments, assessing the ecclesial and missional identity of northern Black congregations, highlighting conflicting modes of Black religious discourse, and finally, using pre-Migration sermons to authenticate that Ransom, Randolph, and Powell were preaching prophetically before the Great Migration. They were addressing issues and bringing them to bear on a northern context that was rendered problematic by the great influx of southern migrants at a defining period in African American history, which made their sermons distinctive in the Great Migration. The chapter demonstrates that prophetic voices need to have some context of freedom in which to express themselves. The rationale for the North being the focal point of this distinctive prophetic preaching mode is based on the reality that if Black preachers raised their voices too stridently against the status quo in the Jim Crow South, the prospect of death by lynching or some other intentional act of violence was much more likely. The text makes the bold claim that one can hardly be prophetic in a significant way if one preaches exclusively to the oppressed, though it is significant for the oppressed to know how to resist their oppression. The prophetic messages of Ransom, Randolph, and Powell are deeply rooted in the spirit and vision of the biblical prophet. Their distinctive style of prophetic preaching confronted social injustice, those issues that are concrete in any particular situation.

Chapter 3 establishes this work's interpretive framework. This chapter shows particular interest in the idea of African American prophetic preaching as a derivative of the message agenda of the Hebrew prophet. Here Old Testament scholarship on the prophets and insights from Paulo Freire, Adisa Alkebulan, Ngugi wa Thiong'o, and Zora Neale Hurston construct a conceptual paradigm of four constitutive marks of African American prophetic preaching. When critical consideration is given to the relationship between basic criteria of biblical prophetic speech, pedagogy (communal praxis), and cultural aesthetics (artistic beauty and power of Black oral expression), an argument takes place to obtain a composite picture of African American prophetic preaching.

Informed by this, chapter 4 analyzes sermons preached in the Great Migration by Reverdy Ransom, Florence Randolph, and Adam Powell Sr. Chapter 5 demonstrates how Martin Luther King Jr. and other social justice clerics of the 1950s and 1960s and Black clerics in the post–Civil Rights era inherited the prophetic preaching tradition of their Great Migration forebears and carried it forward.

In the conclusion, prophetic preaching takes center stage as a predictable mode for truth telling and conduit for confronting injustice as well as providing hope and spiritual sustenance to persons living in America's most vulnerable and imperiled communities.

PART 1

1

THE EXODUS
History and Voices of the Great Migration

The usual charge that the Negro is naturally migratory is not true . . . there is no tendency to migrate but an urgent need to escape undesirable conditions.

—Carter G. Woodson[1]

In the summer of 1917, after hearing the blaring whistle of the Pennsylvania Railroad train that steamed into Augusta, Georgia, twenty-two-year-old Thomas Watson Harvey[2] seized his moment to escape the precarious farm life he had once shared with five brothers and seven sisters. From Thomas' perspective, the Deep South's promise to his people for a better life rang hollow opposite the noisy northbound train's whistle. So Thomas, without delay, gave Burke County his final farewell. He was Pittsburgh bound. Yet, as with many of the archetypal migrants of the first wave—primarily unskilled, young Black males, without family responsibilities—his plans were not set in stone.

Harvey's preparation, as it turns out, did not reflect a concern for gathering personal belongings. He boarded that train in Georgia with his fare, a fish he had received from a local merchant as a token of consolation, and a tentative expectation to find freedom in the North. An air of optimism supported his decision to abandon his agrarian context. But Thomas' quest was not reckless abandon. An uncle's successful transplant from Burke County to Pittsburgh was adequate coaxing to inspire his departure. But on the way,

Thomas changed his course. He never actually made it to Pittsburgh. At the Philadelphia station stop, he disembarked to try his luck on landing a job.

Delaying his decision to enter the changing scene of Black Philadelphia life at this critical time rather than pushing onward to the nation's steel capital might have curbed the rather blithe spirit Thomas, and migrants like him, seemed to possess. Thomas recognized that life in a big northern city would be different, but not completely unfamiliar. Prior to feeling the North's pull, he had fared pretty well in the bustling southern metropolis of Augusta. Gradually advancing to the urban North, Harvey's awakening to the prospect of a better life in the North is emblematic of thousands upon thousands of African Americans who participated in the World War I-era demographic watershed commonly called the Great Migration.

Thomas Watson Harvey's sojourn just prior to the end of the second decade of the twentieth century provides an invaluable resource for those interested in understanding causation, development, and the classic responses from Black religious communities in the years between 1916 and 1918, what is labeled the core experience of the Great Migration. The exodus peaked during that summer Thomas Harvey handed his ticket to the conductor and boarded that Pennsylvania Railroad train. Ironically, Harvey's act of abandonment revealed at least one truth. At his stop, when welcomed by Philadelphia's blistering heat wave, Harvey had confirmed that the community of naysayers down South who had earlier chanted the tune, "Oh what a pity. Don't you know you're going to freeze to death?" were not the sole arbiters of truth.[3] Life in the North did not mean freezing to death. Young optimists like Harvey and others of similar situation went against the conservative advice from southern Black clergy for them to stay put.

Black clergy spoke in two divergent modes. Among ministers who optimistically banked on the fact that a shipment of racial progress would soon arrive, Reverend Charles Thomas Walker of Tabernacle Baptist in Augusta, who was regarded as "the greatest Negro preacher of the time," epitomized the first faction of Black clergy wishing to quell the tide. Harvey described Walker's legend in this way: "They called him the black Spurgeon [since] he was the biggest Negro preacher there was in the South at the time." Noting the manner in which Walker did the bidding of southern Whites, Harvey continued, "And they gave him the courthouse every Sunday, to hold mass meetings and appeal to Negroes to stay home and don't go away."[4] Pastors such as Walker applied traditional preaching methods first introduced to

Blacks, namely Black Baptists and Black Methodists, during the religious revivals of the early nineteenth century. They stressed the importance of developing a personal relationship with God in Christ, keeping to devotional practices, regularly attending Sunday worship, being justified and redeemed through Jesus' atoning works, and being sanctified by the Holy Spirit. Black clergy who spoke out of this domain of experience put disproportionate emphasis on both moralistic concerns and the individual's spiritual well-being over temporal, social justice matters.

Spiritualistic preaching, which operated on different premises, represented the second mode of discourse. Black Spiritualist clergy coiled "communication of the spirit"—relaying messages and spirits through mediums—with elements of Baptist, Holiness, and Pentecostal storefronts. Wisconsin native Mother Leafy Anderson established the first Spiritualist congregation in New Orleans, but moved to Chicago around 1918 to establish the Eternal Life Christian Spiritualist Church to expand the group's reach.[5] Among a host of things, Anderson claimed contact with the spirit of the Native American Sauk war chief Black Hawk, who had lived in her home state.[6] Preaching in Spiritual churches possessed a strong disjunctive orientation toward the temporal world and, in almost all cases, was extemporaneous.

Typically, preachers who rose to the status of bishop, minister, or elder claimed to have the gift of divine healing and prophecy. In the sacred cosmos of Black southern life, these divergent preaching modes could, at best, only provide a channel for parishioners to cope with existing socioeconomic norms. Field-weary migrants with the Promised Land in view heard these messages as acquiescing to the status quo, and thus severed their anchor's rope and set sail for a new world. And though no one could really exit the South without some feelings of social dishonor, the Great Migration signified a new beginning for countless thousands. So when the whistle sounded, Harvey wasted no time. He later remarked, "To be honest, the main reason why I came to Philadelphia, and I think I'd have went almost anyplace, was to get away from the South . . . I didn't feel as though I wanted to take the abuse, you know, that was usually leveled at Negroes. This wasn't healthy for me. So, I welcomed the chance."[7] The city of Philadelphia, for interwar period transplants like Harvey, served as a metaphor for anyplace other than the racially rifted and economically depressed South. By implication out-migration meant more than mustering up courage to leave one's family behind; it was tantamount to staking it all in the search for freedom and human dignity—God's intention for all creation.

The Great Exodus: Roots, Routes, and Reasons

After the 1914 assassination of the archduke of Austria, the relations between Italy, France, and Britain had reached a tipping point and war erupted. The politically fragile relations in a decades-old diplomatic conflict among the esteemed Great Powers of Europe meant political and economic destabilization for all of the major players in the global community. Desiring to protect the United States' European interests, President Wilson gave the nod for U.S. troops to join the chorus of nations in the war. As a consequence of Wilson's declaration, the outbreak of war had a substantial impact on northern industry and the lives of opportunity seekers who fueled the majority of its workforce. The war halted immigration and reduced the supply of unskilled workers who had migrated from Europe several years prior. With the war on, America, a nation that once welcomed 900,000 immigrants to its shores annually, had reduced its European workforce to roughly 100,000.[8] With northern captains of industry and finance in desperate need of replacement workers to supply allying nations abroad with weaponry, they reached southward to respond quickly to the nation's labor shortage. The war effort and northern pull provided an opportunity for Black migrants to earn bread for their families. Coming to the North not only meant earning a better living wage, but also it meant greater social freedoms would be assured. Labor agents traveled deep into the South, calling on workers to staff their factories. Blacks heard this call and responded enthusiastically. Though clearly a signpost of progress, a tragic fact accompanied their eager responses. Content to put purse before principle, northern captains of industry had no real interest in leveling the playing field between America's White and Black citizens. Nevertheless, the pull North for the courageous Black sharecroppers eager to leave meant overturning their quasi-contractual status as low cost tenants scraping out a living.

Migrants flowed out of the South. Some came north by train, some by bus, and others came up the eastern coastline by ship. They followed three major travel routes. Those traveling in lane one—the Virginias, Carolinas, and through Florida—moved up the Atlantic coast and typically ended in Pennsylvania, New York, New England, and sometimes as far as Canada;

those departing from Kentucky, Tennessee, Alabama, and Mississippi, in lane two, usually landed in places like Chicago and Detroit; and finally, Texans and Louisianans, in the third lane, traveled along the Pacific slopes and fed places like California.[9] Hopeful migrants pressed toward the Promised Land in five movements: leaving an isolated farm; moving to a plantation center; then to a small southern town; later to a southern railroad center; and finally purchasing a ticket for Chicago, Milwaukee, or another city.[10]

Labor agents and Black newspapers such as the *New York Amsterdam News*, *Chicago Defender*, and *Pittsburgh Courier*, ubiquitously, played up the advantages of living in the North. Their importance, especially during the first wave, cannot be overstated. Together they captured the hopeful imaginations of southern Blacks caught in the vicious crossfire of racial and economic oppression. Better wages and a decent life in the North proved a more sensible prospect for African Americans than the predictable misery from peonage labor in a depressed, rural southern economy. Higher wages in northern munitions plants, railroad construction, stockyards, and factories outpaced southern wage earnings. Black factory workers in the North could earn $3.00 to $4.00 a day in comparison to the meager southern wage of seventy-five cents. The $2.50 daily wage of Black domestic workers in the urban North was more enticing than the $1.50 to $3.00 per week earnings paid in the South.[11] The important pull factor of higher wages and the promise of new beginnings may have been the impetus for the exodus, but the dominant pre-WWI view was that Blacks should not leave the agrarian context. However, the North, despite its problems, provided a better context for Blacks to mount a human dignity campaign.[12]

From 1916 onward, step by step, southern Blacks pressed their way to Canaan. They vacated their shotgun shacks, left their livestock and tools in the fields, and in some cases left their children behind (to be reared by relatives or friends) as they went in search of freedom. In spite of the long, chilling winters in the North, Blacks had grown weary of the hostilities perpetrated against them in the South. Psychological intimidation through grotesque acts of public lynching even found religious sanction in many quarters of the Deep South. Orlando Patterson, glossing W. Fitzhugh Brundage, points out that not all lynching could be classified as blood rituals of sacred expression committed by White mass mobs. But those who sought simply to instill fear by demonstration had focus in "'the highly ritualized choreography' of the chase, the careful selection of the sacrificial site, the sadistic torture and burning (often alive) of the victim, the collection of mementos from the victim's body, and [finally] the post-sacrificial ritual of the kangaroo 'coroner's jury' verdict."[13] No set of reasons measured higher. To put it succinctly, Black people abandoned southern society because they yearned for a taste of human dignity. Relocation meant greater social freedoms would be assured. Thus, in haste, Blacks steadily emptied out of the South, replacing mule and plow for factory forklift. Northern metropolises created an air of optimism as it invited agrarian Blacks to achieve a higher level of personhood. Over the course of two decades, northern metropolises had gained nearly a million new transplants. Blacks left and headed north to secure a dream too long deferred.

Though the strongest provocation promoting quick departures from the South centered on the hostile social climate and economic situation of Blacks in southern society, immediate environmental causes precipitated them as well. Carter G. Woodson pointed to one in specific—the infestation of the Mexican "boll weevil" that began destroying cotton crops in Texas in 1892 before spreading its reach across the Deep South. This little insect chewed through the cotton fields at a rate of between 40 to 160 miles annually, invading all the cotton districts except that of the Carolinas and Virginia.[14] From the arrival of the boll weevil up to the time of the 1917 release of Woodson's volume, the estimated damage caused by these insects was around 4.5 million bales or roughly $250 million worth of cotton.[15] Failed crops proved especially dreadful for White planters and particularly burdensome for Black tenants working under a single crop planting system in places like Texas, where "cotton is king." Black sharecroppers could never recoup their losses in the South's peonage system. Such vexing realities, coupled with White supremacist intimidation tactics like lynching, caused Black migrants to abandon their plows and cotton bales and strike out northward and westward.

Ironically, southern Black migrants set out for Kansas first, not the urban North. In the wake of a failed Radical Reconstruction, Tennessee coffin maker Benjamin "Pap" Singleton, convinced that Blacks could only prosper away from the South, ushered a band of southern Blacks westward several years before the twentieth-century exodus. Singleton's profession put him in close contact with death and the realities of southern racism. In 1873, after appealing to his comrades who were initially reluctant to leave their southern homes, he prevailed, persuading his band of opportunity seekers to purchase real estate in Cherokee County Kansas.[16] Though never wanting to leave the South, Singleton, who carried the moniker "Father of the Migration," seemed more devoted to a sense of duty to be freed of economic oppression than to "cast down buckets," to use Booker T. Washington's metaphor, in the South's restrictive and unstable waters.

Exodus Faith: Seeking Signs and Refuge

With the passage of the Thirteenth Amendment following the end of the Civil War in 1865, the United States formally abolished slavery. However, most Blacks and Whites, irrespective of their regional home base, held the popular assumption that the South was the natural home for African Americans. Of a total U.S. population of just over seventy-five million in 1900, African Americans comprised seven million of its citizens. This is particularly noteworthy because only 2 percent of America's Black population lived in the North at the turn of the century. Nine out of ten Blacks remained below the Mason-Dixon Line just before WWI, and four out of five Blacks lived in rural areas.[17] A little more than a decade after the Civil War, newly freed Blacks found themselves in an all too precarious situation once again. Life for African Americans in southern society quickly went from bad to worse during the Postbellum-Reconstruction period.

Reconstruction, also called the Black Nadir, represented a time of dismal failure for Black progress. Blacks found themselves abandoned after the withdrawal of federal troops. Their loss of social protections and political clout was felt in earnest around 1877. Southern Dixiecrats capitalized on the North's laissez-faire, postwar rebuilding program, and with President Rutherford B. Hayes at the helm as the commander-in-chief, the idyllic picture of a new South faded, revivifying principles of White supremacy. Stripped of their legislative powers, Black nationally elected officials lost their seats in Congress, and the nation soon ushered in "the strange career of Jim Crow."[18] Blacks faced unscrupulous intimidation tactics at voting polls. Election officials crafted literacy tests, used unlabeled ballot boxes, and in some cases even resorted to violence to protect the status quo. The rise of Jim Crow laws, which was firmly strengthened by the *Plessy v. Ferguson* doctrine in 1896 of "separate but equal," reminded Blacks that regardless of their personal achievements or behavior, "they were still in Egyptland."[19]

Jim Crow segregation statutes established a permanent system that con-
signed Blacks to an inferior station; ironically, "the determination of the
Negro's 'place' took shape gradually under the influence of economic and
political conflicts among divided white people—conflicts that were eventually resolved in part at the expense of the Negro."[20] The psychological
effects of slavery and the dismal failure of Reconstruction, after the defeat
of the Populist Movement by southern Democrats, had left a legacy of racial
bitterness. And this, materially speaking, meant that southern Blacks were
barred from any significant political participation.[21]

Southern planters had not only secured the Hayes administration's
blessing, they had also essentially double-stitched a knot in America's already
stained social fabric. Hence, with the resurgence of White supremacy in
the South, any hopes of ex-slaves acquiring social freedom and full-fledged
political rights looked futile. The fact that southern White conservatives
endorsed the argument that Blacks should make no effort to abandon the
South seemed clearly paradoxical but came as no surprise. Under such an
oppressive system, Blacks knew that however separate the races remained in
the South, things were hardly equal. For many, to remain in such a nefari-
ous social world could only mean sure social death.

Still, the intense resettlement phenomenon had its fair share of dis-
appointments. In many instances the trek north left many hopeful Black
proletarians disheartened upon their arrival. The romanticized picture
of a northern Promised Land appeared barren for nearly all those travel-
worn migrants who landed in crowded ghettos to live in dilapidated flats
and seedy kitchenettes, with few prospects for stable employment. Though
afforded greater social freedoms and opportunities to earn higher wages
than they had previously garnered in the South, Black southern transplants
experienced considerable racial and gender discrimination. Their lives constantly hung in the paradoxical balance of gaining access to industrial or
domestic work while not having any reliable structure for maintaining their
employment.[22]

In matters of faith and spirituality, most but not all Black migrants
were religiously astute, a quality that was passed on from enslaved forebears
who prayerfully petitioned God to hear their somber cries for help. For this
reason alone, the Black migrants' struggle for human dignity involved much
more than the classic push/pull factors. Much like the children of Israel,
Black Christian migrants often waited for a sign from God before leaving

the South.[23] Their quest was spiritual and economic salvation. Those who saw the Great Migration as a religious event put their trust in the sovereignty of God to guide them out of their southern wilderness to the urban North. As carriers of culture, these "exilic" northern transplants had indeed brought certain expectations about the movement of God with them. In the first place, many Blacks viewed the Great Migration as a providential event—God's hand providing them the opportunity to flee oppression. Furthermore, most African American participants' exodus from the South to the industrial North, in the interwar period, had more than material ends in mind. Participants were on a campaign for human dignity and thus had construed their escape from the South as the "Second Emancipation."[24]

Despite the fact that many migrants trusted God to ensure successful resettlement, migrants such as Thomas Watson Harvey and other first wavers had little or no interest in establishing church ties.[25] This, however, did not preclude the fact that countless thousands of Black parishioners overwhelmingly flooded the sanctuaries of historic African American denominational churches in the North. These churches possessed a touch of the familiar, and to the dispossessed migrants in particular, these were places to call home away from home. Scores of Black migrants sought refuge in northern Black churches. Though obviously fewer in number compared to the white, low-steeple, shotgun southern Black churches, northern Black churches had shared an enduring obligation to be a haven for dispossessed migrants who entered their doors.

Large historic Black congregations in the North were dubbed the principal guides in the work of acculturation and adjustment, despite the special efforts of the Urban League and other secular agencies. Churches saw their memberships skyrocket. The mass exodus stimulated a new awareness in African American congregations that required many of them to redefine their missional objectives and refashion their ecclesial identity, not only as the principal caregivers to migrants but also as theologically robust and physically adaptable environments, to respond to complex social problems. The more that northern Black congregations reminded the migrants of home, the more such congregations seemed like safe havens in a strange land. Still, migrants could not assume a happy ending upon their arrival in the North.[26]

The statistical impact of the arrival of the migrants varied from city to city and congregation to congregation. The unparalleled growth of

northern Black churches in this boom time helped the church to see phenomenal strides and innovations in its worship practices and community
outreach. Yet owing to unprecedented institutional change, northern Black
congregations were unprepared to deal with the migration's distressing
effects. Its suddenness and size placed new and uncommon demands on the
preexisting operations and structures of northern Black churches. Between
1915 and 1920, Chicago's Olivet Baptist membership grew from four thousand to nearly nine thousand.[27] Prominent clerics took every opportunity
to boast of rapid church membership increase while overlooking the high
turnover rates of their congregations. Problems mounted for Black churches
in the Great Migration in terms of preparedness, fruitless parochialism,
and long-term effectiveness. Nevertheless, a few Black urban pastors found
creative ways to confront the varied exigencies brought on by the migrant
crisis by proclaiming the gospel's concern for social justice.

Exodus Churches: Sanctuaries of Hope

A few daring Black preachers serving northern congregations at the time of
the Great Migration saw a more imminent need to advance a kingdom of
God agenda. They met crisis issues in creative ways by relating and appropriating the Christian faith in service to the physical and social needs of Blacks.
The Great Migration brought about contrasting expectations concerning
the mission and ecclesial identity of the African American church that came
together in the urban North, and from which materialized a culturally mixed
religious ethos.[28]

Though the migration produced an array of religious options, two leading Black church perspectives existed almost everywhere migrants settled.
The first group, the so-called traditionalists, viewed the church primarily as
a spiritual oasis, and on practical terms considered the institutional church
as a sacred theater for exercising "old-time folk religion." Charles Thomas
Walker and others, whose ecclesiastical vision aligned with famed preachers such as slave preacher John Jasper, the unmatched elocutionist of Richmond, Virginia, represented this first group. Conversely, progressives or
so-called instrumentalists, such as Virginia Seminary and Temple University alumnus Reverend Junius Caesar Austin of Chicago's Pilgrim Baptist,
saw the church as the principal agency for social regeneration.[29]

However, several deficiencies in the interpretation of Black church instrumentalists are noteworthy. Ranked among the Black intelligentsia, and usually disciples of W. E. B. Du Bois and Carter G. Woodson, instrumentalist Black pastors set high expectations for Black churches. Skillful proponents of social reform, Black instrumentalist clerics, regrettably, burdened the church by perpetuating the myth that the Black church was the single most important institution on which Blacks could rely. And following this was the belief that the pew would never rise above the pulpit, that is, the educated and consecrated Black pastor was the hope of the race. This exclusionary mentality of an all-purpose core institution and pastoral leadership mirrored the segregated southern Black church mindset and organizational dynamics. Accordingly, when it became obvious that the migration north was not equivalent to total freedom, in line with instrumentalist doctrine, by default, the Black church shouldered the brunt of the criticism.[30]

Historic Black Protestant churches in the North had a critical responsibility to meet the complex needs of Black resettlement. Migrants were more likely to join congregations that tangibly assisted them in making the transition from the South to the North. Sadly, on the whole, established Black churches were devoid of a specific missiology that their local congregations could rally around to address the multiple social and economic needs of their parishioners. Instead, many of these churches developed ad hoc operational missiologies that included anything from bake sales to church-effectiveness campaigns to denomination building to church renewal and church growth efforts in pursuit of spiritual and physical transformation in African American communities.[31]

The first operational objective was the task of aiding migrants to find decent housing and employment. Abyssinian Baptist Church in Harlem, then the largest African American church in the nation, for example, had several outreach programs that sought to bring renewal to Harlem ghettos. Among them was the creation of a Community House and Home for the Aged. Charles Albert Tindley, a prominent Black cleric in a White parent denomination at East Calvary Methodist Episcopal Church in Philadelphia (renamed Tindley Temple United Methodist Church), boasted a membership of over five thousand. Tindley combined preaching and music with social action to draw southern transplants. Erecting a social vision at Calvary "demonstrated his interest in the welfare of the migrants by appealing to church members to take in lodgers, who were invited to worship where they could hear the Tindley Gospel Singers."[32] By the same token, some Black ministers worked as labor agents, going into the Deep South to recruit migrants for industrial employment in the North. In cities like Detroit, a number of Black clerics were expected to function as job promoters for industry giants such as Ford Motor Company.[33]

Church-engineered assimilation programs to help migrants adjust to urban life as smoothly as possible represented a second operational missiology. Chicago churches like Pilgrim Baptist, which was the third largest church in the National Baptist Convention by 1930, offered participation in more than a hundred auxiliaries to promote small church intimacy.[34] However, assimilation techniques were not without their drawbacks. On the one hand, competition between auxiliary organizations in these historic congregations would often further marginalize urban newcomers. On the other, in the Black community at large, old settlers generally considered it their racial duty to be cultural "gatekeepers" in order to lessen the risk that they would suffer loss of status in their churches and neighborhoods. Naturally, many of their strategies were met with bewilderment and opposition. Established urbanites did not seem truly interested in incorporating southern Black "folkways" into their religious and social customs or preparing newcomers for community leadership.[35]

The third and final missiology involved the coordinated efforts of local congregations to raise money to offer practical relief to disheartened migrants. Aid rendered to address the migration crisis was viewed as a necessary extension of the traditional practice of benevolence.[36] The well-financed and politically influential pulpits of Lacey Kirk Williams' Olivet Baptist, Junius C. Austin's Pilgrim Baptist of Chicago, and Adam Clayton Powell Sr.'s Abyssinian Baptist in Harlem represented rare exceptions as Black church institutions in the North. They had the purchasing power to expand their structures, reorient their services, establish food kitchens, and command influence in local urban politics. In the 1920s Williams' Olivet, for example, had "42 departments and auxiliaries, 512 officers, 23 salaried workers, a congregation of 8,743 members, a Sunday School enrollment of 3,100, two buildings, and five assistant pastors."[37] These churches were major power brokers in the work of meeting the physical and spiritual needs of their parishioners. Still, historic Black denominations were largely restricted in respect to missions for migrants due to their inability to develop a coordinated strategy to put money at the disposal of local churches.[38] With the steady flood of Black migrants to the urban centers, social outreach assumed great urgency for congregations that had not made it a priority. Probing the deeper meaning of the exodus as a religious event shows that migrant participants came north with their own understanding of God and distinctive worship styles. The Black church was refashioned during the Great Migration: "with a migrant people came a migrant church."[39]

Despite the state of health of historic African American denominations and churches in the interwar period, few Black clergy modified their homiletic practices once they settled in the North. The mainstream of Black preachers tended to embrace a theological conservatism adopted from White Evangelicals, who saw the urban environment as inherently iniquitous. Rather than coming to terms with the unique demands of urban ministry, most Black preachers usually applied their literal readings of the Bible as solutions to complex social problems. The vast majority of sermons heard from Black pulpits were salvation centered. Not only did the sermons in many Black churches focus on deliverance from the wages of sin and the redemption of individuals, they fell manifestly in sync with the sermons of their White Protestant counterparts.[40] Though preaching leading with the social dimensions of the gospel became a catalyst for the revitalization of the church, hardly any preaching done in northern Black congregations during the period demonstrated an unequivocal merger between spiritual strivings and social justice.

The Great Black Exodus had indeed signaled a crucial turning point for African Americans. The complex matrix of dilemma, promise, and opportunity had not only transformed an African American "agrarian peasantry into a diversified urban proletariat," but it also aroused radical changes to worship practices and infrastructural operations of one of the most important institutions on which African Americans could depend—the Black church.[41]

Exodus Preachers: A Cadre of Hope

The majority of established Black churches had not developed institutional mechanisms to address the multiple social and economic needs of Blacks whose church ties were weak or nonexistent.[42] Yet in light of the grave dilemmas the exodus produced, a small group of strident northern Black preachers provided a pocket of hope. These clerics rose up within the most prominent Black Protestant denominations of the twentieth century to give prophetic witness in their sermons, reforming theologically facile understandings of the church's witness to the world. In response to the dehumanizing political and socioeconomic conditions brought on by the particular matrix of social and ecclesial factors instigated by the Great Migration, Bishop Reverdy C. Ransom, Reverend Florence S. Randolph, and Reverend Adam Clayton Powell Sr. culled out a distinctive mode of prophetic preaching that spoke directly to the Black-lived experience in the United States of America. Their prophetic discourse sought to achieve three major objectives: to expose and provide criticism to the multiple contradictions affecting Black life; to create a channel of authority for listeners to exercise hope and maintain their dignity and humanity; and to provide fitting assistance for large numbers of Blacks in the period who sought to rebuild and restructure their lives in the urban North. Fundamentally a rhetoric of humanization, Ransom, Randolph, and Powell's prophetic preaching met the period's crisis points in creative ways, trumpeting a certain sound within and beyond the church sanctuary's four walls to convey an outlook of divine intentionality that related to freedom and justice for all humankind.

Reverdy Cassius Ransom (1861–1959)

With the words of poet Thomas Carlyle, Reverdy Ransom described his calling to preach as "the conflux of two eternities"—the fateful moment where two ways meet, each leading in a different direction.[43] But prior to receiving his license to preach, he felt bewildered. The patchy quality of his seminary experience had left him questioning his call to ministry. Dr. T. H. Jackson's[44] unbending literal interpretation of the doctrine of the Trinity was so disheartening to young Reverdy that he characterized this theology professor as one "so orthodox that to him the science of evolution was anathema."[45] Despite this and other spiritual and intellectual frustrations during his seminary years, Ransom developed a profound appreciation for the way in which the message and meaning of the gospel become incarnated within the existential situation of African American life. In contrast to a theological orthodoxy narrowly determined by matters of personal piety, he believed one's philosophical experimentation with other pragmatic approaches could be patently more useful for Black social and moral uplift.

For Ransom, preaching consisted of much more than exposition of doctrines through sophistry and eloquence. Ransom perceived the preaching
task as "risk and wager," to borrow Paul Ricoeur's expression.[46] Dominant
themes arose in Ransom's sermons that reveal his convictions about scriptural authority. Given the complex challenges faced in the interwar period,
Ransom's reading of the times and preaching about Christian hope within
them was characterized by his reflection on a certain set of values derived
from both scripture and his tradition. Stating one's theological convictions
in a value-free way or interpreting the biblical text as hermetically sealed
and thus incapable of addressing present-day horrors was far too imprac-
tical for Ransom. Still, Ransom's extensive career in ministry revealed
that preaching is fundamentally an assignment in faithfulness, inextrica-
bly bound to the work of Christ and his kingdom. After his death at age
ninety-five, one reporter's high eulogistic tribute labeled Ransom, "the last
and, by all means, the greatest of that vanishing generation of electrifying
Negro preachers who surpassed all ministers of the past nine decades, by
far, in expounding the principles of Christ crucified."[47]

Though identified as a radical cleric, a deep sense of piety accompanied
Ransom's prophetic vision. Ransom believed that a preacher's piety and the
goal of orthopraxis (right action) were inseparable realities. He creatively
synthesized, within the same vision, the roles of preacher-pastor, politician,
editor, bishop, and parole board member. Since his early years at Wilberforce, the reputed Black Athens of his day, Ransom epitomized Bishop
Daniel Alexander Payne's ideal educated African Methodist cleric, though
Payne himself was a centrist, politically and socially, "more inclined to see
the good in America and the power establishment."[48] The highly influential
and controversial Payne, however, demanded wide-scale educational reform,
despite the fact that he faced bitter opposition from a growing southern faction of AME's who favored a thaumaturgical-folk style of worship. While
Ransom followed Payne's educational vision, Ransom was certainly more
an ecclesiastical democrat.[49]

By the time Ransom transferred to his second major congregation,
St. John's in Cleveland, immediately after his brief tenure at North Street in
Springfield, a conspicuous homiletic methodology emerged.[50] Ransom did
not preach verbatim from a completed sermon manuscript, but delivered
all his sermons extemporaneously, preferring the use of sermon outlines
(written on half sheets, some dated others not).[51] Stenographers took down

his early sermons, which were published as Sunday evening lecture sermons to Black youth in *The Disadvantages and Opportunities of the Colored Youth.*[52] And since Ransom "could write as eloquently as he preached . . . his written sermons were as articulate and as moving as his spoken ones."[53]

Because his earliest ministry assignments were in the industrial North, Ransom's notoriety did not begin in earnest until his tumultuous and productive eight years in the city of Chicago.[54] In fact he had no true acquaintance with the ensuing migration frenzy until the third phase of his career in the pastorate, when in 1896 he was assigned to Bethel AME in Chicago, at the age of thirty-five.[55] The historic Bethel AME Church signified the basic starting point for his experiment with Social Gospel methods and homiletic practice (discussed further in detail in the next chapter). The congregation drew both the poor and privileged, but at the time, Bethel mostly attracted Black elites. While serving at Bethel, business, political, and educational leaders such as Clarence Darrow, Jane Addams, and Ida B. Wells-Barnett became Ransom's close associates. However, the changing demographics at Bethel, namely conflicting ideals between established Black Chicagoans and a growing migrant community, prompted Reverdy and his wife Emma to take action to address the problem.

Although Ransom preached to standing-room-only audiences in Bethel's nine-hundred-seat sanctuary, it perplexed him that Bethel had no true interest in shedding its "silver stocking" image to become the kind of church that responded to the needs of those flowing out of the South to make Chicago home.[56] Ransom had early on realized that just as Blacks were being drawn to cities at rapid rates, so too would worship practices and habits of hospitality in the majority of Black urban churches need obvious revamping. Lamenting both his unfulfilled vision at Chicago's Bethel and the crippled state of cooperative action among Black clerics in Chicago, due to petty jealousy, Ransom voiced a temperate evaluation of the impact his preaching had on the people and on their set practices in a changing religious ethos. He said, "I flattered myself that the crowds of people were drawn hither by my preaching, but the chief contributing cause was not my preaching but the fact that Chicago's filling up with Negroes from the South, brought up there to work chiefly at the stock-yards and other industrial establishments."[57]

Because of the swelling tide of southern migrants flooding into northern Black sanctuaries, Ransom and other Black clergy soon recognized that given the infrastructure of their churches, in spite of their academic preparations and ecclesiastical experiences in vision and mission, they were ill-prepared to cope with the exodus' effects suddenly heaped upon them. He commented, "I soon realized that the old stereotype form of church services practiced in all Negro Churches fell far short of meeting the religious, moral, and social conditions that confronted them."[58]

Ransom's final stepping away from the politically secure Bethel pulpit to create and organize the Institutional Church and Social Settlement catapulted him onto the national stage. He had long believed that the AME Church could rise above its alienating and idiosyncratic assumptions about class within the African American community. But he grew disenchanted that his denomination had not developed adequate programs, regionally or nationally, to address the social and industrial conditions of Blacks in the Great Migration.[59] Ransom's work at the Institutional Church defined the course of his subsequent commitments to reform church practice within and beyond African Methodism. He carried forth the idea of the Institutional Church to successive ministry appointments in Boston and New York.

Florence Spearing Randolph (1866–1951)

Sociologist and African American Studies professor Cheryl Townsend Gilkes described Florence Spearing Randolph as an "advocate of the spirit." Like many African American women of her day, Randolph placed high emphasis on the importance and power of the Holy Spirit in her ministry. Whether identified by her role as reformer, suffragist, evangelist, or pastor, Florence Randolph advanced the cause of freedom and justice within the church and beyond its borders.

Randolph obtained full clergy rights in the AME Zion Church,[60] receiving ordination and pastoral appointments to several churches in New York and New Jersey within the denomination between 1897 and 1901. Not atypical of connectional churches, she began her preaching career as a supply pastor for two small, struggling churches in New York, Little Zion in Poughkeepsie and Varick Memorial. She later became pastor of Pennington Street AME Zion, now Clinton Memorial Church in Newark, New Jersey. Following this, for two years Randolph pastored a congregation in Rossville, Staten Island, before sailing abroad for ministry work in Liberia and the Gold Coast for eighteen months.[61]

Florence was born in Charleston, South Carolina, in 1866. She was the daughter of Anna (who died early) and John Spearing, a prosperous cabinetmaker and painter, who subsequent to Anna's untimely death, was left with four children to rear on his own.[62] Ironically, Randolph could trace her free Black lineage back almost two generations before the Civil War. Her socioeconomic status afforded her important learning opportunities. After graduating from Avery Normal Institute in Charleston, she pursued a career in dressmaking, one of the few professions available to women of color at the time. By 1885, however, Randolph was northbound.

Following an older sister who had settled just outside of New York City, she migrated to Jersey City, New Jersey.[63] In harmony with the spirit of most southern transplants who departed the South before the high tide of migration, Florence was in search of a better life. She desired a change in her particular set of circumstances. Compared to Charleston's fifty cents a day, the going wage for a day of dressmaking in Jersey City was as much as a dollar fifty. But not only this, her working arrangements in the North came with freedoms in the workplace she could have never anticipated in the Deep South.[64] In Jersey City she met and married Hugh Randolph, a railroad cook who worked for the Pullman Company. To this union, Leah Viola was born in February 1887. Sadly, Hugh's untimely death in 1913 left Florence a widow, which she remained throughout the remainder of her lifetime.

In the late 1880s, Randolph began her theological preparation at Monmouth Street AME Zion Church, studying the Bible under the instruction of the Reverend Eli George Biddle, while teaching youth in Sunday School. Biddle was an AME Zion Holiness minister who had earned a bachelor of divinity degree from Yale and was proficient in Greek and Hebrew. Biddle's tutelage, combined with the Holiness teaching of Julia Foote, who was the first woman to be ordained a deacon (1894) and second to be ordained an itinerant elder (1900) in the AMEZ, profoundly influenced Randolph's preaching. Having access to Biddle's extensive library, Randolph became a lead organizer of Holiness meetings, a role in which she functioned as an exhorter and as an assistant to her early mentor. After a short time, Biddle invited her to assist the distinguished Reverend Julia Foote, who had already gained some acclaim preaching and teaching Holiness in Black as well as White churches.[65] Following her apprenticeship with Biddle, she completed a "synthetic Bible course." She surveyed the major doctrines of scripture at the Moody Bible Institute of Chicago, Illinois, and later in Summit, New

Jersey. She also audited courses as a nonmatriculating student at Drew Seminary, Madison, New Jersey.

In the course of her theological training, other defining events coalesced to form her ministry career. First, she became a member of and organizer for the Woman's Christian Temperance Union (WCTU). This organization led in the work to pass the Eighteenth Amendment. Her affiliation with the WCTU earned her the title "militant herald of temperance and righteousness." Consequently, Randolph devoted many of her early years of preaching and public speaking to addressing the injurious effects of alcohol on the moral advancement of American Blacks.

Like other activist women, she exercised leadership in a web of multifaceted affiliations. She assumed the state presidency of the Woman's Home and Foreign Missionary Society, served as a member of New Jersey's Executive Committee Suffrage, and, in 1915, founded the New Jersey Federation of Colored Women's Clubs. As a result, she became deeply involved in the work of the National Association of Colored Women's Clubs, a high profile organization outside the church, which created a gateway for many African American women to gain leadership experience in local chapters and at the national level. Even though Randolph had risen to the "unusual and distinctive role of pastor in a mainline African American denomination," her involvement beyond the sanctuary was unequaled.[66]

Though hopeful to see the day when her efforts would be viewed equal to her male counterparts, as a woman pastor, ordained a deacon in 1901—a year after Foote's elder ordination—and two years later ordained an itinerant in the AMEZ tradition, she served a string of pastorates without compensation. Nevertheless, when Bishop P. A. Wallace appointed Randolph pastor of Wallace Chapel in Summit, New Jersey, her ministry influence widened, though not without controversy. Some leaders in her denomination opposed this charge. Despite the fact that in her first twelve years of ministry she was assigned to lead churches in fiscal straits with only a handful of members to support her efforts, she successfully grew their budgets and kept open their doors. Typically, "once the[se] churches became solvent, she would be replaced by a 'nice young man' and reassigned to another 'problem.' "[67] However, throughout her twenty-one years at Wallace, which would be her final charge, her public voice achieved some recognition locally and statewide.

Randolph synthesized into one vision her tasks as preacher, missionary, organizer, and suffragist, which distinguished her as pastor and voice of the people. Undeniably, under her leadership a Black "institutional church" was forged. Consistent with the spirit of Ransom's institutional model, she merged her congregation's worship life with social service and political activism. By her retirement in 1946, Randolph had led Wallace from its humble thirty-five-member mission church beginnings that initially met in a local YMCA into a newly constructed facility, which included a one-hundred-seat chapel, a new sanctuary, parsonage, and community center.

Florence Spearing Randolph esteemed the preaching life. Her preaching was overt, clear, and direct, and yet womanly in another sense because of her feminine demeanor. Bettye Collier-Thomas quotes one writer who observed her preaching: "Her sermons, lectures and public addresses are all the more attractive and impressive because of the demure womanly manner in which they are delivered. In the pulpit or on the platform she is always a woman, and when she speaks [she] has something to say."[68] But even if Randolph was perceived as a practitioner of pulpit modesty, her preaching did not abide social injustices, especially those related to sexism, racial discrimination, and maltreatment of the poor.

Despite her tendency to reflect on spiritual issues relating to morality and holiness, she crafted prophetic sermons criticizing church and society while imagining a hopeful reality for her listeners who continually anticipated a word of God's address in her sermons amid the perplexing realities of the Great Migration. Because Randolph was a preacher and a pastor in a mainline Black denomination and remained at the forefront of Black women's activism, her life makes a vital contribution to the understanding of "the way in which women and religion combine to create a motivating force in African American religious history."[69]

Adam Clayton Powell Sr. (1865-1953)

For nearly a quarter of a century, Adam Clayton Powell Sr. was regarded as the "Patriarch of the Negro Pulpit."[70] Born to a family of sharecroppers in Franklin County, Virginia, twenty-five days after the Civil War ended, Powell quickly learned the value of hard work and opportunity. At age six he seized his opportunity to escape his poverty-stricken existence. After he demonstrated his ability to read the entire Gospel of John, his father made good on his promise to send him to boarding school. Powell's exceptional abilities as a student had opened wide many doors since his childhood. Hence, after accepting his call to preach in the summer of 1888, he enrolled in Wayland Seminary and College in Meridian Hill, District of Columbia, now Virginia Union University. Later, in 1904, Wayland bestowed upon their alumnus, Powell, the doctor of divinity degree.

Two pastorates followed: Ebenezer Baptist Church in Philadelphia, Pennsylvania (1892), and Immanuel Baptist Church in New Haven, Connecticut (1893-1908), after which Powell became senior pastor to the 1,600-member, one-hundred-year-old historic Abyssinian Baptist Church, then located in New York's red light district. Observing in 1916, at the outset of the migration, the conspicuous collapse in real estate values in the Fortieth Street area of Manhattan's West Side, Powell successfully spearheaded the relocation of his congregation uptown to 132 West 138th Street in Harlem. The opportune move came at a good time because Blacks invaded Harlem by the thousands, and "this army of Negroes," as Powell expressed, "scared the white people almost to death."[71]

Much like his colleague Reverdy Ransom, who pastored New York's Bethel AME from 1907 to 1912 and then founded the Church of Simon of Cyrene in the city's tenderloin district, Powell's ministry saw the direct effects of southern migration on their northern Black congregations. He said, "There was hardly a member in Abyssinian Church who could not count one or more relatives among the new arrivals."[72] In Harlem Powell became a household name and earned national acclaim, in large part due to the mass exodus but more so by what he did in anticipation of it. Built on the institutional model, Abyssinian Baptist functioned not only as a center for religious life, but under Powell's leadership the church also developed far-reaching social service arms, and still today the church continues to wield enormous political influence. Notably, martyr and theologian Dietrich Bonhoeffer visited the Abyssinian Church from 1930 to 1931 to observe the church's ministry and to hear Powell's preaching. According to Ralph Clingan, Powell's social gospel left an indelible imprint on Bonhoeffer and his theological vocabulary. The terms "cheap grace" and "world come of age," later used by Bonhoeffer, were first coined by Powell.[73]

Powell nonetheless insisted that no pastor should ever build a church around himself. However, to consider the gifts of evangelism, administration, and social outreach he brought to Abyssinian is to know that he became an authentic spokesman for the people. At his retirement services in 1937, one parishioner acknowledged that "Dr. Powell's sermons worked wonders" because they "moved the membership to build and equip the church and community house at $335,000, of which every dollar was paid within four years . . . to buy and equip a home for our aged members at the cost of $40,000, which has been paid off . . . to establish the Chair of Religious Education at Virginia Union . . . to pay salaries of missionaries to Africa."[74]

While Powell's successor at Abyssinian, his son Adam Jr., who also became New York's first African American congressman, exceeded his father's public fame, it was the senior Powell who paved the way civically and religiously.[75] Most sermons delivered by Blacks in the southern and northern regions of the United States during the period were entertaining and soul stirring, but patently disregarded social justice engagement in the public sphere. Notwithstanding this truth, like his contemporaries Ransom and Randolph, Powell's preaching sought spiritual and social salvation for Blacks politically, economically, and educationally. Despite serving a nationally recognized church, his preaching drew wide criticism from Black clergy and even death threats. On one occasion, the Black Baptist Ministers' Conference of New York fought Powell's vision to establish a community house in Harlem to meet the religious, social, and educational needs of Blacks. Instead of working to lift up the standards of Black people, those "Black ministers scrapped the idea of a community house, saying 'We don't want nothin' like that. We want a place where folk can git religion.'"[76] Such narrow-minded thinking, thought Powell, was the bane of Black progress. For Powell, the church had to do more than "preach souls into heaven"; it must speak to human suffering and concern itself with the whole individual. But even here its objective was partly realized. Powell believed that the church had to purify itself from within and from without if it was to be a standard-bearer for God and for the people.[77]

True to form, within this vision of purifying the church, Powell's prophetic voice was most palpable. For the modern church, according to Powell's reformist vision, the Sermon on the Mount, Matthew 5–7, was his curriculum, and the spirit and organization of the ancient church in Jerusalem was his model.[78] In *Against the Tide*, Powell defends his biblical hermeneutic for conceiving the church on an institutional model. He said, "I can understand how people, even ministers of the Gospel can differ on

political, social, and moral questions, but I cannot for the life of me understand how anybody, especially the Shepherds of Christ can fight a man
because he feeds them. Jesus never allowed anyone who followed him to go
away hungry." According to Powell, what was largely absent in modern-day
Black churches was its New Testament legacy. "The gospel of supplying people's physical needs was preached and practiced by the church during the
lifetime of the first apostles," he said; "therefore, any church that would bear
Christ's name must make this New Testament model their own."[79] This
suggests that the New Testament church possessed a power and vitality that
Powell discerned was largely absent in modern-day Black churches.

The homiletic visions of Reverdy Ransom, Florence Randolph, and
Adam Powell Sr. in the Great Migration rose to distinction because they
addressed issues such as housing discrimination, poverty, and prostitution
and brought them to bear on a northern context rendered problematic by
such a great influx of southern migrants at a defining period in African
American religious history. Because the sermons preached in the Great
Migration by these daring ministers were delivered primarily in church
settings, one might argue that these clerics were merely "preaching to the
choir." Nonetheless, despite the size and sudden impact of the migration
upon the northern environment, along with the unprecedented demands
placed on preexisting operations of established northern Black churches in
particular, northern Black churches in the Great Migration remained the
central place for organizing Black life.

Black churches constituted the principal agencies that engineered the
distribution of spiritual and material goods, of which both Christian con-
verts and nonconverts could partake. Representatives of three major Black
denominations, Ransom, Randolph, and Powell were widely heard in the
period, and based on their specific religious orientation and political core
values, their messages reflected a range of interests. Part of the prophetic
message to church people was to accept responsibility for the community
where social needs were evident and should be provided. But the prophetic
message also brought challenges to the larger social system. For example, in
a series of sermons, Reverdy Ransom decried the gambling policy syndicate
that by the turn of the century had become intrepid and unchallenged on
Chicago's South Side.

Ransom was a politically active alderman of his district, and part of
his work entailed arranging private meetings with government officials and

police officers to defy the syndicate. But Ransom's whistleblowing came at a cost. Though physically unharmed at the height of his antipolicy campaign, explosives were detonated in the rear of the Institutional Church and Social Settlement where his office was located. Disturbed by the church's inattentiveness to the social and educational development of young African American girls, Florence Randolph's sermon "Hope" called for the cooperation of both church and civic entities, not only to build churches and race institutions but also to establish in northern states a home of protection for Black girls. Still, Adam Powell spoke truth to power. He addressed New York City officials to do away with the prostitution industry and improve sanitation to enhance living conditions in his Harlem church's neighborhood. In each case the prophetic message was not simply spoken Word alone, but the spoken Word for the sake of justice. Justice always points to concrete practices. The prophetic Word may on the one hand register demands for social services, calling the city or nation to take responsibility for its citizens, or on the other to challenge the church to combat negative forces by community organizational work. Ransom and Powell innovated their respective contexts, organizing, respectively, a settlement house and community center, amid great resistance.

During the Great Migration period of the first half of the twentieth century, a distinctive form of African American prophetic preaching came to prominence. It offered a radical critique of the status quo from the perspective of God's intention for creation, and it created a channel of authority for listeners in northern Black congregations, which allowed them to maintain their dignity and humanity within the dehumanizing political and socioeconomic conditions of the Great Migration period.

2

THE PROMISED LAND
Social Crisis and the Importance of Black Preaching

Then the Lord said, "I have observed the misery of my people who are in Egypt:
I have heard their cry on account of their taskmasters. Indeed, I know their suf-
ferings, and I have come down to deliver them from the Egyptians, and to bring
them up out of that land to a good and broad land, a land flowing with milk and
honey."

—Exodus 2:7-8a

Blacks being pulled north faced their fair share of dilemma and dis-illusionment. Antagonism and hostility met the large segment of Blacks moving into cities. The Great Migration incited racial warfare. Many ethnic Whites in the North feared job competition. With the war in motion, a surplus of industrial jobs had opened up. European immigrant laborers returned to their homelands to fight in WWI. But upon the return of these workers to the States in postwar years, hostility ensued. In East St. Louis, Illinois, Blacks were given the harshest and most undesirable work in industry. Industry moguls used Blacks to threaten publicly and, if necessary, to replace White workers who attempted to unionize. Despite the nature of politics in this industrial suburb, White employers still remained aware of the issue of race, and they also desired to promote segregation in East St. Louis neighborhoods. For example, when a Black person attempted to move into a White neighborhood, a city official would contact the Aluminum

Ore Company or some other factory. Both government and industry officials would conspire together against the Black person's employment if he
did not return to a Black neighborhood.[1] This political dilemma contributed to a number of violent outbreaks. Riots erupted in East St. Louis in
1917, in Chicago in 1919, and in other cities.

The urban atmosphere was riddled with racial-ethnic tension. Due to
racial prejudice, many Whites feared that interracial neighborhoods would
spur both an escalation in crime and the lowering of property value. First-
and second-wave migrants, an amalgam of skilled and unskilled workers
and Protestant Christians and unchurched, were culturally homogenized.
Thus, discriminatory practices and segregation increased for Blacks. To further complicate the settlement crisis, migrants, who themselves were "carriers of culture," often resented the varied assimilation techniques of their
northern Black hosts. The old settlers, in some cases, thought it was their
sacred duty to civilize and amend the "common" ways of their Black southern sisters and brothers. To default on this obligation, they believed, could
only encourage criminality and community chaos. Many northern Blacks
were far more interested in the prevention of neighborhood deterioration
and their community standing than either incorporating southern Black
"folkways" into their social customs or preparing newcomers for community leadership.[2]

Communal Crises: Broken Churches, Divided Loyalties

Northern Black churches and their leaders were largely unprepared to deal
with the migration's acute social and religious impact on existing organizational structures. Notwithstanding the longstanding Black church tradition
of vigorous evangelism to bring prospective members into the proverbial
"ark of safety," based on the data, in the migration "there is no strong evidence that black churches in the North were proselytizing migrants and
encouraging them to come boost their growth."[3] Despite escalating membership rolls, the northern Black churches' priorities before WWI followed the assumption that allocations of personnel and money ought to
be expended on preserving southern Black institutional structures, where
the majority of African Americans lived and were thought likely to remain.
Even White northern denominations that had long histories of supporting
Black church and school building projects held the assumption that the

South was the natural home for Blacks. Consequently, southern Whites gradually rescinded their support, leaving the preservation, maintenance, and responsibility of Black denominations like the African Methodist Episcopal and Colored Methodist Episcopal and educational institutions like Tuskegee University in Alabama and Hampton University in Virginia in their own hands.[4]

Tuskegee, established in 1880 under the leadership of Dr. Booker T. Washington, offered Blacks the highest caliber of agricultural and industrial education in the South. Washington brought the school to national prominence in 1895 after his famous "Atlanta Expedition" address, which exalted the virtues of education and entrepreneurship over directly challenging Jim Crow segregation, as National Association for the Advancement of Colored People (NAACP) lead spokesperson W. E. B. Du Bois had advocated. Though initially considered by Du Bois and other prominent Blacks as a revolutionary moment, Washington's philosophical opponents would later refer to his speech as the "Atlanta Compromise." Throughout his long tenure from 1881 until his death in 1915, Washington helped to achieve Tuskegee's institutional independence from the state of Alabama, an accomplishment that earned him the moniker "The Wizard of Tuskegee."

Washington's alma mater, Hampton University, originally opened its doors in 1868 as Hampton Normal and Agricultural Institute. Its mission was to prepare African American men and women to teach newly freed slaves. Aided by the American Missionary Association, Hampton drew great support from the Freedmen's Bureau. Both Tuskegee and Hampton cherished the financial resources of northern philanthropists. Eventually, however, these two schools suffered from the steady withdrawal of monetary contributions from Whites, just as other historically Black schools had. But because Tuskegee and Hampton were classified as progressive Black schools with operations vitally connected to southern society in the pre-World War I era, they were fairly well supported. Notwithstanding weakened White philanthropy in the South, with fiscal precedence given to southern memberships, the mass exodus posed fundamental problems to deprived Black denominations in northern cities.

A lack of ecumenism and infrastructure support among and within traditional African American denominations made it difficult for Black churches to expansively confront the migrant crisis.[5] Black Methodists seemingly had a church planting advantage over Baptists. Their structure and polity would have bolstered their ability to garner and redistribute resources in the northern context. But the hope of a unified Black Methodism (AME, AMEZ, and CME)[6] quickly fizzled during the migration due to petty jealousy and denominational rivalry. AME bishop Reverdy Ransom suggested that such trivial wars sabotaged any real possibilities for pre-exodus, intradenominational cooperation among Black Methodists.[7] Both the lack of denominational superstructure and the privileging of local church autonomy among Baptists make the Black Baptists' story more difficult to reconstruct.[8]

Organized in 1895, the National Baptist Convention (NBC), with its aggregate membership and resources devoted to the South on the eve of the crisis, gave little attention to organized mission work and social service in northern cities before WWI. Given the polity of Baptists, separation from White churches was easier for Black Baptists than Black Methodists. However, efforts at forging a national denomination proved considerably more difficult for Black Baptists. All-Black Baptist associations actually began in the West, specifically Ohio in 1834, not in the South. These associations were early forerunners to a series of efforts toward a national organization. From the demise of the Consolidated American Baptist Missionary Convention, the first effort at national consolidation, which lasted from 1867 until 1879, emerged three new bodies: the Baptist Foreign Mission Convention of the United States of America, originally headquartered in Richmond, Virginia, and concerned with African missions and use of alcohol and tobacco; the American National Baptist Convention, which convened in St. Louis in 1886 and claimed over 9,000 churches and 4,500 ministers among its one million constituents despite northern White Baptist resistance; and the National Baptist Educational Convention of the U.S.A., formed in Washington, D.C., in 1893 to train and equip clergy and missionaries. Between 1894 and 1895, a motion was proposed and passed by a joint committee to consolidate these three bodies into one convention, and so the National Baptist Convention, U.S.A., was formed with the Reverend Elias Camp Morris elected as its first president.[9]

At the time of the migration, it was obvious that NBCUSA's efforts at home mission had been "snared [by] racial and denominational politics."[10] The Black Baptist schism of 1915 drained resources that could have been directed toward the migrant crisis. The schism originated from the acrimonious dispute between NBC president Reverend E. C. Morris and publishing house mogul Reverend Henry H. Boyd; it ultimately split the convention and gave birth to the smaller National Baptist Convention of America, also known as the Boyd convention. Albeit, in 1895, the Southern Baptist Convention agreed to match dollar for dollar the money the National Baptist Convention raised for domestic missions, the use of the funds was restricted to the southern states. The Boyd-led convention further restricted funds for the development of helpful mission efforts during the migration crisis. Boyd's group had blamed their ineffectiveness, in part, on White Southern Baptist favoritism shown to their rival NBC—the larger convention.[11]

The major African American denominations, with the exception of Colored Methodist Episcopalians, had their historical roots in the North. These denominations experienced their greatest membership increases in the rural areas and small towns in the antebellum South.[12] But to the contrary, Bishop Charles H. Mason's Church of God in Christ (COGIC) in Memphis, Tennessee, the largest Pentecostal denomination in the United States, sprouted several congregations in major northern cities, adding to the denomination's strong base of support. Though based in Tennessee, through his travels and church planting efforts in the North, Mason's influence was more widely known in places like Chicago and Philadelphia, where the new denomination had fewer Baptist bodies to compete with for members. For Mason, 1897 signaled his break with the Black Baptists. His rejection was incited by his passionate interest in calling worshipers back to old-time religion and the spiritual phenomenon of slave religion. Over the course of Bishop Mason's leadership, COGIC transformed from a primarily rural-based denomination to an urban-based one.[13]

Urban-Based Theology: The Social Gospel

For a variety of social and theological reasons, Black denominations before the Great Migration had not developed extensive social programs, as did the White institutional churches that grew out of the Social Gospel Movement.[14] White liberal Protestant denominations were the first to come to terms with the unique challenges of church life in an urban environment. White theologians like Washington Gladden and Walter Rauschenbusch affirmed the potential good of humans and believed that God was actively working to create, eventually, a kingdom of heaven on earth.[15] The classic

Social Gospel Movement formed a theological basis for a new and more vigorous Social Gospel, which took account of Black life in America. But the primary reason early Social Gospel leaders exacerbated the problem of racism, despite the fact that most were in favor of humane treatment of Blacks and others, involved their teleological understanding of mission. In their quest to transform a Christian culture, White Social Gospelers had seemingly little interest in the work of alleviating social, political, and economic problems and were in reality only committed to incremental improvement, a form of gradualism for implementing social justice. In addition, they misunderstood the basic problem of the color line, which invariably affects other societal problems.[16]

Theoretically, what this meant in practice was that God's will on earth would presumably be achieved through White paternalism. One goal of the Social Gospel Movement was "achieving the assimilation of nonwhites into an orderly submissive minority in which they would not differ in any appreciable way from the majority."[17] Consequently, Black leaders, such as Ida B. Wells, Reverdy Ransom, and Nannie Helen Burroughs, were not only routinely ignored by the Christian Social Gospel Movement powerbrokers, but Black clergy, at least initially, were wary of the Social Gospel Movement. Black denominations tended to settle on a more theological conservatism inherited from White Evangelicals, who saw the city as a place of iniquity.[18] But preachers in the vein of Ransom, who was a neglected voice in the broader movement, at the level of Social Gospel praxis, added depth and eloquence to the message of the Social Gospel. In such a White-dominated society, it is more accurate to distinguish between two distinct movements: one where Blacks and Whites fought for differing visions of the "kingdom of God in America," which revealed the pervasiveness of White racism, and the other where White Social Gospelers lacked the inherent resources to be self-critical.[19]

Black institutional churches, such as Ransom's converted railroad chapel in Chicago, took a different tack. Created for the purpose of responding to the Great Migration's remarkable challenges, nontraditional churches recovered the symbiotic relationship that began much earlier between Black churches and mutual aid societies in the late eighteenth and early nineteenth centuries. Whether growing out of mutual aid societies themselves or incorporating such societies after later establishment, Black churches in urban centers immediately saw the value of this dialectical union. African

American churches and mutual aid societies were the earliest social institutions created by the Black community. Mutual aid societies assisted in the establishment of Black urban churches and contributed to the unique formation of Philadelphia Black clergy luminaries such as Richard Allen, founder of Mother Bethel AME Church in 1794, and Absalom Jones, the nation's first Black priest who served the predominantly Black St. Thomas Episcopal Church. Since its origins in slavery, the symbiotic relationship between Black churches and mutual aid societies propagated the tendency of Black congregations to expect their Black ministers to take on more than traditional ecclesiastical roles.[20] Ralph Luker's description of these nontraditional communities of faith is enlightening. In the African American experience, missions, institutional churches, and settlement houses are generically related institutions.[21] Two factors distinguish the three institutions from one another. First, institutional churches ministered primarily to members; missions and settlement houses ministered to a constituency. Second, worship often occurred at settlement houses, but it was a secondary activity among many such activities. At missions and institutional churches, worship was the central act of the community's life together.

To infer causation of prophetic Black preaching on the grounds that a few Black clergy were committed to the Social Gospel Movement, though a clear association exists, is perhaps exaggerated. With their generally "conservative biases in race relations" and heavy reliance upon the home missions movement, early Social Gospelers did not directly challenge mechanisms of social control in the public sphere that dehumanized Blacks. In terms of advocacy for freedom and equality of opportunity for Blacks, to borrow Rayford Logan's phrase, Whites experienced "the astigmatism of the social gospel." These prophets of the Social Gospel, ironically, were so preoccupied with the discomfiting woes—brought on by industrial ills—of the supposed socially progressive, urban North that the fight for Black freedom in the hostile White South went virtually ignored. The racism of Josiah Strong, the faithlessness of Lyman Abbott, and the complicity in silence of Washington Gladden, Walter Rauschenbusch, and others serve as an indictment of the Social Gospel.[22]

Through Christian auspices, these late nineteenth-century, reform-minded White Social Gospel advocates sought to address social problems they believed were produced by urban and industrial growth. White Social Gospelers did not, however, consider African colonization to be a means of alleviating racism in America, and they were divided over whether the franchise was a natural right for Blacks. In general they appeared indifferent to the hostile terrain of race relations.[23] While it is true that the Social Gospel Movement's conception of urban reform influenced the thoughts and actions of a few Black clerics, it is nonetheless incorrect to see these influences as central to Black prophetic discourse. In fact the social ideals espoused by Rauschenbusch and Gladden were neither uniquely American nor exclusively Protestant. David Levering Lewis explains:

> The social ideals expressed by Pope Leo XIII in the encyclical Rerum Novarum also contributed to its [SGM] development. In reaction to excessive laissez-faire capitalism, the German philosophers Adolf von Harnack and Albert Ritschl had formulated basic ideas several decades before they were evangelized by Washington Gladden and expositorily presented by Rauschenbusch and George D. Herron.[24]

The indigenous and contextual forces that shaped Ransom, Randolph, and Powell's theological methods to revise and expand the Social Gospel in the urban environment were much more significant to the prophetic preaching mode. In the hands of certain Black preachers, the Social Gospel was refashioned to become something of a "tertium quid"—something distinctly different from any of its major contributors. In this case, it was a complex fusion between the elements of White Evangelicalism in Black faith and African Traditional Religion (ATR).[25] White Evangelicalism in Black faith and ATR, dialectally related, were institutionalized in historically Black churches and were linked to their surrounding communal associations. Blacks did not use Christianity as Whites first introduced it to them. Instead, they made certain substantive changes that took into consideration their oppressive condition and other contextual factors.

Equipping the Saints: Institutional Churches and Social Settlements

By contrast, a stronger correlation appears in the relationship between prophetic Black preaching and those few Black clergy that adopted the institutional church model. Reverdy Ransom's initiation of Chicago's Institutional Church and Social Settlement (ICSS) of the AME denomination in 1900 represents a classic example of the nature of such an association. Black clergy who designed the institutional church model developed their programs to suit their own particular educational and theological sensibilities. Reverdy Ransom combined methods from Jane Addams' Hull House and Richard Wright Jr.'s reformulated Social Gospel principles, taught to him by Shailer Mathews and other faculty at University of Chicago Divinity School, to address Black concerns in Chicago.

In contrast to the general stream of Black worship practices that focused almost entirely on interior or spiritual concerns, the institutional church model created a strong base for Black ministers to preach prophetically. Ransom's institutional church brainchild was established to meet and serve the spiritual, moral, social, and industrial needs of Black people. Ransom's ICSS in Chicago included "kindergarten, cooking and sewing classes, nursery, social club, employment agency, and manual training classes."[26] Even the famed sociologist W. E. B. Du Bois hailed Ransom's experiment as the "most advanced step in the direction of making the church exist for the people rather than the people for the church at the turn of the century." Du Bois claimed that apart from Ransom many African American Methodists had not yet come to terms with the unique demands of an urban ministry.[27] Ransom's pioneering theological methods and prophetic social message earned him the title "the foremost spokesman for the social gospel of this generation."[28]

Though appointed to a string of churches throughout his ministerial career, Ransom carried forth the institutional church concept to subsequent posts—Charles Street AME Church in Boston and New York's Church of Simon of the Cyrene. Simon of the Cyrene, located in the heart of New York City's tenderloin district, though operating on a much smaller scale than his Chicago settlement church, reflected his selfless character and ability to launch and cultivate prophetic ministries. Ironically, Ransom's radical acts of compassion toward New York's dispossessed took place during and subsequent to his appointment as editor of the A.M.E. Church Review and continued until his elevation to bishop in 1924.

Despite Ransom's growing public and denominational reputation in Chicago, his pioneering vision of a Black institutional church had repeatedly placed his life in danger and put his preaching on the periphery of traditional AME piety and homiletic practice.[29] The most notable event occurred when someone damaged Ransom's ICSS with dynamite after he organized a campaign and preached sermons against the "policy gambling racket" that began to flourish among the poor and underprivileged on Chicago's South Side. He was eventually reassigned, which meant departing the institutional church ministry he founded in Chicago. Ransom's church work and increasing involvement in racial protests and electoral politics angered Bishop Abraham Grant, his ecclesiastical overseer, to such an extent that he prohibited Ransom from preaching on Sundays. To contextualize this situation, from 1896 to 1900, Ransom had been the celebrated preacher-pastor of Bethel AME in Chicago.

Ransom left the historic congregation to form his institutional church. Ransom later claimed that upon leaving Bethel, his successor Reverend A. L. Murray, along with Reverend A. J. Carey of Quinn Chapel, had so bitterly opposed him organizing his institutional church that they persuaded Bishop Grant to silence him from Sunday morning preaching. They reasoned that it would affect the Sunday attendance at Bethel as well as other churches throughout the city. As a result, Ransom was restricted to preaching on Sunday nights or on weekday nights. He reportedly complied with the restriction until Bishop Henry McNeal Turner, a senior bishop, paid his ICSS a visit a few weeks later. After hearing the news, Turner quickly overturned Grant's prohibition and requested that Ransom announce his church service for the following Sunday, which Bishop Turner would attend. Turner, in the pulpit with Ransom that following Sunday, impulsively turned to Ransom and said, "I am not going to preach this morning, these people came to hear you—you preach." According to Ransom, when he had finished his sermon, Turner professed, "Great God!! Just think of anybody trying to silence a voice like that on Sunday morning."[30] Subsequent to this restrictive order, Ransom received word that another bishop was about to transfer him to Indiana. Shortly after, it was arranged for Ransom to head to Boston's Charles Street AME. Despite the denomination's professed aims of racial uplift and an educated and consecrated clergy in African Methodism, inner city Black clergy rivals united with certain powerful bishops to create constant frustration for the reform-seeking Ransom. Deep suffering accompanied Ransom's prophetic Christian vision. He resigned after his brief tenure with ICSS in Chicago.[31] Though his work in Chicago would be short-lived, Ransom, nevertheless, never abandoned the mission principles of the institutional church. His innovative ideas germinated in other arenas—ecclesial and political—throughout his ministerial career during the Great Migration.

Furthermore, notwithstanding slow development in the South, by the time of the migration, Black urban congregations in the North were adopting the institutional church model. Prominent New York churches—Abyssinian Baptist, Bethel AME, St. Phillips Episcopal, and African Methodists in Philadelphia and Detroit—had built on and furthered Ransom's ecclesiological vision.[32] For urban Baptist congregations in the twentieth century in particular, institutional churches functioned "as centers of religious life to be sure, as social service agencies, and as bases of political power."[33] To be sure, African American institutional churches were the exception rather than the rule on the eve of WWI, but it seems that these pulpits were indeed fertile soil upon which prophetic Black preaching could sprout.

Black Religious Discourse: Divergent Modes and Responses

Black religion became exponentially diversified in the urban environment during the Great Migration. The migration made readily available a variety of oral-based discourse options from which Black religious leaders could seize upon and customize to fit their agendas and programmatic approaches. African American oral-based culture and oral consciousness prized judgment and decision-making message formulations that could speak to exigencies that could arise at any given time over rhetorical methods, placing logic and empiricism at the center.[34] Therefore, in contrast to methods based on rationality found in traditional or classical Greek rhetoric, northern transplants were drawn to African American rhetorical discourse options that possessed intuitional qualities fluid enough to help common people make sense of their plight.

Priestly-Evangelistic

Seldom did sermons preached by Black ministers in the Jim Crow South directly challenge the status quo. Freedom to voice dissent in public was virtually nonexistent. However, one civic-minded southern activist, Reverend Dr. Henry Hugh Proctor of First Congregational in Atlanta, stood out as an anomaly. The brazen Proctor, and White southern attorney Charles T.

Hopkins, called together twenty African American men and twenty White men to form the Interracial Committee. They assembled the men in hopes of easing the city's racial tension after Atlanta's bloody race riot in 1906. Proctor's church was an important agency for Black self-improvement. It housed an employment bureau, library, and counseling service agency, and provided home economics classes for women.[35] Still, even if Proctor's "big city preacher" progressive inroads and social standing insulated him from hostile forces directed at Black leaders, the majority of Black clergy were sociopolitical quietists who invested their time and attention on the priestly affairs and interior concerns of the church.

Nearly all Black clergy in the South preached sermons and used methods that exalted the virtues of humility, good will, and patience to curb migration fever. Augusta's leading preacher, the Reverend Charles Thomas Walker (nicknamed "The Great Black Spurgeon"), for example, held mass meetings in the city courthouse and made it a point of duty to dissuade Blacks from making their northbound trek.[36] Obviously, as was the case in the colonial period, when most Black preachers rejected the prophetic role for a politically passive realism, little had changed by the time of the interwar period. As migrant Thomas Harvey observed, "The preacher was always making it a point of duty to warn you not to leave. And they would go on and tell you how good the white folks was in the South . . . you got it every Sunday."[37] Though Walker might be regarded as a progressive minister respected in rural and urban locales in the South, rather than encouraging social criticism, he and other southern Black Christian pastors primarily preached sermons that urged their listeners to enhance themselves morally by integrating elements of personal piety (i.e., daily prayer and abstention from cardinal sins). Overall, the mood, mind, and message from the southern Black preacher encouraged a strategy of patience and acceptance over and against social criticism. It is important, however, to remember that the priestly political strategy of patience itself was neither inherently wrong nor in favor of maintaining the status quo; rather, on the continuum of options available, the priestly political strategy for finding reasonable and actionable ways to address the problem of racial injustice alone was limited and inadequate. Without the protected freedom to voice their righteous indignation in open air and level their assault on the status quo, exemplary and ethical forms of prophetic preaching simply were not and could not be sustained in southern society.

Nationalistic–Jeremiadic

Marcus Mosiah Garvey's nationalistic message had great appeal to the masses of poor Black tenants crammed into overcrowded, land locked northern ghettos. Following his Back-to-Africa forefathers Henry McNeal Turner and Edward Wilmot Blyden of the late nineteenth century, Garvey introduced his lofty vision of an autonomous Black nation-state in Africa into the platform of his United Negro Improvement Association (UNIA). His plan captured the hopeful imaginations of Promised Land–seeking migrants and even several Black Protestant ministers and laypersons, who had journeyed north to access the ever-elusive American dream. At odds with W. E. B. Du Bois' assessment that the race problem could be mitigated through access to higher education, Garvey was absolutely convinced that because "the white man universally has lost control of himself in the Fatherhood of God and the brotherhood of man," the only beneficial solution to the race problem was for African Americans to redeem Africa as their homeland.[38]

Enthralling his captive audience of Black listeners around the rallying cries "Up you mighty race" and "One God, One Aim, One Destiny," Garvey declared that the Black quest for justice in America would not roll in on the wheels of inevitability, to use Martin Luther King's phrase. Instead they must take action like "Trotsky and Lenin [who] took the sword and freed the oppressed millions of Russia . . . [and] George Washington [who] took the sword and freed America. What they have done you must do or you must die."[39] For many of the oppressed hopeful adherents to Garvey's message, this was not utopian fiction. Garvey's organization had wide tentacles. With its 814 branches in thirty-eight states and 215 in other parts of the globe in 1926, UNIA not only dwarfed the membership of the NAACP, but also its organizational structure greatly influenced two other highly visible twentieth-century protest movements—Father Divine's Peace Mission Movement and Elijah Muhammad's Nation of Islam.[40] Though ideologically similar as a matter of principle, Garvey's brand of nationalism was different from the classical Black Nationalism ideology of his nineteenth-century forebears. Classical Black Nationalists had not shed the notions of "progress and civilization," cultural ideals of European and White Americans, and had failed to embrace an indigenous African or New World African understanding of African redemption and freedom objectives of the Black nationhood.[41]

Conversionist-Renewalist

Holiness[42] and Pentecostal storefront churches flourished in northern migration hubs such as Philadelphia, Harlem, Detroit, and Chicago. They were likewise personality-driven cults.[43] Baptist-raised Georgia native Elder Lucy Smith was a vastly popular Holiness preacher during the Migration. In search of the familiar, Smith left Olivet Baptist Church and joined the predominantly White Pentecostals at Stone Church, where her folk-style worship sensibilities were supported. Eventually she departed to establish All Nations Pentecostal Church. At first a one-room church, it quickly became a hot spot for those disenchanted by northern Black traditional congregations on Chicago's South Side.[44] Though one could make sundry lists of Black cultic religious leaders whose African oral-based homiletic formulas drew inspiration from Black Baptists, Holiness, and Methodist store-front churches, a select group is particularly noteworthy. The spiritualistic preaching that emerged from Black Spiritualist congregations led by Black women, such as New Orleans-native Chicago pastor Mother Leafy Anderson's Eternal Life Christian Spiritualist Church, established around 1918, and Mattie L. Thornton's Holy Nazarene Tabernacle Apostolic Church, established nearly a decade prior, for example, combined elements from the religious mainstream to those of Spiritualism.[45] With uninhibited religious expression, Spiritualistic preachers relied heavily on "communication in the spirit" through mediums, who typically possessed gifts of divination and healing, and séances. Some Black Spiritualists even professed an ability to communicate with the dead.[46]

Popularly known as and affectionately called Charles "Sweet Daddy" Grace by his legion of followers, Bishop Marcelino Manuel da Graca's United House of Prayer for All People (UHOP), like the Black Spiritualists, employed faith healing, Holiness, and Pentecostal methods to earn the hearts of Blacks of the inner city. Headquartered in Washington, D.C., Grace's churches, which appealed to Blacks and a few Whites, spread far and wide in cities with large concentrations of Black residents, like Philadelphia, Charlotte, and Newark, New Jersey. In these churches followers worshiped the venerated Grace himself as a religious paragon, in the sense that the congregation concentrated their thoughts toward him as "grace incarnate." In the UHOP ritual, first the preacher read from the Bible, inserting remarks, and then this was followed by an exposition of the text with reference to a bestowal of some aspect of grace in the lives of the bishop's disciples. The sermons were basically a catalog of the hearer's cardinal sins of adultery, fornication, stealing, and backbiting, which were brought into the sphere of the bishop's grace-filled pardoning power. Nonetheless, pardoning was not free; all worldly possessions had to be relinquished to Daddy Grace to obtain true membership.[47]

Whereas Grace's church carried the Christian moniker, Rockville, Maryland, native George Baker Jr.'s (Father Divine) Peace Mission did not. The only preaching worthy sacred text for the Peace Mission was Divine's self-aggrandizing oracle—published as the *New Day* magazine. It was the Mission's sole authorized canonical correspondence. Father Divine discouraged Bible reading and counseled his followers to forget all else save his teachings. Like UNIA, the Peace Mission Movement (PMM) experienced phenomenal growth before its precipitous decline following Father Divine's death.

The PMM was first organized in New York and then moved its headquarters to Philadelphia. In the group's Depression-era heyday, counting the PMM's multiple branches, called "extensions," demographers estimated that membership ranged between several thousand and several million. In the Peace Movement cult, Divine not only was the organization and its message, but also, according to his followers, he was God. Divine's hand-selected, multiracial network of secretaries transcribed, codified, and distributed the *New Day*. Of course, given the cult's philosophical stricture that Father Divine was God, any renegade or unauthorized "extension" carrying the name without Divine's divine sanction welcomed his vociferous disdain.

Whether message formulations came courtesy of Holiness and Pentecostal preachers, or unorthodox, personality-driven, religious charismatics, such as Prophet Cherry, who castigated White Jews in favor of an endogamous approach to recover Black presence in the Bible, or through the spell-binding oratory of North Carolinian ex-railroad worker and founder of the Moorish Science Temple Noble Drew Ali, who took inspiration from Islam, Buddhism, and Christianity, each Black religious figure who made decisive inroads in the context of Black lived experience during the Great Migration borrowed from a rich, oral-based African American rhetorical tradition. Applying rhetorical strategies of this same tradition, but having dissimilar objectives, the prophetic preaching of Reverdy Ransom, Florence Randolph, and Adam Powell Sr. sought not to abandon American society but to reform it through biblically based Christocentric justice proclamation.

By the same token, their prophetic preaching eschewed systems that enlarged the "cult of personality." Whether their prophetic proclamations rang through the corridors of their Chicago, New Jersey, or New York congregations, Ransom, Randolph, and Powell adeptly conceptualized the Black existential predicament in theological fashion and articulated messages of God's kingdom agenda. At the same time, they rejected any line of reasoning that claimed God was not involved in Black political and socioeconomic liberation.

Though a few other modes of Black religious discourse could be considered, what these divergent preaching orientations held in common was an agenda that sought to address the social dislocation of Blacks in the urban center. To understand the nature of prophetic Black preaching, this prophetic homiletic discourse needs to be inspected in relation to divergent modes. The vista of Black religious speech in the period reveals that prophetic preaching not only occurred in rare instances but also was in fact divergent in message content from other contending Black rhetorical modes.

PART II

3

PREACHING AS EXODUS
Prophetic Imagination, Praxis, and Aesthetics

A prophet is one who interprets in clear and intelligible language the will of God . . . a prophet is one who doesn't seek popular causes, but rather the causes he thinks are right.

—Benjamin Elijah Mays[1]

During the Great Migration, a small cadre of courageous voices in northern Black congregations proclaimed messages of judgment and hope to the countless thousands of uprooted African Americans from the South who flooded into their sanctuaries. Clerics Reverdy C. Ransom, Florence S. Randolph, and Adam Clayton Powell Sr., hailing from Black institutional churches within their respective urban communities, rose up in the spirit of the Hebrew prophet. They addressed Black social dislocation by fashioning a rhetoric of justice and divine intentionality. In order both to retrieve the essential characteristics that define the functional role of the biblical prophet and to establish a sufficient basis in which to interpret these characteristics in our times, an evaluation of key facets is necessary to disclose the genuineness of prophetic authority. In reflecting theologically on the prophets in this way, two important matters must be acknowledged. First, although all of Israel's prophets were primarily interpreters of the torah, one must take into consideration the historical period and religious environment in which certain individual prophets did their work. Preexilic prophets, such as Moses, Elijah, and Elisha, confronted a very different theological landscape than did their sixth-, seventh-, and eighth-century successors—the so-called "writing prophets"—Amos, Hosea, Habakkuk, and Jeremiah. In Yahweh's dealing with Israel, the biblical prophet's message changed based on his particular audience. As compared to Amos and his successors, preexilic prophets more frequently confronted individuals, particularly the monarchial leadership in place (Samuel confronted Saul; Nathan confronted David; Elijah confronted Ahab/Jezebel). During and after the Babylonian exile, the prophets' proclamation of Yahweh's words of judgment and salvation more directly addressed Israel as a nation for their apostasy or in response to their contrition.[2]

Second, since prophets such as Jeremiah and Ezekiel lived and worked at the beginning of and during the exile, specific matters of true and false prophecy, for example, were foremost in their concerns. With prophets holding contrastive judgments of divine speaking, the one who spoke on the Divine's behalf to the exilic community assumed great significance. Consequently, those labeled as false prophets in the Old Testament were not necessarily charlatans and swindlers. Rather, many were so judged because they preached messages of salvation without demanding obedience and covenantal obligation.[3] The showdown in Jeremiah 23:28 between Jeremiah and the false prophet Hananiah illustrates clearly two prophets sharing radically different discernments on the question of salvation and divine retribution. Prophets like Jeremiah interpreted the history of and divine happenings in the life of Israel as a new dialogical encounter between God and Israel. Such encounters continue through the postexilic period with the prophet Deutero-Isaiah, whose words of salvation signal "a new exodus was to take place, only this time the departure would not be in haste."[4] This reorientation will show not only the incongruent features between the preclassical prophecy of Moses and the classical prophecy of the eighth century, but also that seeking to determine the authentic nature of the false prophet versus the true prophet poses a problem for biblical scholars.

With an intrusive mode of homiletic speech, the Great Migration clerics made decisive inroads into their social landscape both within and beyond the church. In contrast to sermons that preached patience and humility with Whites and mirrored the hermeneutical concerns of White Evangelicals, which emphasized individual sin and redemption while disregarding the social evils caused by economic and political structures of American society, their specific mode of prophetic preaching offered a radical critique of the status quo. Using the rhetoric of divine justice, it empowered listeners in their congregations to maintain their dignity and humanity during that tumultuous time. Their prophetic sermons addressed issues ranging from unemployment to classism within their churches. Tapping into the biblical prophet's spiritual reservoir, a few Black urban clergy of interwar America understood their preaching to be as much a courageous and challenging Word as a gracious Word. To them their prophetic discourse was no less sacred than the prophet's because its aim was to encourage listeners to struggle with the meaning of faith, which meant exploring the revelation of God in Scripture at its intersection with human experience.[5]

The Life World of the Hebrew Prophet

Prophetic Call and Assignment

The most basic task of the Hebrew *nābî'* (most often translated as *prophet*), meaning "one who is called" or "one who calls forth" in the Hebrew scriptures, was to hear and disseminate God's instruction.[6] Through the human channel of prophetic mediation, God addressed God's people. Exclamations of justice, ecclesiastical reform, moral and ethical responsibility, and redemptive hope for peace tinted the speech and work of the Israelite prophets. Prophets pointed to events in which God was at work and told why God was active in them. For example, Jeremiah and Ezekiel's call narratives are comprised of vision reports of future occurrences and night visions. Hence, the context of the prophet's social world was intrinsically related to the prophet's prescient task. Furthermore, the prophet's cosmological surroundings constituted the arena for prophetic demonstration. Functioning within particular sociocultural boundaries, prophets were expected to announce with great certainty God's connection or absence in specific events. As spiritual intercessors for the people, prophets assumed the insufferable task of proclaiming divine justice that criticized the corruption of the established government and the idolatrous practices of temple worship.

Israelite prophecy consisted of both ecstatic and deeply reflective forms of oracles and narratives. Prophets spoke as oracles of salvation and judgment to the ruling powers of the state and to religious leaders. Analogical and metaphorical symbolism shaped conceptions of the Divine in the ancient Near East. Within this religious world, symbols created a bridge to interpretation, concealing and revealing characteristics about the nature of God and God's active relationship with humankind. Emblematically, the image of the potter's wheel in Jeremiah 18:1-12, for example, characterizes the process of how the divine-human relationship is to be understood. In this sense, the prophet's work was to proclaim to the people Yahweh's desire to reform and reshape them. Jeremiah is not depicted as an intermediary without need for personal and spiritual formation but as an individual in spiritual process alongside the community into which he was called to serve. The prophet's speech was addressed to and worked out in public, not in isolation. The depiction of a divine potter at work molding and forming community provides symbolic imagery of the divine council or council of Yahweh—a place understood to be ruled by the gods, a pantheon as it were, that acted as an assembly to make decisions about the structure and order of the world.[7]

To comprehend the complex nature of the prophetic role, understanding the cosmic-political significance of the divine council, takes on crucial importance.[8] Even though the religious world of the prophet in the context of Mesopotamian religion in the ancient Near East was not imagined as vast and unchanging, a political understanding of a governing divine council of nature and human affairs existed. In Israel's case, Yahweh sat on the throne as king, judge, and warrior, and a nameless host of divine beings surrounded the Lord. In this divine assembly, the prophet served as Yahweh's human instrument, carrying out Yahweh's instruction in the social realm. Accordingly, words received at the council always preceded the prophet's authorization to act in spaces of temporality. This dichotomous relationship is seen in Jeremiah's proclamation to the inhabitants of Judah, when he denounces the false prophets of hope:

> Thus says the Lord of hosts: "Do not listen to the words of the prophets who prophesy to you; they are deluding you. They speak visions of their own minds, not from the Lord. They keep saying to those who despise the word of the Lord, 'It shall be well with you' . . . they say, 'No calamity shall come upon you.' For who has stood in the council of the Lord so as to see and to hear his word as to proclaim it?" (Jer 23:16-18)

Speaking the divine Word, Jeremiah announces:

I did not send the prophets, yet they ran; I did not speak to them, yet they prophesied. But if they stood in my council, then they would have proclaimed my words to my people, and they would have turned them from their evil way, and from the evil of their doings. (Jer 23:21-22)

Whether arising from passionate personal concern or out of strict obedience to God's decree, or some combination of the two, readers can only speculate the interior motivations of the prophet. Notwithstanding this, the passage reveals that the prophet was entrusted with a message and was held accountable for its contents in two worlds—the eternal and temporal.[9] The consent to speak the divine Word, according to Jeremiah, is not based on a prophetic title conferred. Rather, the entitlement to speak the prophetic Word remains contingent upon his access to the council of God, his ability to hear a voice from one other than his own, and his proclamation of a credible Word. In this case, the credible Word calls God's chosen ones to turn from evil. With respect to human responsibility, prophets, on the one hand, carry a functional role as the religious community's spokesperson. On the other hand, they understand their task in a particular way though their prophetic broadcasting always answers to some authority.

The book of Jeremiah illustrates a distinctive self-awareness. Jeremiah's own anxiety about proclaiming the Word conveyed his intense regard for message accuracy over message popularity. More than an obvious plea for God's address, the cosmological inquiry, "Is there a Word from the Lord?" served a political function. This question authorized the prophets to speak divine decrees and public announcements in a volatile social realm. Sometimes words of judgment rejoined the query, and other times hope was the response. In any case, however, as evidenced in the prophetic literature, the truth-bearing task of the biblical prophet secured him a kind of clout; and while mostly met with an ungracious reception, as in Jeremiah's circumstance, his reformist agenda that urged repentance for their apparent apostasy expressed a continuous and credible claim. Truth proclaimed always necessitates that the prophet secures access to the presence of Yahweh and Yahweh's divine assembly.

No bifurcated worldview existed in the ancient Near Eastern culture. Moderns today conceive the world on a compartmentalized basis, dividing life activity into categories of sacred and secular. Life was not so easily dichotomized in the world of the prophets. Thus, the prophetic role theologically was just as critical as the social one. Competing ideologies existed. The issue of Baal worship looms as one example of Israel's disloyalty to the demands of the law. Yet, the more subtle theological tensions like those between Jeremiah's adherence to the conditional "if/then" covenant, as detailed by Moses and the dominant temple ideology of the day, positions the prophet in a confrontational and challenging role. The inescapable tension between prophecy and kingship always remained present within Israel. For example, Hananiah's embrace of tradition for the sake of self-preservation and King Zedekiah's immoral and socially egregious behavior repeatedly earned Jeremiah's admonition and disdain.[10]

Prophetic Agenda in a Dangerous Social World

The Hebrew prophet Jeremiah is paradigmatic in that he accepts an appointment from God to a work of "building up, and tearing down" (Jer 1:10). Jeremiah's prophetic announcements, peculiarly enough, functioned to subvert the religious and social establishment's perception of reality. And greater still, drenched in its uncommon demands, the prophet announced a radically new future despite the pronouncement's ungracious reception within the community of ancient Israel. Prophets were clearly products of their hostile environment, though not much is known about the "psychology" of the prophet. Called into communities that often stood against their work, they were obligated to remind individuals that human life that disregarded God was not life at all. The prophetic assignment typically coexisted with some degree of protest from the prophet. Akin to Jonah's rebellion and short-lived escape to Tarshish and Elijah's search for a safe house fleeing Jezebel's wrath, Jeremiah laments his call and cries out to God in chapter 20, "O Lord, you have enticed [meaning deceived] me, and I was enticed; (v. 7) . . . I have become a laughingstock all day long; everyone mocks me" (v. 7b). Despite this, God instructed the prophet to speak the divine Word to the people of Israel whether they heard or refused to hear. But as noted in verse 19 of Jeremiah's text, God's promissory Word accompanied the prophet's calling and task. That Word claimed, "They will fight against you; but they shall not prevail against you, for I am with you, says the Lord, to deliver you."

Speaking the divine Word in concrete terms, prophets addressed "injustice and social oppression, crises of military invasions and the barbarities of war, creation of political alliances, religious apostasy, monarchical pretensions . . . tyranny,"[11] and the like. Prophets were in constant contact with the political establishment, whether on the periphery or in the king's entourage. But as messenger of Yahweh, the prophet's responsibility was to represent the divine king to the earthly king, proclaim justice and the requirements of the covenant, and announce and interpret God's interventional acts within human community.[12]

Thus, to be prophetic meant having great concern about the integrity of the spoken Word. Authentication of one's authority to speak prophetically, on the one hand, depended on whether or not the prophecy came true. On the other hand, and perhaps on a flimsier basis, credibility was established by the prophet's professed association with the heavenly assembly or was confirmed by the prophet's call narrative.[13] Because the prophet was "neither a 'singing saint' nor a 'moralizing poet,' but an assaulter of the mind,"[14] to use Abraham Heschel's vintage phrase, who spoke truth to power, ironically, telling the truth in a dangerous social world ultimately secured the prophet's prophetic clout.

Evoking Alternative Worlds

Acts of utterance are acts of imagination that carry generative power to evoke new perceptions of reality. In spoken Word, prophets rise up to engage life-and-death matters. Whether functioning as crisis addressers or crisis evokers, they carry the divine response into a material reality. This idea runs as the central thread throughout all of Walter Brueggemann's work on prophetic speech.[15] The focus of his landmark classic, *The Prophetic Imagination*, is the prophetic consciousness of Moses, and how that consciousness continues in the work of other prophets, derivatively, and consummates in Jesus of Nazareth. For Brueggemann the rejection of the status quo and speaking words of resistance constitute the two determinant factors for developing and nurturing a prophetic or "alternative consciousness" based on the Mosaic outlook. When dialectically related, these elements call for both a healthy suspicion of power and a self-awareness about the seductive influences of culture. Against commitments to imperial consciousness—the politics of silencing revolutions and criticism suppression in Scripture—Israel's prophets waged a poetic war to negate the dominant imagination through image and metaphor—symbol-laden discourse spoken concretely and directed toward spaces of particularity.[16]

Speaking prophetically offers hopeful symbols, mines the memory of the people, and educates them to use the tools of hope, while recognizing the powerful way in which words, speech, language, and phrase shape consciousness and define reality.[17] Through figurative medium, prophets articulated, in a concrete manner, their rejection of totalizing claims that disallowed counterpoise.[18] Hence, the venue for prophetic truth telling, by definition, resides in an arena of contestation, where daring utterances always invite conflict in a taken-for-granted world. Even still, Hebrew prophets dared to cast a hopeful vision and an alternative perception of reality that affirmed God's power to transform reality itself.

Prophetic Continuities and Discontinuities: Ancient and Contemporary Lines

Two noteworthy considerations require discussion before attempting to draw parallels between the biblical prophet and the prophetic preaching of representative Black clerics in the Great Migration. The first consideration recognizes the implausibility for anyone in modern times to function precisely as did the Old Testament prophet. The Hebrew prophet did not preach from scripture based on his witness as the contemporary cleric does to discern and proclaim how God works in current times. The second consideration acknowledges that Christian preaching in the modern sense qualifies as prophecy insofar as it points to God's work, but only in a secondary manner because the full Word of God has now been spoken and incarnated in Jesus Christ, and the reconciliation between God and humankind has commenced.[19] Therefore, determined by Christian faith commitments, the prophetic Word is "not only communication or proclamation but also the putting into operation what is announced. Not only a Word about judgment and salvation but also a power that initiates and brings them both to reality."[20] In Christian tradition that announcement of hope is revealed in the person of Jesus Christ, whose incarnational salvific, redemptive, and reconciling presence offers life to a deathly world. Whether explicitly named or presupposed in the prophetic sermon proclaimed, at the heart of prophetic preaching is the gospel of God in the person of Jesus Christ.

In a less than perfect world, prophetic preaching becomes a Word of glad tidings to the poor and a liberating Word for the physically and spiritually infirmed. In Jesus' norm-setting vision to his Galilean audience in Luke 4, he proclaims himself the fulfillment of Isaiah's prophecy with the declaration, "Today the scripture has been fulfilled in your hearing" (v. 21). The oracle speaks a prophetic Word of interrogation; it calls into question social arrangements that protect Roman interests, exploit the poor, and baptize the status quo. To the members of the Galilean community for whom hope seemed improbable, the embodiment of God's concern for society has arrived in the person of Jesus. The living Word entwines with history, and prophetic hope becomes an incarnate reality for society's hope, especially for those Galileans for whom the communal predicament of human suffering had endured for generations. For purposes of this text, the idea of justice concerns the distribution of material resources, fairness to one's neighbor, righteousness toward God, the proper use of the created order, and personal responsibility for communal wellness.[21]

Interpreting the gospel with regard to what justice demands is to remain attentive to the law of love, the pursuit of human dignity and freedom, and the active resistance to moral evil. Understood and appropriated as an alternative to hopelessness, two essential characteristic marks of Exodus preaching are revealed. African American prophetic preaching interprets *to euangelion* ("the gospel") with regard to justice ideals and the active pursuit of hope for emancipatory ends. More specifically, corresponding with the Old Testament prophet's vision and message of justice and hope, this mode of discourse (1) unmasks systemic evil and opposes self-serving, deceptive human practices and (2) remains interminably hopeful when confronted with human tragedy and communal despair.

In Paul's correspondence to the Corinthian church, the apostle speaks of "handing over" the gospel to the Corinthians as it was shared with him (1 Cor 15). Based on this text, James F. Kay sees in 1 Corinthians a reminder that humans do not invent the gospel. Rather, the preached gospel transmits tradition that came from God. Kay asserts, "Paul characterizes this good news by the noun 'gospel' [*to euangelion*] and the verbal form 'gospeled' [*euengelisamen*] so that the good news becomes not only 'the message' proclaimed, but also entails the act of proclaiming it. The gospel [therefore] embraces both word and act."[22] In essence, the gospel proclaimed is pressed into service of divine purpose.

Emboldened by the biblical prophet's message and the prophecy's culmination in Jesus Christ, the daring Black migration clerics offered

words of judgment against an unprincipled democracy, words of admonition to church communities for ethical dubiousness and moral laxity, and
words of salvation to the poor and downcast Black southern migrants who
exchanged their Jim Crow existence for life in the urban ghetto. At one
with the speech of the biblical prophet, the prophetic sermons of Reverdy
Ransom, Florence Randolph, and Adam Clayton Powell Sr. naturally arose
out of specific situations. Their strident messages unmasked systemic evils
and deceptive practices that stifled human flourishing. With subversive
intent, these preachers confronted human tragedy and communal despair
with tools of hope. In the same way that the biblical prophet's message
revealed the divine plan in spaces of temporality, these innovative Black
ministers felt similarly entrusted as instruments of God. The influence of
their homiletic context on the shape of their preaching is paramount. To
mediate change within their specific congregations and communities, these
preachers took seriously the immediate sociohistorical situation of listeners.
As a result, African American prophetic preaching came into existence as a
response to the situation that needed and invited it.[23]

The Praxis and Aesthetical Dimensions of Exodus Preaching

The African American prophet has traditionally had a certain affinity for
creative rhetoric and poetic imagination brought to bear in the American
context. Beginning in slavery, Black churches have institutionalized the prophetic principle in many distinctive ways, recognizing injustice far and wide.
However masked the prophetic principle is in much of African American
preaching today, these characteristic themes of the prophetic Word establish basic criteria for drawing ancient and contemporary parallels.

Naming Reality

Paulo Freire's stronger emphasis on context and praxis strengthens Brueggemann's claim that prophetic speech is always "concrete talk in particular
circumstances where the larger purposes of God for the human enterprise
come down to the particulars of hurt and healing, of despair and hope."[24]
Freire illustrates the pedagogical dimension of prophetic speech by noting
the extreme importance for oppressed people to find their own voice in

order to name their own reality. Otherwise they may name their oppressor's reality as their own and therefore contribute to their own oppression. In the way that slaves sang spirituals in the cotton fields to evoke an alternative reality and in order to keep hope alive, their hope was rooted in an eschatological vision that linked song to circumstance. Ransom, Randolph, and Powell were doing this in their prophetic sermons. Their determination to transcend oppression in thought and imagination, as the biblical prophets had done, meant their prophetic messages gave voice to the disinherited masses who sought equal protections under the law in America, irrespective of their regional home. Specific to this concern is Freire's principle of *conscientization*—from the Portuguese term *conscientaçacao*—which refers to the process in which people develop a deepening awareness (consciousness) of the contradictions of the sociocultural reality shaping their lives and their capacity to transform that reality.[25] Conscientization points to the significance of dialogue and critical reflection on concrete historical reality.[26] Freire's pedagogical theory originates from his own experience as a political exile from his native Brazil. In 1964 he lived in Chile during a military coup. In his major work *Pedagogy of the Oppressed*, first published in 1970, he advances a critique of education born out of his concern for poor illiterate migrant workers. Freire's relevance to this textual subject matter, however, lies not in the formal tenets he proposes in his educational philosophy, but rather in his theorizing about "critical dialogical reflection on concrete historical realities and action for humanization."[27]

Theologies reflecting on African American contexts share themes with Latin American philosophies and theologies of liberation. Both are concerned with justice issues pertaining to oppression and liberation. Yet, these contexts have different sociohistorical questions and concerns. African Americans, for example, have remained particularly conscious of the long history of slavery in this country and its repercussive effects.[28] In spite of the differences, Freire helps here because he connects speech with prophetic actions as concrete praxis. Praxis, defined as "reflection and action upon the world in order to transform it," is a dialogical activity.[29] In the process of conscientization, praxis opens up possibilities for oppressed people to combat their own "cultures of silence" (dehumanization). Such praxis "is set in thoroughly historical context, which is carried out in the midst of a struggle to create a new social order."[30] To the disheartened migrant masses flooding into northern cities in the first half of the twentieth century, the prophetic preaching that took place in northern Black congregations literally spoke into existence a new way of being in the world.

According to Freire, dialogue acts as an essential prerequisite for the creation of a new social order.[31] Dialogue can only make a difference in the world if love is its foundation; it is an act of humility; it possesses intense faith in humankind to become more fully human; it takes place in a context where hope is present; and it promotes critical thinking—thinking that is at once inseparable from action and constantly immersed in temporality without fear of risks.[32] Critical thinking becomes tantamount if one is to be aware of self, the world, and one's activity upon the world. The upshot of this critical dialogical reflection not only affirms dialogue as an existential necessity but also implies from the standpoint of praxis that, in order for people "to exist humanly," they must be free to participate in naming reality so that they can change it. The freedom to speak "is not the privilege of some few persons, but the right of everyone."[33]

> Human beings are not built in silence, but in word, in work, in action-reflection . . . But while to say the true word—which is work, which is praxis—is to transform the world, saying that word is not the privilege of some few persons, but the right of everyone. Consequently, no one can say a true word alone—nor can she say it *for* another, in a prescriptive act which robs others of their words.[34]

Through dialogical action, Freire rightly observes that the dehumanized can begin to commit themselves socioculturally to the work of conscientization, "by means of which the people, through a praxis, leave behind the status of *objects* to assume the status of historical *Subjects*."[35] Through the process of conscientization, the culturally despised discover their voices by learning to perceive the extent to which their lives have been formed and socially determined by social, economic, and political contradictions.[36] Transforming one's lived reality entails a dedicated allegiance to a struggle for ownership of one's personhood at both an individual and social level.

The praxis of naming reality to transform it is what prophetic Black preaching achieved in the Great Migration. For the interwar period, a daring few Black preachers named the power of God to overcome dehumanizing political, economic, and social forces in their prophetic sermons. These preachers were guided by a vital hermeneutic of God's good intention for creation and the resolute conviction that listeners in their northern Black congregations needed a way to articulate their misery and be freed from America's created "cultures of silence." Black preachers such as Adam Clayton Powell Sr., Reverdy Cassius Ransom, and Florence Spearing Randolph rose up to name the dehumanizing political and socioeconomic realities (substandard housing, racial and gender discrimination, unstable employment) stirred by the Great Migration, and simultaneously offered a word of hope, which possessed the power to topple despair.

Naming one's own reality to transform it happens when speech-acts link with prophetic actions as concrete praxis to open possibilities for voiceless oppressed people. Although Freire sculpted his pedagogy in Brazil, a similar pedagogy issued forth in the prophetic voice of the African American preacher in the United States. In their prophetic proclamation of the Word, they dared to connect that Word to the concrete social conditions of the listener. In the way that slaves sang spirituals in the cotton fields or exhorted the courageous in the "invisible church" to evoke an alternative reality in order to keep hope alive, hope was rooted in an eschatological vision that linked song and spoken Word to circumstance. This is what a few African American preachers during the Migration were doing in their prophetic sermons.

Randolph, Ransom, and Powell connected speech with cultural memory to assist exodus participants in naming their reality by (re)membering, that is, seeing themselves as scattered-to-be-rejoined destiny seekers belonging to a cultural womb, uniquely African and southern, in spite of their communal dislocation and subsequent relocation in the North. Moreover, prophetic Black preaching involves much more than truth telling. As a language of relentless hope, prophetic Black preaching operates as the means, carrier, and clarifying medium of memory.[37] Gloria Albrecht argues that the "beloved community" is actualized at the site of one's dangerous memory of struggle against domination and acts of resistance. Through the dangerous memory of suffering and resistance, she writes that "the subversive hope for justice" is nourished.[38] Human survival rests on the fact that persons find transformative ways to articulate their misery and name their identity-shaping reality.

The Will to Adorn

In his 1989 publication *Finally Comes the Poet: Daring Speech for Proclamation*, Brueggemann focuses on the poetic character of prophetic speech. Not only does he reiterate the notion that prophetic speech evokes an alternative world or perception of reality, but also he claims that the practice of preaching itself must be "subversive fiction"—a poetic construal of a world beyond the one taken for granted. This poetic speech is not about romantic caressing, moral instruction, or problem solving, but the intense, unsettling proposal that the real world in which God dwells, and where God invites us, is not the one overcome by worldly powers.[39]

Brueggemann invokes biblical authority for this aesthetic dimension of prophetic preaching, and one would not expect him to ground his discussion of this dimension in an awareness of the particular issues of social and ecclesial injustices in African American contexts. Zora Neale Hurston's observation of the aesthetics of Black church worship as a way of talking about the poetic side of prophetic Black preaching provides a clear example of African American prophetic preaching.

The aesthetic quality of African American prophetic preaching is often perceived through contrasting lenses, in which both "the awesomely beautiful and the tragically ugly"[40] are held together. The homiletic upshot to this union reveals that hope and promise bear its fruit, and from this coupling God establishes a new order for the people. Cultural aesthetics is the basis of the imaginative genius and furtive power of the prophetic preaching of legendary preachers, including Vernon L. Johns, Lacy Kirk Williams, Elijah John Fisher, Junius C. Austin, Howard Thurman, Ella Pearson Mitchell, Sandy F. Ray, Josephus P. Barbour, Prathia L. Hall, and Samuel D. Proctor. They took scripture and culled out a hope-filled discourse about God's will to transform church and society, and for the individual to "make a way out of no way."

African American prophetic preaching soars not only as concrete and particular speech but also as daringly poetic speech. At the heart of prophetic sermons lies the African American preachers' ability to draw on cultural-aesthetic principles to communicate the gospel. The Great Migration preachers in their respective northern pulpits were creative poets who possessed the "will to adorn." This aesthetic impulse runs counter to preaching cultivated by contemplative, inner pietistic styles of worship. As a carry-over of colonialist legacies, contrasts in aesthetic visioning, as Willie James Jennings maintains, call attention to the immense challenge for Blacks to affirm and confirm cultural identity within a White (Eurocentric), universalizing framework, where cultural narration and human worth are based on false perceptions of White nobility. Thus, the cultural activities such as the preaching of non-Whites would instinctively be judged against processes that narrate "the true, the good, the beautiful, the intelligent, and the noble around white bodies."[41] While this did not necessarily lead to a loss of agency of indigenous Black preaching traditions, it did, however, mean that in the pursuit of establishing its nomenclature and own set of norms, traditions of this kind would inevitability struggle with or against White approximation.[42]

In practice, prophetic Black preaching could involve a variety of homiletic approaches, that is, differences in delivery style and sermonic structure, depending on the specific needs of the listening community and the preacher's theological, political, or educational formation. The aesthetic impulse is what furnishes the preacher's imagination and speech with subversive power, which is a valuable asset to the preacher to make lateral leaps linguistically where linear flattened prose cannot.[43]

In her essay "Characteristics of Negro Expression," African American novelist and folklorist Zora Neale Hurston illustrates the speech-act inclination to adorn speech. With metaphor and simile, double descriptive words, and verbal nouns, Hurston says, "The American Negro has done wonders to the English language . . . but it is equally true that he has made over a great part of the tongue to his liking and has his revision accepted by the ruling class."[44] Bishop Ransom and Pastors Randolph and Powell represented a rare company of Black clerics who had substantial formal education for their times. Thus, the great use of metaphoric language in Hurston's portrayal seems most indicative here. Hurston rightly affirms that the search for beauty is subjective—human beings have different standards of and different interests in art. Most are thus incapable of passing judgment on the art concepts of others.[45] The aesthetic impulse to create is always at work in the African American speech-act:

> The stark, trimmed phrases of the Occident seem too bare for the voluptuous child of the sun, hence the adornment. It arises out of the same impulse as the wearing of jewelry and the making of sculpture—the urge to adorn.[46]

Fundamentally, Hurston shows that the will to adorn in the speech-act is "a desire for beauty."[47] Insofar as prophetic Black preaching makes use of language and culture and carries this impulse for beauty, aesthetics become a way of talking about the speech-acts in the prophetic sermons preached during the Great Migration.

Hurston enables the audience to see and hear the evocative power of language and rhetoric; she communicates how particular cultural-aesthetic principles that convey artistic beauty emerge as a result of the intermingling between African and American culture. Though Hurston argues from an essentialist point of view, she accurately picks up on the power and beauty of Black oral expression. She affirms that through symbolism and the use of "extended" metaphors and verbal nouns, Blacks creatively adorned their speech in attempts to recreate their lives. In prophetic Black preaching, "language becomes a vehicle for transforming meaning, for translating behavior into words and for converting every-day life drama into written texts which are also performances."[48] Instead of relying on expository prose, the preacher-poet communicated in signs and symbols that "extend the spatial and temporal boundaries of prose" to multiply the dimensions through which a listener may encounter God in the preached Word.[49] Hurston's idea about poetic language carrying an impulse for beauty helps elucidate the fourth and concluding characteristic. African American prophetic preaching carries an impulse for beauty in its use of language and culture.

The Exodus Preaching Paradigm

Four constitutive marks exist that together establish a paradigmatic model of prophetic Black preaching that is both biblical and contextual. Interpreting the gospel in a present-future sense based on the principles of justice, African American prophetic preaching, representing the paradigm, (1) unmasks systemic evil and opposes self-serving, deceptive human practices, (2) remains interminably hopeful when confronted with human tragedy and communal despair, (3) connects the speech-act with just actions as concrete praxis to help people freely participate in naming their reality, and (4) carries an impulse for beauty in its use of language and culture.

Three regulative features govern the conceptual construction or paradigmatic understanding of the idea that African American prophetic preaching derived its message and agenda from the Hebrew prophet.[50] The prophetic Word of God begins with stunned, unjustified, and unargued speech of affirmation and celebration; it insists on naming places where ambiguity, intrusion, and gift are present; it dares speech that specifies concrete places where the reality of God's otherness is at work decisively in the human process; and, finally, it gives to these concrete happenings the name of holiness, either holy graciousness or holy judgment.[51]

The first feature that governs this conceptual construction insists that prophetic Black preaching is God-summoned speech that runs counter to the tendency to reduce the prophetic Word proclaimed to positivistic history or modern rationality. Preaching of this kind rejects the assumption that every justifiable assertion can be scientifically proven or disproven, which means that the historical process is closed off, rendering God incapable of intruding decisively in the human process and reenacting the impossible. Prophetic preaching is epistemologically distinctive. In contrast to attempts to render God as deferential to Cartesian ideals or to make God some spectral figure, prophetic preaching begins at a different place and in a different mode of discourse, which insists on naming God as an emancipating interventionist actively involved in the human process.[52]

Prophetic Black preaching at the time of the migration moved in a similar direction. Rather than distort the reality, prophetic Black preaching identified numerous social and political obstacles thwarting freedom and pointed where God was at work in a particular community.[53] Insofar as prophetic preaching is highly contextualized speech often found in subcommunities, it may be considered as socially distinctive. By not retreating from daunting issues of the public sphere, prophetic Black preaching sought to expose America's failed promises to its Black citizens. To listeners in northern Black churches, the prophetic Word, fueled with energy and surprise, conveyed both the judgment of God and the consolation of God's promises. Because a few Black clerics dared to preach prophetically, many heard the promise of a new and hopeful future in their urban Promised Land.

A second limit imposed is similar to the first. Prophetic Black preaching dares to speak about God's presence in the places where pain, oppression, and neglect are all too apparent. Throughout the migration, it undeviatingly proclaimed that God was available and active in, with, and among displaced migrants in northern cities. In the atmosphere of industrialization and wartime, some Black preachers dared to tie their subjective experiences to scripture to conceive of a God who operates sovereignly as "other" and yet is freely and intimately at work in human processes to bring about new social realities. The sermons considered take a particular tack in naming their reality.

And finally, a third limit imposed relating to this constructed paradigm is that this distinctive form of prophetic discourse names experiences within concrete and temporal spaces as holy. These spaces are deemed either holy graciousness or holy judgment,[54] which means that prophetic speech tended to reiterate themes of judgment and deliverance. In the case of prophetic Black preaching, a few Black ministers during the Great Migration addressed issues ranging from unemployment to classism within their churches. They understood this type of preaching to be as much a courageous and challenging Word as a gracious one. As a Word that calls into question the oppressive society on behalf of the people, prophetic Black preaching, to borrow from J. Philip Wogaman, is sacred speech because it aims toward helping listeners to struggle with the meaning of faith, which means exploring the revelation of God in scripture at its intersection with human experience.[55]

With this critical understanding of African American prophetic preaching as consisting of four characteristic features and as derived from biblical prophetic speech, chapter 4 examines in detail selected sermons preached in certain northern Black churches immediately prior to and during the Great Migration. Looking specifically at a representative sampling of sermons from Bishop Reverdy Ransom, Rev. Florence Spearing Randolph, and Rev. Adam Clayton Powell Sr., chapters 4 and 5 demonstrate how their prophetic sermons formed a distinctive discourse that flowered in the period, forming a venerable tradition inherited and carried forward into the Civil Rights period and virtually abandoned thereafter. Not only does the African American prophetic preaching paradigm reveal a composite picture of the nature and function of African American prophetic preaching, but also it makes evident the urgent need for a roadmap to rehabilitate the prophetic voice that calls American preachers to reclaim in spoken Word the voice of the prophet that speaks justice, divine intentionality, and hope.

4

EXODUS PREACHING
Gospel and Migration

The deep confidence that life will not ultimately sustain evil is a part of the distilled wisdom of the prophet and the door of hope through which generations have passed into the city of God.

—Howard Thurman[1]

Reverdy Cassius Ransom, Florence Spearing Randolph, and Adam Clayton Powell Sr. were supported by different denominations in distinct contexts but faced similar challenges in the migration.[2] The question of the color line in their White-dominated society constituted a deep-rooted problem for them. A racially hostile social world circumscribed their labors as Christian preachers no matter how effective they were in their own contexts in addressing matters of freedom and justice. But in contrast to their set of circumstances, Ransom, Randolph, and Powell seriously imagined a different reality.

Their prophetic sermons show an unfettered use of resources that were components of African American northern church traditions. Their finely honed prophetic sermons worked to call specific congregations to their true identities as participants, informing and transforming the ethos and conscience of church and nation. By merging praxis and race consciousness (without extremism) to focus on the latent problems and possibilities of wartime America with its rapidly expanding industries, their prophetic preaching played a crucial role vis-à-vis the social progress of urban Blacks. The Black clerics of this study were interminably hopeful that God would act on the behalf of migrants faced with a suffering present; the subversive intent of the sacred rhetoric they proclaimed sought to help migrants name their own reality as God's good creation. Through metaphor and word picture, their aesthetically rich discourse proposed social change for emancipatory ends. And while they were not the lone creators of prophetic Black preaching,[3] nor could the whole of their preaching be construed as prophetic in character and function, their sermons showed a dominant tendency toward the prophetic. These early twentieth-century clerics, molded by their unique experiences and the rituals of their specific subcommunities, became prophetic voices of the people, exposing the contradictions of Black life.

Primed for Prophetic Preaching in the Promised Land

African American clerics Ransom, Randolph, and Powell did not collide with the perplexing effects of migration fever unprepared for action. In contrast to the majority of Black clerics in the North or the South, they preached a word of hope to the neglected, leveled criticism to social and economic power structures, and unequivocally affirmed the legitimacy of present human experience as a vehicle for participating in God's redemptive plan. That which these preachers understood about the Black societal condition had profound consequences upon their homiletic readiness. The following selected sermons preached before the high tide of Black migration reveal their keen awareness about the structures and trends of their social reality.

Pre-Exodus Sermons

REVERDY C. RANSOM

*Thanksgiving Sermon: The Industrial and Social Conditions of
the Negro, 1896*[4]

Thou hast multiplied the nation and not increased the joy.

—Isaiah 9:3 (KJV)

Sermon Fragments

In the years that are past and gone we have played a marked part in the industrial development of this country and it is no less true today than it was in the past. But we have been forced in the north, in Chicago, as well as in the south, into a condition that may truly be termed industrial serfdom . . . it is the unwritten law in almost every avenue of life, that the Negro shall perform those tasks and engage in those enterprises which are distasteful to white men, and whenever the Negro aspires to a position in life which is thought desirable by white men he is felt to be an intruder, to be aspiring out of his place and above his plane. We are accused of being poor, but no man can ever become wealthy or save money until he makes money.[5]

Our race is a race of workingmen and workingwomen. There are no capitalists among us, no millionaires.[6]

There has been, so far as I know, during the past year no abatement of the crime of lynching which has swept through this land. There is too much indifference by some of us who are up here in the north, but yet you are not safe up here: if you go too far they would swing you right here in Chicago: they did try to do it some years ago. We are not safe here, although a little more so than our brethren in the southern section of the country.[7]

Our so-called leaders rise up and say those white people will make it hard for us. What more can they do? They are killing us in the south: taking our votes away when they get ready: they have declared it constitutional to compel us to ride-in "Jim Crow Cars": they have forced industrial serfdom on us, and yet when a voice stands out and pleads, some, because it is not their voice, some because they are not getting the glory, some through fear . . . will sink the interest of the race for their own personal gain and personal safety for the time.[8]

While our numbers are being increased we must take a stand demanding recognition, for the destiny of our race is one.

The thing we must do is to force from the hands of American Christianity and American civilization, that proper recognition which is granted to us by the bible, which American Christianity comes to us holding in her hands. I believe that it should be one of the missions of the colored churches in our land to take their stand against American Christianity and compel recognition at its hands and the doctrine which it preaches in the name of God and heaven: that she should recognize the fatherhood of God and the brotherhood of man: that she should recognize that which she professes with hypocritical lips—the communion of saints at the altar which Jesus Christ has purchased with His blood.

Reverdy Ransom's 1896 Thanksgiving sermon "The Industrial and Social Conditions of the Negro," delivered at Bethel AME in Chicago, addressed the issue of Black social dislocation. The sermon deplores the continuation of Black poverty and socioeconomic discrimination in urban America. Based on Isaiah 9:3, "Thou has multiplied the nation and not increased joy," Ransom criticizes a nation of such great wealth and industrial might for its gross practices of inequity along racial lines and seeks to know why inequality of opportunity between Black and White laborers continues. Appealing to the witness of scripture and strict belief in the doctrine of the fatherhood of God and brotherhood of man (a recurrent theme in his sermons), Ransom seeks to persuade his listeners that American Christianity and American civilization have an obligation to assist Blacks in negotiating their survival in the industrial age without Blacks fearing violence and discrimination.

———

REVERDY C. RANSOM

Thanksgiving Sermon: The American Tower of Babel; or, The Confusion of Tongues, 1909[9]

Therefore is the name of it called Babel; because the Lord did there confound the language of all the Earth.

—Genesis 11:9 (KJV)

Sermon Fragments

The Negro and the Negro question have passed through many phases, dating back nearly three hundred years ago when he first set foot upon this soil. The Negro question first came up for discussion at the time the foundations of the Government were laid.[10]

The confusion of tongues over the Negro question in this country is illustrated by the attitude of the most intelligent and progressive Negroes. We have on the one hand Dr. Booker T. Washington and his adherents; on the other hand Dr. W. E. B. Du Bois and his adherents; while outside of these there is a great unclassified host. Now, the adherents of Dr. Washington speak one language and the adherents of Dr. Du Bois speak another; neither can understand the other. Therefore, like the confused tower builders of the Plains of Shinar, they go into different camps and take their separate ways, while the unclassified host to which I have referred, stand hesitant and halting between the two conflicting bodies of opinion.[11]

If we turn to the Government itself, the Constitution of the United States speaks one tongue and the United States Supreme Court another.[12]

America is based not only upon the ethics of Jesus, but upon democracy, as set forth in the spirit of the Declaration of Independence. This means all men should be permitted here to achieve the highest possibilities of which they are capable.[13]

I see, as from the tower of Babel, the scattered groups returning from the confusion that has so long kept them separated and divided. They have learned that despite all differences of speech, they have at all times had one word in common—that word is MAN. Now we learned to articulate in unison another word—that word is BROTHER. Now standing face-to-face they say—"MAN AND BROTHER." The recognition is instant. Barriers are broken down, the confusion is silenced, and in brotherly cooperation they set themselves the task of building their civilization a tower of strength, because all men who toil and strive, who hope and aspire, are animated by a common purpose that is peace, happiness, and the common good of all.[14]

Ransom's "Thanksgiving Sermon: The American Tower of Babel; or, The Confusion of Tongues," delivered before the Bethel congregation in 1909, expounds on the social progress legacy of African Americans. He finds the Genesis account of confused tongues a fitting parallel to the confusion that abounds in the attitudes of Black national leadership, the Supreme Court, the legislature, science, literature, and religion over the Negro question. "If we turn to the realm of religion the confusion increases. *When the pulpit is not hesitant or incoherent, it is absolutely dumb* . . . There is no speech or language which is common to the different denominations, or even to the various pulpits of the same denomination," laments Ransom.[15] Confusion will continue within the nation, he contends, until the ethics of Jesus, as set down in the New Testament, are understood not as iridescent dreams but as reality in brotherhood based upon the Fatherhood of God. Black brothers and sisters seek fraternity and equality.[16]

As these selected sermons allude, clearly etched in the fabric of Ransom's premigration preaching was the appeal to uphold the human dignity of all God's creation and the belief that Christian faith could promote social transformation.

———

FLORENCE S. RANDOLPH

Hope, 1898[17]

And now abide faith, hope, and charity, these three; but the greatest of these is charity.

—1 Corinthians 13:13 (KJV)

Sermon Fragment

Hope, says Dr. Pierson is the last thing in the world; when all else has gone out of life, hope is still left; and being left, all else becomes possible. Paul says, "We are saved by hope, which hope we have as an anchor for the soul, both sure and steadfast."[18]

As hopeful for the spiritual, we should also be hopeful for the temporal; for life while it reaches throughout all eternity, begins in this world; and if we would make this life what it should be, a foretaste of the heavenly, we must encourage a hopeful disposition; for with such a disposition the head and heart [are] set to work, and one is animated to do his or her utmost. And by continually pushing and assuring, a [seeming] impossibility is made to give way.[19]

Florence Randolph's 1898 sermon "Hope" endorses the creation of a safe home for African American girls, to help them develop skills for womanhood and to participate in a growing industrial economy. Devoting much of her attention to the repercussive effects of society's ills, Randolph drives home a Social Gospel message derived from the three Christian graces recorded in 1 Corinthians 13—faith, hope, and charity. Hope does not center on blissfully longing for heaven.

Rather, the hope which Paul describes is one that remains "hopeful for the spiritual. . . . [And] should also be hopeful for the temporal; for life while it reaches throughout all eternity, begins in this world."[20] Randolph makes clear that the work of God assures African Americans a progressive future. Not glossing over the many social problems and disadvantages Blacks face, she refuses to accept that race, nationality, and gender are to be determining factors of racial advancement. She boldly declares, "We must try and hold up our women, if we desire to see the race rise to a higher standard; for it is not the Negro's color but his condition that is the most detrimental; it is not a man or woman's color, but their merit, character and worth, and this has been proven by many of the race."[21] Notably, what is at stake in her late nineteenth-century milieu finds powerful articulation in her understanding of the character of the divine and human relationship in the context of Black life in the United States.

On the one hand, advancement requires perseverance. Knowing that if we cannot be geniuses, we all ". . . can do something for the elevation and future progress of the race: for the day of small things is not to be despised." But on the other, Randolph affirms God's purposive will: "The Negro has a history which God intends [that] shall never be blotted out though his Caucasian brother would try to rob him of it, and bring about a problem."[22] And finally, Randolph returns her focus to the issue that occasioned her sermon: the establishment of an industrial Christian home for African American girls.

> Let us cease to find fault and [to] feel discouraged, for as a race we are (either blessed or cursed, which ever you are [of] a mind to term it) with a large number of critics or fault finders, and only a few who are willing to go into the hedges and highways into the attics and tenement houses, into the homes of the poor and the desolate, endeavoring to take a ray of sunshine; who can take a poor miserable, unfortunate girl by the hand and call her sister, thus trying to lead her to a purer life. This is a real Christian's duty.[23]

Here she admonishes her listeners that Black people cannot rest on simply building churches because that is a delusion of Black progress. Rather, she says, "We must build race institutions of every kind and endeavor to support them independently."[24]

———

ADAM CLAYTON POWELL SR.

A Graceless Church, 1911[25]

Sermon Fragment

> There are about 50,000 colored people in Greater New York who do not attend church. If these non-churchgoing thousands could be assured that they would be given such a warm reception as the one described they would pack and jam every church in this city inside of six months. People delight to go where they know they are wanted and where they are cordially received. When strangers are met by smiling ushers and given a warm welcome by the members of the congregation, in ninety-nine cases out of one hundred they will come again, and if they are not followers of the Lord Jesus Christ they will soon fall in love with Him.

Powell's sermon "A Graceless Church," published in the *New York Age* in 1911, brought criticism to greater New York institutional churches for failing to aid the social development of men and women. In the sermon Powell acknowledges his personal distress over potential church newcomers finding more hospitality and cordiality beyond the four walls of the church. When people discover more kindheartedness in a lounge or pool hall than the average church, then that church ceases to be characterized by grace:

> The church has almost lost the grace of hospitality and cordiality. It has neglected to entertain the strangers that come within her gates and the strangers have gone to places where the environment is impure looking for social warmth. The church must recognize that man is a social being, that if the church does not treat him cordially he will go elsewhere seeking social gratification . . . If they stay in stuffy flats they die with consumption. Not a single colored Baptist or Methodist church in Greater New York has made any provision for the social development of men and women.[26]

To neglect the obligation to demonstrate kindness to the stranger is unchristian, declares Powell. Therefore, the ushers, who in many respects are the most important officers in the church, must not take their duty lightly.

The usher plays a critical role in inspiring people toward conversion. Powell continues, "He can do more to restore the lost grace of sociability than anyone connected with the Christian organization . . . We all know that first impressions are usually the best or at least the hardest to overcome."[27]

> Christianity means more than piously ramming the word of God down the throats of men twice a Sunday and to secure from them a confession of their faith in Jesus Christ. To save a man is to get him out of a bad environment and put him in a good one with Jesus Christ as his example, ideal and inspiration.[28]

Inspired by British sociologist Benjamin Kidd's principles of power, en route to transforming church and society, Powell preached Christian unity and church reform to large scores of African American hearers before the high tide of migration.

The social issues taken up in Ransom, Randolph, and Powell's sermons in years prior to the exodus, in many ways, only intensify after the United States' entry into WWI. Continuous throughout, each preacher holds a deep appreciation for the mysterious divine initiative and theological presupposition behind their prophetic preaching, showing that God is affected by the conduct of those whom God has brought into being.[29]

Great Exodus Sermons

Two sermons by Reverdy Cassius Ransom expose the exodus' effect on prophetic preaching. In Ransom's sermons "The Church That Shall Survive" and "Heralds and Prophets of a Changed Order and a New Day," a voice resides alternative to the destructive realities scourging early twentieth-century Black life within and peripheral to the church. In humanizing words of proclamation, Ransom reminded Black listeners of their worth to God despite their suffering. Akin to the biblical prophet's message, Ransom's mediating prophetic speech helped listeners to perceive and to name the contradictions of their sociocultural reality. And because Reverdy Ransom, as Anthony Pinn notes, "merged worlds and brought to his Christian commitment a full range of resources that gave little distinction between sacred and secular,"[30] his preaching cultivated an authentic perception of hopefulness for interwar-period Blacks in a range of ecclesial contexts.

———

REVERDY C. RANSOM

The Church That Shall Survive, 1936[31]

Sermon Fragments

Now, a sermon should always be placed upon the revelation of God through Jesus Christ, His Son. The occasion asks not only for a sermon, but for a quadrennial sermon (that is, one which should look both backward and forward). It should look backward at least to the things through which we have come for the past four years, and these things have naturally derived from the things in [the] past which make history of our church up to this hour. But more than this, it should look forward, facing the future as it relates to our opportunities, our duties, and our tasks.[32]

. . .

No institution, whether church or state, can stand still without beating a retreat or moldering to decay. It must go forward. I do not mean that activity is synonymous with progress. There is much activity which is engaged in threshing old straw or simply beating the air. We should be active by forever enlarging our vision to meet the changed moral, social, and spiritual conditions of the succeeding generations in which our lot is cast. We must always have in mind that widening our activities through engaging in work on behalf of schools, hospitals, Y.M.C.A., temperance, world peace, and in forms of work for help and mercy do not constitute a church. They may, and should, grow out of its life and spirit; but the church is now, as of old, a body of believers however large or small, who are united through saving faith to Jesus Christ as Redeemer, Lord, and Master of their souls.[33]

On May 6, 1936, Ransom, now bearing the well-worn stripes of bishop, delivered the Quadrennial Sermon at the Palace Casino on Tea Street and Eighth Avenue in New York City before the thirteenth session of the AME General Conference.[34] He took his text from Exodus 14:15: "And the Lord said unto Moses, Wherefore criest thou unto me? Speak unto the children of Israel." Bishop Ransom stood in "his tall, Indian-like . . . stringy, gaunt, and lean [form], [which] filled the pulpit . . . [and] immediately there was close attention to his shrill, musical voice."[35]

If the AME Church is to survive, proclaims Ransom, it cannot grow complacent, romanticizing the days of Paul, Wesley, Allen, Turner, Payne, or even Booker T. Washington. Rather, it must strive to find relevance in a rapidly changing atmosphere. Moreover, if it is to survive, according to Ransom, "We must furnish our own redeemers and prophets to lead us to go forth and walk with the tireless and ageless God." Still, there is another problem. Regarding the church's present state of health, Ransom could only believe that there were just as many formidable foes to progress within the church to contend with as forces without:

> Where past and present meet the future begins. We have arrived here today largely through the impact of the inertia of the past that has come from our fathers, rather than any power or foresight we have achieved ourselves. He who clings to the past, without at the same time going forth in the light of the present to meet the future, is bound to a body of death. This is why we now call upon God to meet us in this place as we now stand at the conflux of the past and future, to give us vision, courage, and faith to meet the new age--a challenge that cannot be evaded or ignored.[36]

The sermon's central theme is that the church always lapses into idolatry when institutional sacredness is based on age to the disregard of its ability to confront present-day crises and serve humankind. Ransom hoped to penetrate resilient attitudes and traditional ideals. Urging listeners toward a new and unsettled future, Ransom charges: "God changeth not, but the methods by which His servants meet the changing society must keep pace, changing with God's unfolding plans to bring men near to Himself through the procession of yes."[37]

The church that shall survive is a self-critical institution. Ransom points to three key barriers to progress that demand modification and the church's attention. In the first place, he believes AME established schools that once served a real need as the only opportunity for Black education should earnestly reevaluate their fitness in a marketplace where education is increasingly state supported. To meet modern-day standards, the AME Church, he professes, is in truth only viable enough to support two or three colleges and one theological seminary. In like manner, the church should rethink its continued use of outmoded foreign missions methods: "Africa knows now that the white nations who send her missionaries are really there to subjugate her people and exploit the land."[38] He radically reframes the church's traditional question about mission when he asks: Are present missionaries equal to the task to know how to heed Africa's cry?

Third, he wagers an appeal for unification of all Black Methodist bodies: "Will this General Conference revive it [the issue of unification] and pursue it until it becomes an accomplished fact?" For Ransom this question implied more than an ecclesial or religious concern. Implied was consciousness about the economic, political, and social welfare of millions of Blacks. Given the AME Church's vibrant heritage, Ransom believed his denomination should lead the way in the unification process. Other important themes emerge in this sermon, though without detailed elaboration. For example, justice appeals calling for material and political gain for Blacks are mentioned outright, and the persistent query about anti-lynching laws is raised.

Ransom believed that the church's survival could only be secured if it was furnished by courageous and prophetic leadership, but no less empowered and supported by "the angels and all the hosts of Heaven led by the Son of God."[39] One captures the poetic biblical imagery of the heavenly realm. But apart from this, Ransom explains what the church must do to survive and be faithful to the gospel:

> The bishops and ministers that lead this church must have their call and commission from God, and the geniuses of their credentials and the divine authority with which they are clothed must be witnessed by the power and faith to proclaim and uphold the gospel message in an evil time. It must be a prophetic church, not only beholding the Lord and lifting up, while the cherubim cry "Holy, Holy, Holy" round his throne; but while the church is marching through the wilderness, they must point to the realm of hope and promise that lies just beyond. They must proclaim liberty to the captives—those that are socially, economically, and politically disinherited—with authority of a divine justice that will not rest until every fetter of injustice and oppression is broken.[40]

In this brief segment of the sermon, one finds an aggregate picture of Ransom's prophetic voice. "The Church That Shall Survive," at each turn, displays the characteristic features distinctive of prophetic Black preaching. This sermon, in relation to the others considered later, stands out as the archetype displaying the paradigm of the prophetic Black mode. "The Church That Shall Survive" speaks against idolizing the AME Church's past heritage and educational accomplishments. It encourages the church toward flexibility and direct action in view of the impact of actual dehumanizing social and economic conditions affecting Black life as the church moves forward into a hopeful yet unsettling future.

In concrete terms, Ransom addresses human suffering, specifically lynching and the absence of voting rights, as an obstacle to liberation. Moreover, he criticizes established power, such as the White power structure's denial of citizenship and voting rights to Blacks. But equally important are Ransom's repeated appeals to the church to remain hopeful in finding its relevance and achieving its aims contemporarily despite their collective misery. The strong sense rises to suggest that the sermon is intended to be dialogical. This claim finds support in the realization that the preacher's pen explicitly invokes the language and imagery of the church to help clergy and laity name the strengths of their valiant past, while also supplying the necessary challenge for them to face up to their contemporary limitations. Finally, perceiving, as he did, his message as a poetic construal of God's larger purpose for the human enterprise, in this sermon Ransom's captivating verse flourishes. Forever searching for beauty, he was a true artisan of the speaking art. He demonstrates a hopefulness when he proclaims: "Let . . . American Christianity in the United States, practice what it preaches but for a single day, and its cruel features would be wreathed in smiles, its ruthless spirit would be so transformed as to envelop the world in the folds of a mantle of good will."[41]

———

REVERDY C. RANSOM

Heralds and Prophets of a Changed Order and a New Day,
1920s[42]

Sermon Fragment

Our people, with a sense of frustration bordering upon discouragement, if not despair, have listened and are listening now, for a voice proclaiming how and where they can find a door of escape. We have our education, politics and wealth, the churches, emphasizing chiefly [ ] and freedom in a world after [ ]. We do not want to live and leave our children to struggle there in the generations to come. We want some of our paradise now. Each one of us holds the solution within his own [ ]. We confess our inadequacy and hopelessness while the deliverance we seek lies within our own minds and spirits. We have surrendered the dignity and freedom of our own minds and spirits to economic pressure, to political and social barriers, and to religious forms whose withered leaves neither inspire nor perish.[43]

I am here to declare redemption, salvation and deliverance, to come of old. We must pass through our own Gethsemane and bear our own cross. We must cast off the yoke and break the chains which for centuries have made us but mere [ ] and echoes of the white man in social, political, economic and religious affairs. We should take the world that lies behind the barriers to which our race has been confined and make it an empire of triumphant freedom and power.[44]

In this sermon Ransom urges Black people, and Black youth in particular, to find a distinctive voice or face extinction—the kind of retrogression that happens when prophetic voices are silenced. Ransom based this sermon on John 1:23, which reads, "The voice of one crying in the wilderness, make straight the way of the Lord." From this text Ransom articulates his race-conscious appeal for a contextualized Christianity that redeems and uplifts Black culture. Ransom begins the sermon deductively, affirming the work of the Holy Spirit in the lives of those God commissions. He states:

An atmosphere of bewilderment and frustration hangs over Americans of African descent. It pervades their political, economic, social, educational and even their religious life. Their greatest need is not wealth, legislation, schools and churches. There is no deliverance in these things unless the spirit and the voice of the herald and prophet lies within them.[45]

If deliverance comes to African Americans, namely, bewildered Black youth, he argues that these persons must find justification and inspiration for entrance into the cause of protest against injustice. In harmony with his major claim in "The Church That Shall Survive" that inspiration must not simply come from biblical figures, he affirms that revelation flows from people such as Martin Luther and Richard Allen, people who became servants and prophets in their day. More specifically, inspiration should originate from the would-be prophets of the present day. That is why Ransom counsels that "to have vitality, dignity and power, a people, like an individual, must be self-formed and not crushed into the mold of another mind or spirit."[46] Airing his disdain for any false notion that would perpetuate the myth that in matters of politics and education Blacks should take their intellectual cue from Whites, Ransom avers:

Why should an opinion or idea carry more weight with us because a white man voiced it? I reject it or enlarge it, as I perceive its defects or narrowness. But on the other hand, if the voice of truth comes from Mount Sinai or the Acropolis, from Galilee or Mecca, or from the heart of Africa or Asia, I will follow it to the ends of the earth.[47]

Ransom says it is not enough for Black education to copycat the best White colleges and universities. Negro schools must possess their own soul and, like the Negro spirituals, give birth to something unique and distinctive in America. The particularity in his speech becomes so intensely palpable that one senses the deep convictions behind his guiding hermeneutic that seems to govern much of his preaching—the fatherhood of God, the brotherhood of humankind. This means that all humanity is created in the image of God and, therefore, equal in personhood. And yet, Ransom was undeniably a "race man"; his strong theological convictions about the brotherhood of all humanity never assuaged his pursuit of racial justice. He cites the manner in which Jews found strength in prophets and heralds such as Moses, Elijah, and Isaiah in their pursuit of freedom and power. Blacks are to do likewise, similarly finding their own servants and prophets out of their rich cultural bank. Because the mindset of Black inferiority among Blacks is difficult to overcome, would-be progressive Black youth must seek God for prophets and heralds among the race. Ransom illustrates this point by declaring what is at stake if education is not indigenous to one's social reality:

I am voicing no tirade against the body of classified knowledge which is the intellectual inheritance of the world enlarged and enriched from one generation to another, and to which all countries and races have contributed. I simply proclaim the freedom of our own souls from slavish devotion and bondage to the spirit and ideals of another race or people.

What this means educationally is that Black people must participate in naming their reality and their cultural self-worth or risk the humiliating stigma of being labeled a socially and intellectually inferior race. "Heralds and Prophets" encourages a prophetic consciousness by advising listeners to seek God's power as well as to participate in one's own naming of reality to bring about transformation. The sermon's purpose is to both address and transform "cultures of silence" in the Black community. In order for transformation to take place in the religious realm, the Black church, maintains

Ransom, must be foremost an equalizing space for ecclesiastical freedom. For Ransom the church epitomizes that environment where "men were not to surrender their common humanity and manhood, or dishonor God, by accepting a secondary or inferior place in any religious fold bearing the name of Christ."[48]

But Ransom demonstrates in this sermon that he is not only concerned with matters of the ecclesia, he also boldly criticizes American democracy. Correlating the ideals of democracy and Christianity together, he asks, "Is our American Democracy to become an instrument of corruption and oppression, or of freedom, justice of civic righteousness and peace?"[49] Ransom alleges that the United States has retrogressed on its promises of justice to African Americans.

But at the same time, he expresses hopefulness in God's provision of spiritual and material resource to enable African Americans to exit their sociopolitical wildernesses. Ultimately, Ransom seems to suggest that Blacks must do the work of contextualization, namely, cultivating resources internal to their own traditions, particular views, and gifts. Therefore, this means that for Blacks to continually strive for White acceptance and respect is not only idolatrous behavior, it is futile. Black youth, argues Ransom, should not aspire to the religion of the oppressor, that is, follow after "a Christ that stands for American Christianity" devoid of the weight of the cross. To seek after such a version of Christianity in the end is always a "stupendous delusion."[50]

Clearly, two realities of criticism and relentless hope are held side by side. Ransom anticipates divine action in human community. Reflecting on the times, he maintains, "While the white man's world is busy making war . . . intent upon science and invention, and carrying exploitation and oppression to the ends of the Earth, the Negro lags behind and suffers."[51] Yet, while all this may be true, "a yearning for the appearance of the reign of God in the life of men" is obvious. Ransom refuses to despair. Poetically, he concludes the sermon expressing that it will not be enough for American Christianity to preach Jesus Christ "with eloquence and learning, or set it to music, or dress it up in fine churches and lofty cathedrals." For the preaching of Jesus Christ to break the power of sin and death, the fire of divine love must burn within, or "faith dies on the threshold of hollow mockery."[52]

Evident are the characteristic marks of the prophetic Black preaching mode. First, one readily discerns how the sermon functions to confront self-serving and self-deceptive ideologies in a White-dominated society, which claims that "truth" is culturally restricted. A movement toward a new, hopeful, yet unsettling future becomes apparent as Ransom refashions the dominant, White view of Christ. Next, underlying his rhetoric throbs the steady refrain of concern that Black human suffering and social inferiority must forever be seen as incompatible with God's justice. The preacher's sermon is pedagogy for the oppressed, especially in a society polarized along racial lines. Such pedagogy exclaims that to be human and strong is to possess the intrinsic right to name one's own reality. Ransom's oratory takes a critical posture against established power. As the sermon draws to a close, he inquires, "Is our American democracy to become the instrument of corruption and oppression or fortress of freedom?"[53] Ransom consistently deals with this theme, specifically in "The Industrial and Social Conditions of the Negro" and "The Church That Shall Survive." He questions the efficacy and power of American democracy since Black lynching is at an all-time high and Blacks are denied their citizenship rights in the North and the South. Finally, one notices in this sermon Ransom's ability to connect his daringly poetic speech with prophetic actions. To White American Christians and leaders in the nation's democratic experiment, Ransom says, "We want some paradise now."[54] The pursuit of paradise is not some whimsical fantasy. It is the expected fulfillment of the promise of physical and social liberation intended for all persons. Not detached from the Black struggle for humanization, paradise is the embodiment of justice and a people's access to an alternative reality. Ransom's homiletic ability earned him the right to become the voice of the people.

———

FLORENCE S. RANDOLPH

Antipathy to Women Preachers, 1909

Sermon Fragment

Fear not, women, because you are about a great work for I know that ye seek *Jesus*, who was crucified and I am not surprised for you ministered to Him during His life. In death you were not divided. You followed Him to the cross, notwithstanding the danger to which you were exposed and now you have come to weep at His tomb. But weep not. He is not here, for He is risen, as He said. But go quickly and take the glad news, preach the first gospel sermon . . .[55]

Florence Randolph's sermon in 1909 "Antipathy to Women Preachers" asserts that androcentrism and gender discrimination in Christian pulpits illustrate a misreading of Scripture. Though the AME Zion Church was the leader in ordaining Black women, Bettye Collier-Thomas maintains that the goal for most Black women seeking ordination in Randolph's era was simply inclusion in the church polity, not necessarily pursuing the need to transform the patriarchal church.[56] However, in "Antipathy" Randolph takes an unfeigned and critical stance against sexism in the church, naming it an idolatrous instrument of oppression. Citing a litany of texts, she contends that God has irrefutably predestined women to labor as participants in Christian ministry. Women are called to model the fearlessness of the Hebrew prophets Jeremiah, Ezekiel, and Daniel. In the way that Hagar, Deborah, and Mary displayed valiant service to God, women must likewise find courage to face their challenging social limitations.

Randolph hits her stride in the sermon when she claims that after the resurrection, the words spoken to the first preachers (women) were the words, "Fear not ye."[57] Given this departure point, at each successive turn, this sermon argues that to exclude women as laborers in the Christian ministry is antithetical to the report of scripture. Their inclusion, however, carries the promise that women will be rewarded for their sacrifices. Randolph had indeed tackled a host of other social issues alongside the cause of gender equality throughout her career before the mass exodus. Her religious and political involvements, at the local and national level, made it clear that her preaching unavoidably sat at variance with the social status quo. "Antipathy" rebukes the Victorian ideal of womanhood for an all-Black audience. Women, she suggests, should model the biblical figure Deborah:

> [Deborah] shows what is possible for a woman to do, especially a woman led of God and her work [withstands] forever the assertion of some that a woman if she be a wife and mother is only fit to look after her household. Deborah was a wife and mother in Israel yet her capacious soul embraced more than her own family. It reached thousands on the outside and we see her work, both in and outside, sweetly blended together.[58]

Randolph's sermon lacks any overt appeal to a race-conscious ideal. This demonstrates that a broad-minded challenge to the status quo rather than any agenda toward race or gender romanticism shapes the prophetic Black homiletic mode. Thus, in accordance with our formative characteristics of this genre of proclamation, "Antipathy" speaks against self-serving ideologies that claim God does not and will not choose women to labor as gospel preachers. Randolph's interpretation of texts drives the listener toward an unsettling future, one in which ancient biblical figures provide needed justification to affirm women preachers. Moreover, relentless hope becomes obvious in this sense as the preacher Randolph urges her listeners to heed biblical authority exemplified in an intertextual, hermeneutical dance, or more precisely, proof texting. Biblical women are shown as role models for contemporaries, and human suffering is framed in the language of gender discrimination.

In addition, the subject "Antipathy to Women Preachers" itself implies that in the speech-act, the sermon offers criticism to established ecclesial power by addressing androcentric biases in churches, specifically the exclusion of women in positions of church leadership. Beyond the typed manuscript stands the fact that in such a sermon, Randolph's own legitimacy as a preacher and personal security are at stake. Finally, Randolph, as she describes Deborah as a moral exemplar for women, accomplishes two things in the preaching event: (1) she names Black women's reality as oppressive and seeks to transform it, and (2) she adorns her evocative speech in a manner that blends the beauty of language with culture.

———

FLORENCE S. RANDOLPH

If I Were White, 1941

Matthew 7:3-5; 1 John 4:20

Sermon Fragment

If I believed in Democracy as taught by Jesus I would preach and teach it, no difference who differed with me. If I really loved my country and believed that she, because of her high type of civilization, her superior resources, her wealth and culture, should lead the world into a just and durable peace—a peace that would bind all nations together so that wars should forever cease, then I would stress the fact that charity must begin at home.[59]

Quite the opposite of "Antipathy," Randolph's sermon "If I Were White," preached on Race Relations Sunday, February 1, 1941, at Wallace Chapel AME Zion Church, is expressly race conscious. Based on Matthew 7:3-5 and 1 John 4:20, she creatively arranges her sermon as a first-person narrative. This sermon interrogates the promises of American democracy, the deceptive ideology of Black inferiority, and other chronic injustices of the postwar period. Consistent with Ransom's plea in "Heralds and Prophets" that Black inferiority must be seen as antithetical to the gospel, Randolph reminds her listeners of their self-worth and emphasizes that America's Whites who claim to be defending democracy at wartime have an obligation to all American citizens. Randolph says, "Charity must begin at home."[60] In the end she charges that the truth about the incompatibility between Christianity and White dominance is something the majority culture must reappraise.

Randolph begins by locating her congregation's despondency, speaking of "these strenuous war-torn days, when the entire Christian world is struggling to get its bearings as to the Church and its definite place in the world adjustment, when men are in doubt, and thousands are already [losing] faith, not only in Christianity but even in God."[61] Regarding the respect and fairness she urges Whites to show to African Americans, she continues, "If I were white, I would speak in no uncertain language to my own people what I believe to be right."[62]

Then appropriating Matthew 7:3, part of Jesus' Sermon on the Mount, she evokes a sermonic aim: "And why beholdest thou the mote that is in thy brother's eye, and considereth not the beam that is in thy own eye?"[63] Whites must learn to be sincerely self-critical about their attitudes toward minority races if they claim to believe in the message of Jesus Christ and the God of scripture. The persistent realities of racial prejudice and oppression of Blacks, she intimates, are obvious opportunities for Whites to exercise prophetic consciousness. As if to make the point conclusively, she wisely appeals to the wisdom of 1 John 4:20, "If a man say, I love God, and hateth his brother, he is a liar."

By the sermon's close, one notices an understated plea to her doctrinal position concerning holiness through her use of a creative homiletic strategy. All Christians, she affirms, should strive for holiness accomplished inwardly, which manifests itself in one's behavior temporally. Therefore, if one seeks to claim skin superiority, then one must also be superior in love and in personal character. Randolph does not become resigned only to the diagnosis of present-day crises, but she imagines a different reality where the gospel is rightly applied in society. Randolph suggests, "I would recommend as far as possible that Negro speakers of thought and education be invited to speak from white pulpits and [that] white ministers and other workers, who believe the Gospel they preach, [be invited] to speak from Negro pulpits."[64] In this regard, she ties scripture with concrete praxis.

The characteristics of the prophetic mode of proclamation are clearly present in this sermon. As expected, Randolph disputes the offhand, idolatrous notion that God has created Whites superior to Blacks. She speaks in concrete language that the refusal of Whites to act justly toward Blacks, domestically and abroad, not only embraces sin rather than Christ, but also reveals a realistic picture of America's race problem. In her city of Summit, she chronicles numerous exigencies caused by unjust housing situations, mediocre schools, public discrimination, poor medical facilities, and the lack of Black physicians for Blacks, all, she says, meriting the positive response of White men and women who would follow after Christ. Still her sermon presses toward a hopeful future: "If I were white and believed in God . . . I would speak against Race Prejudice, Hate, Oppression, and Injustice."[65] Such words of proclamation imply that a window of opportunity remains open. Finally, despite the sermon's serious tone, in her conclusion one detects the preacher's creative urge to adorn. After citing a litany of human injustices, she appeals to the imagination of her northern Black congregants about dealing with these certain matters of Black hardship. "If I were white," she says, "and acted justly, I would be conscience free before him with whom I have to do." And yet more revealing are her next few lines:

I slept, I dreamed, I seemed to climb a hard, ascending track, and just behind me labored one whose face was black. I pitied him, but hour by hour he gained upon my path. He stood beside me, stood upright, and then I turned in wrath. Go back, I cried, what right have you to stand beside me here? I paused, struck dumb with fear, For lo, the black man was not there, but Christ stood in his place. And Oh! the pain, the pain, that looked from that dear face.[66]

When Randolph calls attention to the plight of Black human suffering, she does so only after her careful theological reflection on God's activity in the person of Jesus Christ, one who himself was degraded and misunderstood in the ancient world. Then comes a push for her Black listeners and overhearing Whites to see an ontological connection between the life of Jesus and that of Black human suffering in America. Accordingly, her hermeneutic of suspicion inquires, "Are whites adequately conceiving who Jesus really is?" Christ stands in place of the rejected ones. Finally, "If I Were White" poetically epitomizes the bold and vitalizing hermeneutical step to tell her congregation what Matthew 7:3-5 and 1 John 4:20 wish to say on Race Relations Sunday.

ADAM CLAYTON POWELL SR.

The Model Church, 1911

Sermon Fragment

In the second chapter of Acts, we have a clear and striking picture of a model church. We are justified in calling it a model church because it was organized by the direction of Jesus and was vitalized and electrified by the burning presence of the Holy Spirit.[67]

I believe that God wants us to model all our churches after the pattern of that first church. Let any local church today compare the qualifications of its members with the qualifications of those who constituted the first church at Jerusalem, and it will have to confess that it falls shamefully below the standard there given.[68]

First delivered in 1911 as part of his campaign to move Abyssinian to Harlem from its previous Fortieth Street address in Manhattan, "The Model Church" stresses the importance of evangelism and stewardship in contemporary church's service to God and mission to the local community. The 1930 published version of this sermon is used in this study, for it addresses social issues pertaining to unemployment, poverty, materialism, and ecclesiastical reform in the World War I context. The "model church," Powell proclaims, is established on six key effects: conviction of sin, saving faith, stewardship, social responsibility, soul saving, and spirit-filledness.

He begins by naming the church's perplexing reality in brazen terms: "To say there is not a New Testament church on earth would be not only a bold and sweeping statement but a discouraging indictment against organized Christianity."[69] Believing that God desires local churches today to pattern themselves after the first church recorded in Scripture, Powell, the consummate reformer, hopes to guide his congregation to a past reality of ecclesiastical faithfulness. First, Powell voices that there was something about Peter's preaching that convicted the members of that first church of their sins and brought them to repentance. Second, as a consequence, the members of the New Testament church experienced saving faith—believing that Jesus was wounded for our transgressions, that his blood cleanses individuals from sin, and that his transforming power is decisive for the new creation of women and men. Third, in addition to a church member's commitment to a saving faith, Powell claims that one must recognize the high call of stewardship on one's life. He says, "God owns us not only through race birth but . . . grace birth."[70] Fourth, as Powell suggests, men and women of the church have the social responsibility to manage what God owns, everything from our (mental) faculties to our facilities.

With this orientation, all members recognize their stewardship in relation to God's ownership. Powell also helps the congregation acknowledge its duty to meet the needs of the community, whether they are social, economic, or spiritual. He continues, "Every New Testament church must discover the real needs of the people in the community in which it is located and do its utmost to supply those needs in the name and in the spirit of the Lord Jesus."[71]

Fifth, a model church is one possessing a passion for souls, a church whose central motivation is to bring men and women out of spiritual darkness into God's light. Again, skillfully adorning his preaching, Powell reports that at Jerusalem "3,000 were converted at the place of worship, but the 5,000 were converted on the street."[72] Finally, the model church is that church experiencing the power of the Holy Spirit. A church living in this power is fruitful and life-giving to the spiritually dead. But on the contrary, a church without the Holy Spirit, he concludes, "is like a tree without sap, a watch without a spring; an automobile without a motor."[73]

"The Model Church" bears out the characteristic elements of prophetic Black Christian proclamation. It speaks against the idolatry of self-serving, ecclesiastical practice that does not put into practice the ministry of hospitality by its evangelism. Powell refuses to absolutize the present but articulates hopefulness about the church's ability to offer something evangelistically to the local community in a present-future sense. Such a word of reform to the church directly challenges the established power of normative, ritualistic practices that work to silence criticism. The frequency with which this sermon was preached indicates that Powell never rested until the sermon spoken became incarnated in the lives of the people. Because this sermon was routinely heard, Powell desired to help his people to participate freely in naming their reality through the implementation of the sermon's objectives. A poetic craftsman of the sermon, Powell, lastly, paints a vivid picture to address the predicament of human suffering, announcing:

> A man hungry and cold will not have much patience with a lecture on spirituality. If a man has no shoes, he would not want to be told about the golden slippers of the New Jerusalem. If he has no warm clothing, it would antagonize him to describe the long white robes and the golden girdles of heaven. If you should go into a man's sickroom and find him in need of physical attention and begin to sing heavenly songs and pray long prayers, the probabilities are that he would never want to see you again.[74]

The church first established by the atoning work of Jesus Christ at Jerusalem was not a do-nothing, pie-in-the-sky, believer's fellowship; instead, under the enduring threat of persecution on account of Christ, it became the ecclesial prototype that would benchmark any future community daring to bear the emblematical badge, "We are Jesus people."

ADAM CLAYTON POWELL SR.

The Colored Man's Contribution to Christianity and When It Will Be Made, 1919[75]

Sermon Fragment

The word soon in this prediction is a stone of stumbling to many Bible readers. Some of them unhesitatingly say that the prophecy is discredited and annulled because it was uttered three thousand years ago. At that time it was proclaimed that Ethiopia would soon reach out after God, and these puzzled readers argue that, since thirty centuries have elapsed without witnessing any united movement of the colored people of the earth toward God, the prophecy has become obsolete or, in the language of the lawyer, has expired by the statute of limitation. These readers forget that our puny methods of reckoning time are vastly different from God's calendar. It is believed by some of the best biblical and scientific students that the seven days mentioned in Genesis represent at least seven thousand years. This opinion is in harmony with the teachings of both the Old and New Testaments which declare that a thousand years with the Lord are but as yesterday. In God's eye-view, then, it was only three days ago when it was said, "Ethiopia shall soon stretch out her *hands* unto God."[76]

Powell proceeds on a foundationalistic, homiletic course in "The Model Church," urging principles of financial, moral, and spiritual progress. But as this next sermon demonstrates, his pulpit speech is also immodestly race conscious. "The Colored Man's Contribution to Christianity," delivered in 1919 at the Abyssinian Baptist Church in Harlem, New York, explores the relationship between religion and race, specifically how members share their particular cultural inheritance in shaping present-day Christianity. Not only does moral progress rank high among Powell's homiletic aims, but also human progress is contingent on changing European-American perceptions of African Americans.[77] Parallel themes among the selected Ransom sermons, Randolph's constructive agenda to have pulpit exchanges between White ministers and Black ministers, and Powell's "Colored Man's Contribution" sermon are obvious. Guided by the premise that African Americans will make their own unique and significant contribution to Christianity when they collectively extend their hands to God, Powell presses the interpretation of Psalm 68:31, "Ethiopia shall soon stretch out her hands unto God," to mean all that it can mean.

At the outset he dismisses any thought that would declare the text's prediction annulled or made obsolete due to the passing of time. As Powell expresses, "In God's eye-view . . . it was only three days ago when it was said, 'Ethiopia shall soon stretch out her hands unto God.' "[78] And for the purpose of Powell's argument, thereafter, Ethiopia signifies Black people all over the world. He affirms that the so-called "white races"—Jews, Romans, Greeks, and Anglo-Saxons—have made their lasting imprint on Christian faith. Then, in a highly reductionist analysis, Powell summarizes a clear picture for his congregation: Jews have nationalized religion and protected monotheistic faith; Romans skillfully brought organization and ecclesiastical order to Christianity; Greeks bequeathed to Christians philosophy of religion; and Anglo-Saxons individualized faith, that is, they sought freedom of conscience and religious liberty. What immediately follows in the subsequent move is the sermon's most pertinent two-part question: "What contribution will the colored man make to religion, and when?" He illustrates:

> I believe that the colored people are going to emotionalize religion. They possess enough emotion to move the world when it is properly confined and directed. The serious religious thinker criticizes colored people not because they are emotional but because of the way they express their emotions. Electricity is the most powerful and useful thing yet discovered . . . When it leaps from its scabbard in the skies, splits trees . . . we are startled and frightened . . . Confine it to batteries, dynamos and wires, and this wild, frightful something runs our trains, drives our automobiles . . .[79]

Powell's use of the term "emotionalize" is not off-putting nor does it fuel the racial stereotyping of Blacks. Rather, he seeks to rescue the Word and clarify its meaning, suggesting that to "emotionalize religion" is to understand emotion as rooted in love. This kind of emotion is consonant with spirit and vitality. Love, and therefore emotion, more than knowledge, he says, is the greatest power in the world.

Next, the sermon discusses solutions to the race problem in America. Powell says that it was once thought that acquiring property and getting an education would make Whites "respect us and treat us as men and American citizens."[80] Here again, as in the previous sermons of this study, arises the consistent affirmation of Black humanization in the face of destructive forces. In another, a group of "colored" leaders are now declaring, "The only way for the colored man to save himself is to arm and defend himself."[81] But Powell earnestly believes that both gaining White acceptance and retreating to violent tactics are wholly inadequate solutions to the race problem. He says, "Even if we were prepared to fight, this method [taking up arms] would not assure us racial permanency. This is not the method proclaimed by the text."[82] A race only will be blessed, he maintains, "by stretching its hands to God."[83] In saying this his appeal broadcasts God's justice and intentionality toward humankind through love:

> I can never be moved from the opinion that the colored man was placed in America by the providence of God to teach the white man the meaning of genuine Christian love and sympathy. In this particular the colored man has shown his superiority to the white man, for the one who loves is

always superior to the one who hates. What the white man's Christianity needs is not organization, not money, not more adherents, not knowledge, but the whole system needs to be fired and energized by that deep and inexpressible emotion called love.[84]

Idols have never saved a nation or civilization.

Powell argues, "Egypt, Babylon, Rome, Carthage and Greece possessed all of these in a marked degree. Only a few pyramids tell of the former greatness of Egypt, and a heap of civilized rubbish marks the location of the once great Babylon."[85] Then, he characterizes the decline of the German race, despite Martin Luther's great contribution to Protestantism, as a lesson to humankind. Powell is convinced that the "signing of the armistice on the 11th day of November 1918, served notice on humanity that mentality, money and munitions of war can never save a race."[86] "White and colored people" surmises Powell, "were deluded into the belief that the war would make the world a fit place to live . . . it has made the world a more unfit place in which to live by stirring up all the latent evil forces. There never were such manifestations of hatred and wickedness as now."[87]

In the sermon's final assessment, he finds the biblical story of Queen Esther constructive. If Black people would seriously read Esther and translate its teachings about fasting and prayer, "a marvelous deliverance"[88] would happen. Equally important, both Blacks and Whites receive a call to action. Whites must see the power of emotion (love) that oppressed people have cultivated in their souls to vitalize religion. Laying "insults, indignities, injustices and all the unspeakable outrages heaped upon their race before God," Powell says Blacks must accept the call to the spiritual disciplines of prayer and fasting.[89] This awareness, claims Powell, "would be the most powerful and effective protest that ever went to Heaven from any continent . . . let the race try God."[90]

In every way this sermon testifies to the ambiguity and gift of God's presence in the human process, namely, in the lives of African Americans. Powell names his congregation's reality and declares that only a free God can transform African Americans into individuals who make lasting contributions to the Christian religion. "The Colored Man's Contribution" meets the criteria of prophetic Black preaching. It speaks against self-deceiving practices, which suggests that Blacks have made no significant contribution to Christianity; it holds a title that is a prime indicator that Powell's homiletic vision refuses to absolutize the present; it addresses human suffering caused by lynching, denied citizenship rights, racial riots, mob violence in major U.S. cities, and the aftereffects of WWI; it takes a critical posture against established power when he argues that violence against Blacks "has silent sanction of the United States government";[91] and it emphasizes Black spirituality with hopeful affirmation. Love (described as emotionalism) is the Black contribution to Christianity. The momentum of the faith is love. Powell instructs his listeners to name it as their contribution to Christianity and as a gift to the world. It is a vitalizing gift to a religious faith that has grown stale. By spiritual means—fasting and prayer—this gift can be received and offered to carry the impulse for beauty. Powell draws on aesthetics to describe "emotionalize[d] religion," making the abstract concrete and practical.

As representative preachers of prophetic Black preaching, Reverdy Ransom, Florence Randolph and Adam Clayton Powell Sr. provide a collective voice. Their prophetic sermons offer a divine outlook within the numerous exigencies of the Great Migration. In their prophetic sermons, they carve out biblical themes, reiterating judgment and deliverance and suffering and hope, while sharing a basic conviction about the dignity and humanity of people as people of God. Part of their challenge came in the call to rebuild lives in a period of intense social crisis. These pastors needed to provide a message of hope but also to direct people to resources. That is why urban Blacks who heard Ransom, Randolph, and Powell witnessed Scripture as "an imaginative text that served the self-revelation of God and as a historical narrative that confirmed God's active presence in human affairs."[92] Against Black dehumanization in the public sphere and discord along the lines of skin color, class, and gender, these Black preachers rose up at a critical time to combat the contradictions of their social reality through the spoken Word.

The unity between their consistent call for Black humanization in a White-dominated society and that of their homiletics, striving to be fitting for the occasion, theologically faithful to Scripture, and relentlessly poetic and hopeful about God's concern, finds utterance in the message content and dialogical character of their sermons. To inquire, then, about why and where such preaching comes into existence becomes only as important as the questions when and how. Crucial to the understanding of the distinctive nature of African American prophetic preaching in northern Black congregations during the Great Migration period is the discourse-shaping historical and social environment through which it was fashioned. Heard in these sermons are echoes of the presumption that certain commonalities exist among Blacks as a consequence of both White supremacy in America and the ethos of Black subjugation it created.

Molded by their theological reflection and active response to the many social and ecclesial conditions stirred up by the Great Migration, the prophetic sermons of Ransom, Randolph, and Powell brought serious challenge to problems in the period: denied citizenship and voting rights, lynching, and economic injustice. Reverdy Ransom's sermon "The Church That Shall Survive" unambiguously insists on ecclesiastical reform within African Methodism (urging the unification of Black Methodist bodies and updating strategies for foreign and local missions) and social reform in the public sphere (securing industrial and economic justice, voting rights, and requesting federal laws against lynching).

During the migration, Black lynching horribly had reached an unprecedented record. Because of his perceptive reading of the times, the preacher Ransom—connecting his speech with prophetic actions as concrete praxis and looking forward to a hopeful future for his denomination—fittingly declares, "We should be active by forever enlarging our vision to meet the changed moral, social, and spiritual conditions of the succeeding generations in which our lot is cast."[93]

But equally poignant, Ransom's "Heralds and Prophets" laments the social conditions of the migration, which he believes has created an "atmosphere of bewilderment and frustration"[94] for African Americans. Not only does Ransom acknowledge the particular contribution of African spirituality Blacks have made to American Christianity as well as raise questions that relate to making Black schools more competitive, but also he lifts up a concrete assessment concerning the state of affairs for Black life in the interwar period. In Ransom's estimation both American democracy and American Christianity have failed their Black constituents. On the one hand, he maintains, democracy has not ensured freedom, justice, civic righteousness, and peace for its Black citizens. On the other hand, Christianity has not held democracy accountable to its promises. On this thought Ransom connects the speech-act to praxis, addressing both church and state, when he inquires: "Is our American Christianity to be voiceless for peace when faced by war, silently acquiescent when challenged by social, economic injustice and oppression and political corruption and tyranny? Or will it stand as the defense and champion of Equality, Justice, Freedom, Righteousness and Peace?"[95] The movement from indictment to hope is glaringly apparent.

This joining of theo-rhetorical discourse to Black social reality in the Great Migration toward praxis is likewise evident in Randolph's sermons "Antipathy" and "If I Were White." This first sermon, directed to the church, speaks to the specific issue of gender discrimination in Christian pulpits. Beyond racial prejudice, Randolph addresses the thorny issue of inclusion and empowerment for women to preach the gospel. To be fully appreciated, "Antipathy" must be situated and identified within its sociohistorical context. Black women clerics who achieve to some extent the same recognition as their Black male counterparts, such as Chicago's elder Lucy Smith and reverend Mary G. Evans, were rare exceptions to the norm. In Chicago, according to Wallace Best, "Smith and Evans provided new models for female urban religious leadership . . . [they were] the first women to head major churches in the city . . . [and] also among a small number of pastors that managed to build a major church edifice from the ground up."[96] Thus, what Randolph was able to develop in Summit, New Jersey, taking a tiny, fraught mission and transforming it into a robust institutional church was no small feat. Similarly, to preach a sermon like "Antipathy," expecting that her preaching would empower women to act in their present reality, assaulted directly the dominant consciousness of the age. As Randolph proclaims, "Fear not, women, because you are about a great work for I know that you seek Jesus."[97]

In "If I Were White," Randolph confronts Black patriotism in the context of a failed democracy for Blacks, unjust housing problems, poor schools, and substandard health care in her city of Summit, New Jersey. The church, Randolph claims, has a responsibility to recognize injustice and to work earnestly to correct social imbalances. Part of the problem, declares Randolph, is the lack of empathy Whites have toward the Black plight and struggle for equality. The sermon further develops the concept of injustice as antithetical to God's intention for creation.

Finally, in "Colored Man's Contribution," Powell labels the war effort as counterproductive to the social progress of Blacks and Whites. The war has made the world "a more unfit place in which to live by stirring up all the latent evil forces."[98] Before rehearsing his litany about the determination of Blacks who have suffered indignities while still moving forward "up from" the South to busy northern cities, he lays out an example of how the speech-act correlates with praxis concerns as prophetic action. Powell, alluding to recent occurrences of mob violence in major U.S. cities sparked by racial hatred, declares that violence is not the solution to the race problem. Black people are the ideal teachers of Christian love and sympathy (and these are greatest of emotions) given their difficult lot in America, said Powell. They must frame the racial reconciliation agenda in America. The solution to the race problem is not found in physical force using razors and pistols. That solution is not taught anywhere in the Bible, but "the race will be blessed and made a blessing . . . by stretching its hands to God."[99] War imagery is drawn on to correlate the speech-act with prophetic actions in Powell's sermon "The Model Church." He encourages his parishioners to be good stewards. "Stewardship," a major sermon subhead, "implies that ownership is vested in another,"[100] says Powell. Using this concept of a steward in relation to wartime as an example, he illustrates the real disparate socioeconomic condition of Blacks in this country. He laments:

> With all our boasted wealth, we learned during the last war that we do not own anything; that we are simply the stewards of our property, our money, our children; that in the last analysis, ownership is vested in the government. During the World War the government demanded not only our money, our houses, our lands, but our children. We had either to go to the front when called or go to a federal prison.[101]

The distinctive features of the prophetic sermons preached by Bishop Ransom, Reverend Powell, and Reverend Randolph show not only that the sermons of these representative Great Migration clerics constitute a radical departure from other distinctive proliferating modes of religious discourse on the scene, but also how their prophetic preaching, in concrete expression, attended to the manifold exigencies of the Black rhetorical situation. Hence, it is unsurprising to see that the prophetic messages of these gallant voices of social change were indeed rooted in and governed by the normative traditions of Black churches and the Black community. Since the rise of the independent Black churches during the revivals of the late eighteenth century, this normative Black Christian tradition, or what Peter Paris refers to as the prophetic principle of nonracism, insists on human equality under God.[102]

In light of the grave dilemmas the Great Migration produced, the essential argument of this book claims that a specific mode of prophetic preaching flowered within the African American church. Three distinguished representative preachers responded to the perplexing conditions evoked by the migration crisis. Their words offered a critique of the status quo from the perspective of God's intention for creation, and by addressing the dehumanizing political and socioeconomic conditions of their listeners, they encouraged their listeners to maintain their human dignity and empowered them to name their reality in order to transform it.

Given the eschatological outlook observed in the sermons of these Black clerics, African Americans could by no means cling to disjunctive pie-in-the-sky convictions. Their hopeful speech was at once a refusal to escape reality and absolutize the present. Their preaching literally spoke into existence a way of being in the world that concerned itself with divine intentionality and the power to transform the present. Ransom trumpeted the prophetic message, affirming his regard for the "fatherhood of God and the brotherhood of man" principle; Randolph championed women's rights and righteous living (holiness) to encourage social responsibility; and Powell attended to the work of evangelism, purifying the church and fighting for equal opportunity for Blacks in American society. In each case these preachers demonstrated unequivocally a shared concern for justice, for without justice no ecclesiastical and social reform was possible.

These preachers of the Great Migration awakened a different reality. Discovered in their prophetic sermons beyond their African Methodist Episcopal, African Methodist Episcopal Zion, and Baptist contexts, respectively, are complementary voices that taught scores of people to actively practice hope and to seek spiritual and social salvation, politically, economically, and educationally. These preachers aspired after this salvation in unique and creative ways from institutional churches, which appear to be the seedbed and outgrowth of their prophetic preaching mode of discourse.

Having demonstrated how four characteristic elements of prophetic Black preaching came to light in the early twentieth-century sermons of three representative Black ministers during the Great Migration, application of the prophetic Black preaching paradigm to sermons preached in the Civil Rights, post–Civil Rights, and postmodern eras will show how Martin Luther King Jr. and other contemporary Black preachers inherited this tradition and carried it forward.

5

EXODUS AS CIVIL RIGHTS
King and Beyond

In fact, if the trumpet makes an unclear sound, who will prepare for battle?

—1 Corinthians 14:8 (CEB)

Three hundred years of humiliation, abuse and depravation cannot be expected to find voice in a whisper. . . . Negro haves must join hands with Negro have-nots. Our society must come to respect the sanitation worker. He is as significant as the physician, for if he doesn't do his job, disease is rampant.

—Martin L. King Jr.[1]

Black prophets of the interwar period earned distinction based on their recognition of social injustice and how they brought the prophetic Word to bear on the distressing picture of Black life in North America. Reverdy Ransom, Florence Randolph, and Adam Powell Sr. were linking agents; they proclaimed messages of hope but also directed people to resources. Speaking provocatively of God's presence in concrete places where pain, oppression, and neglect reared their menacing heads, from one generation to the next, prophetic preaching in African American church contexts has been the mediating apparatus for translating the message of God's abiding love and hope for humankind.

Though a distinctive mode of prophetic preaching emerged in the Great Migration period, the power of the prophetic-preaching paradigm did not remain fixed in interwar-period America. Rather, in the voices of Black ministers who would daringly speak to African American exigencies in subsequent eras, one discovers that African American preachers addressed operationally a broader canon of issues than previously observed. The matrices of concern in subsequent eras may exhibit more complexity in terms of circumstances, but the paradigm's four constitutive marks are not only enduring in their relevance. These characteristics of prophetic Black preaching delineated in the third chapter of this book can also guide and awaken new expressions of prophetic preaching today.

Civil Rights Voices-Sermons

The clerical heirs of the Great Migration preachers are the linking agents for their times. Similar to his prophetic preaching forebears who pointed out America's political establishment's inability to provide basic citizenship rights for Blacks, Martin Luther King Jr. brought forth the prophetic interpretation of America's enduring problem of racism, which he later conjoined with the problems of militarism and poverty. Great Migration clerics were not the first and will not be the last to protest against injustice and point out America's conspicuous failure to live up to its creed of democracy. In 1963 Martin L. King Jr.'s famous "Letter from the Birmingham City Jail" reminded a group of White, "liberal" Alabama clergymen that nonviolent demonstrations did not create social tension in Alabama. Rather, the Civil Rights movement's tactics sought to expose social relations that suppressed justice. King's poetic retort to the admonition of White moderates that the movement wait for a "more convenient season" spoke beyond his Alabama audience:

> We who engage in nonviolent direct action are not the creators of tension. We merely bring to surface the hidden tension that is already alive . . . bring it out in the open where it can be seen and dealt with. Like a boil that can never be cured as long as it is covered up but must be opened with all its pus-flowing ugliness to the natural medicines of air and light,

injustice must likewise be exposed, with all of the tension its exposing creates, to the light of human conscience and the air of national opinion before it is cured.[2]

King knew that silence and passively waiting would only topple the aims of people on the move, but as a Christian minister of the gospel, he also recognized that the pursuit of justice was fundamental to the Hebrew prophet's agenda. King's own critical awareness and understanding of the prophetic Word as timely speech naming God's presence or absence in human experience becomes instructive for African American preaching in contemporary times.

MARTIN LUTHER KING JR.

I've Been to the Mountaintop, 1968[3]

On February 12, 1968, following a racial incident that involved the dismissal of twenty-two Black sewer maintenance workers from their post while their White counterparts stayed on the job, a 1,300-member cadre of mostly Black Memphis sanitation workers banded together to demand recognition as a legitimate union. They insisted on a 10 percent wage increase and workers' benefits. Following three days of failed negotiations with city officials to redress the problem, Black protesters took to the streets demanding racial and economic justice and donning signs that read "I AM A MAN" inscribed in bold black ink. Eventually, the city imposed injunctions to end the protests. Dr. Martin Luther King Jr. and his associates heard the cries of the strikers and decided to join in their struggle. Ironically, King's Southern Christian Leadership Conference (SCLC) had been drumming up support for its own next major campaign—the Poor People's Campaign. This event was to draw 3,000 of the nation's poor from all races and backgrounds to Washington, D.C., in late April in an effort to call to the nation's conscience America's poverty epidemic.

King came to Memphis on March 18 at the invitation of Congress of Racial Equality (CORE) director Rev. James Lawson, and addressed a fervent crowd of 25,000 strike supporters gathered at Mason Temple of the Church of God in Christ.[4] There, King discussed the planned demonstration that would take place in downtown Memphis, insisting on nonviolence and peace. However, three blocks into the march, hopes for a peaceful protest ended in rioting and looting. Supposedly initiated by a group of militant Black youth called the Invaders, the botched march rendered King more vulnerable to critical backlash from skeptics who believed his nonviolent, passive resistance strategy had run its course. King knew he would have to return to Memphis to conduct a successful march if the Poor People's Campaign to the nation's capital was to be tenable. They changed the date to April 8, 1968, for what was to be called the March on Memphis.

An exhausted King and his comrades arrived in Memphis on April 3, 1968. They checked into room 206 at the Lorraine Motel. Eager to march again, more than 2,000 strike sympathizers streamed into Mason Temple. The weather was rainy, but the people were undaunted and anxious to hear from King regarding their next steps. King had not intended to address the crowd that night. More than anything, he desired rest. So he commissioned Reverend Ralph Abernathy to stand in for him. But the gatherers wanted to hear King. Compelled by their expectation, King succumbed to their wishes. Once there, King followed his escort to the pulpit. Then as Abernathy's protracted introduction concluded, King mounted the speaker's desk to deliver his final sermon, "I've Been to the Mountaintop."

King's final sermon is hauntingly similar to the picture of Moses descending Mount Horeb with the Decalogue in hand. Like Moses, King, not yet forty years old, is divinely retained to mete out the hard facts of sacred revelation and moral instruction to a road-weary band of American wilderness travelers in search of their American Promised Land. Casting out vivid globetrotting imagery in prosodic Black Baptist fashion, King first urges his captive listeners to join him on a mental flight through the ages.

> If I were standing at the beginning of time . . . and the Almighty said to me, "Martin Luther King, which age would you like to live in?" I would take my mental flight by Egypt . . . and I would watch God's children in their magnificent trek from the dark dungeons of Egypt through, or rather across the Red Sea, through the wilderness on toward the Promised Land. And, in spite of its magnificence, I wouldn't stop there.[5]

King marshals epistrophe with the steady refrain "I wouldn't stop there" in the sermon's opening lines to clarify his intent to move forward unimpeded. Creatively expanding the trope, King contextualizes the present moment for his listeners, traversing the ages from the Greco-Roman era to the second half of the twentieth century. Then the sermon shifts.

King's melodic refrain comes to a sobering punctuation when he announces the late 1960s as the uppermost limit of his request to live. This prescient remark would come to pass as King was felled the next day by an assassin's bullet.

If one considers the optics of King lying at the feet of his disciples in a pool of blood on the hotel balcony, the moving scene brings to mind the ill-fated termination of Moses' trek to Canaan at Mount Nebo's summit, Pisgah, Canaan's edge. The familiar picture of King's stunned footmen pointing in the direction where the fatal gunshot rang out also recalls the biblical story of the Hebrew spies sent to reconnoiter Canaan's fertile land with its presumably hostile inhabitants.[6]

With King's repeated line "I wouldn't stop there" from "I've Been to the Mountaintop" now firmly fixed in the listener's consciousness, he sums up his sermon in two sentences: "The nation is sick. We want to be free." In dialectical fashion, antithesis and thesis are worked into a true synthesis as the skilled and oftentimes-castigated pulpit master rehearsed the epic struggle of Blacks in America for the charged assembly.

Next, in an obvious attempt to hearten the hopes of his listeners, King indicts the establishment men—the modern-day pharaohs Bull Connor, George Wallace, and Memphis' Democratic mayor Henry Loeb—as hard-nosed perpetrators of crimes against humanity. Although King was confident that their struggle would end in victory, he knew that there were detractors among the listeners who wondered if the movement was heading in the right direction. Not long before King's sermon, as his biographers note, he had harbored deep psychic pain and depression, particularly after expressing his vocal opposition to and pacifist stance on the Vietnam War. Many feared King had stepped out of his lane. Fearing an onslaught of endless demands, the prevailing sentiment of White segregationists went as follows: Short racial victories, "we will concede." Antimilitarism. "Preacher, you are meddling and treading on thin ice." And now, standing in yet another southern city, upsetting the carefully drawn racially gerrymandered maps, declaring that the haves of American capitalism must share their bounty with the poor, the establishment's message for him was clear: "Nigger, you've crossed the line and must be stopped." King's earlier burning bush revelation, which came in prayer at his kitchen table years prior, had reached its Gethsemane moment.

At the sermon's second quarter mark, King, the poet, now tactical strategist, asserts, "Now what does this all mean in this great period of history?" The plan he put forward was threefold: maintain unity by sticking together; stay focused and keep the issue of injustice at the forefront; and finally, anchor external direct action with the power of economic withdrawal. This crucial prescription in the face of the modern-day giants of White supremacy and racial segregation made evident that the people's success would not roll in on the wheels of inevitability, as King so often expressed. Opposite liberal theology's misplaced optimism, King's Niebuhrianism enabled him to see Christian hope and collective social misery evenly. Biographer David Levering Lewis noted that King's hope was not an embrace of false optimism; his was "a progressive view of society and sanguine view of human nature."[7] Thrown against this biblical backdrop of the Exodus saga, King knew that the tactics of engagement were different, and yet he believed the rallying cry of the oppressed Israelite and the American Negro to be virtually identical: "We want to be free. . . . We mean business now and we are determined to gain our rightful place in God's world . . . and we are determined to be men . . . people." This passionate cry of divine intentionality and hope epitomizes the essence of prophetic preaching.

King insists that his hearers fix in their minds that they are God's children and, because of this, according to God's law, social and economic deprivation, poverty, racism, and other social ills that create and foster unjust suffering are morally and ethically wrong. Taking no notes to the pulpit, King delivered the sermon entirely unscripted. The first two-thirds of King's message is his replay of the milestones that have propelled the movement to this defining moment. The sermon's prophetic markings are conspicuous. King first recognizes the positive efforts of Black ministers leading the charge. Resisting the temptation toward self-deceit and falling victim to the trappings of the cult of personality, King asserts, "I want to commend the preachers [present tonight] . . . because so often, preachers aren't concerned about anything but themselves. And, I'm always happy to see a relevant ministry." Undoubtedly his compliment was an indirect indictment on clergy who were unwilling to practice their religion outside of the church sanctuary. Rather, by contrast, as King implies, one's prophetic witness signifies more than criticism of the body politic; prophetic ministry is as much a criticism of pastors who only talk about "long white robes over yonder" and "the new Jerusalem" while disregarding the poor who "want some suits and dresses and shoes to wear down here."

King's critical stance against Memphis' dictatorial mayor is couched in adorned repartee that hearkens back to past hard-fought victories. Amplifying the cumulative effect of using prudence to resist forces of evil and injustice with deliberate speech, King refuses to absolutize the present situation, but helps his audience to see the larger scope of their reality. He wants strikers and their sympathizers to see that their future success would not be secured based on enthusiasm for the cause; rather, their success, declares King, is contingent upon honoring careful planning while working on God's clock:

> I remember in Birmingham . . . when we were in that majestic struggle . . . by the hundreds we would move out, and Bull Connor would tell them to send the dogs forth, and they did come; but we just went before the dogs singing, "Ain't gonna let nobody turn me around." Bull Connor next would say, "Turn the fire hose on." And, as I said to you the other night, Bull Connor didn't know history. He knew a kind of physics that somehow didn't relate to the transphysics that we know about. And that was the fact that there was a certain kind of fire no water could put out.[8]

In captivating metaphor the water of which King spoke pointed to the fact that Black people's identity and capacity to endure suffering had all to do with their intimate connection to a God who saves the oppressed without human means.

King's sermon, at each turn, addresses human suffering and pairs that suffering and despair with the refusal to relinquish hope in the democratic experiment. God is aware of our Black misery, maintains King. He says, "We mean business now, and we are determined to gain our rightful place in God's world"; a public demonstration of nonviolent protest will "force everybody to see that there are thirteen thousand of God's children suffering, wondering how this thing is going to come out . . . sometimes going hungry . . . and, we've got to say to the nation: we know how it's coming out." God is actively at work. "Something is happening in Memphis; something is happening in our world."

Shuttling down with dramatic pause, King connects the speech-act with concrete praxis, affirming his conscious regard for and continuing commitment to peaceful demonstration. King attaches promise to fulfillment, collapsing the biblical narrative into modern-day parlance, and urges the crowd to believe their victory could be achieved without resorting to violence: "We don't have to argue with anybody. We don't have to curse and go around acting bad with our words. We don't need any bricks and bottles. We don't need Molotov cocktails. We just need to go around these stores, and to these massive industries in our country."

Finally, as King draws the sermon to its climax, he advises his listeners to envision a Promised Land that would not be denied them. He names his reality and also their stake in knowing what it means to come to terms with death. Similar to Moses' view of Canaan's fertile fields from Mount Nebo's lookout point, King would also get a glimpse of a radically changed America, though materially it would elude him. Brought to the precipice of a new day, King confidently voices: "I may not get there with you. But I want you to know tonight that we, as a people, will get to the promised land!" With these words, King's imprint as prophet of the movement became eternally fixed.

SANDY FREDERICK RAY

Journeying through a Jungle, 1979[9]

The Reverend Dr. Sandy F. Ray was born in 1898 in Stranger, Texas, a rural farming community in Falls County. Prompted by a series of crop failures, the young Ray and his family relocated to Palestine, Texas, and then to Ft. Worth, where he finished high school. He soon became active in Mt. Zion Baptist Church, where he was licensed to preach at twenty-five and apprenticed to Rev. Dr. M. K. Curry Sr. Though initially encouraged to attend Arkansas Baptist College in Little Rock, Ray caught the attention of Rev. Dr. W. L. Dixon at a district Sunday School convention, for which he spent all of his funds to attend. After informing Dixon of his desire to prepare formally for the ministry, Dixon urged Ray to enroll at Morehouse College in Atlanta, and there Dixon paid his expenses for his freshman year and the beginning of his sophomore year. Before his graduation from Morehouse, Ray began pastoring at First Baptist Church in LaGrange, Georgia ,for a brief period. Three other pastorates followed: First Baptist Church in Macon, Georgia; St. Luke Baptist Church in Chicago; and Shiloh Baptist Church in Columbus, Ohio (while working on a doctorate at Arkansas Baptist College).[10] Ray was called to his final pastorate, Cornerstone Baptist

Church in Brooklyn, New York, in 1944, where he would serve for thirty-five years.

Sandy Ray was a role model for Martin L. King Jr., and King affectionately called him "Uncle Sandy." Rising above their impoverished upbringing, "Daddy King" and Ray became best friends and classmates at Morehouse College in the 1920s. In fact, after Martin L. King Jr.'s 1958 stabbing by a deranged woman at a book signing in New York, King spent three weeks recuperating in the Ray family's parsonage. King frequently visited Cornerstone when he traveled to New York, and in 1966 King delivered "Guidelines for a Constructive Church," one of his most famous published sermons, from the Cornerstone pulpit at the dedication service of its new community center. Before going to New York, Ray served as the first Black representative elected to the Ohio state legislature. In addition, serving as a member of SCLC's steering committee, Ray also raised funds to support King's organization.[11]

Ray's sermon was published the year of his death as *Journeying through a Jungle*. Its subject matter and content suggest it was delivered before a gathering of ministers. Based on Matthew 3, Ray's narrative sermon focuses on John and his wilderness preparation for ministry. Moving in and out of first person, Ray begins his sermon hypothetically imagining the embarrassment John's strange appearance, behavior, and captive call to the wilderness must have appeared to his family since John's father, after all, was a highly regarded priest in their community. As most gifted storytellers, Ray's descriptive adornments paint a vivid picture of Matthew's record.

> His father was established in the community. He, no doubt, expected that his son would succeed him in the priesthood, but John had no interest in the formalities of the priesthood. He probably rebelled at being an altar boy. His father may have felt he was losing his son. His father and mother may have agonized that their son had this weird behavior. He was caught up in some far-out expectation of a coming Messiah. Their hopes, plans, and prayers could not restrain their son. He was a captive of a call to the wilderness.[12]

Ray uses this move to establish for the listener a clear understanding of what it means to answer God's call. God calls preachers into peculiar places. More than the wilderness, the context of John's preaching, Ray suggests, was a moral and spiritual jungle. In John's life-world, he declares, "There was exploitation and oppression of the poor from the Roman Empire . . . corruption and hypocrisy in the church leadership . . . dire poverty and misery among the masses of poor . . . [and] bold, brazen sin in the land in all its ugly forms."[13] Then Ray quickly segues to his sermonic proposition, which is almost entirely rendered metaphorically:

> I submit that we are journeying through a jungle at this period of our history. Through our various skills and technology, we have penetrated the physical jungles of this nation . . . We have fairly successfully mastered the forest and jungles of the land . . . but morally and spiritually we are journeying through a jungle.[14]

But this declaration is too obvious, he contends. The jungle is now the front office, where certain evils are allowed anonymity. Directing his criticism toward the economic engines of Wall Street, the prostitution industry, and the drug culture of the urban metropolis, he avers: "The jungle is often financed by millions of dollars and protected by bribery. Pimps and prostitutes walk our streets brazenly, daringly, and defiantly without shame or fear. Narcotics has become . . . a death-peddling industry."[15] "The captains who control the jungle," he continues, "oppress the poor, underprivileged, underpaid, exploited, ghettoized, and untrained."[16] Reminiscent of Ransom's opposition to the policy racket and Powell's attack on the prostitution industry in New York's tenderloin district, Ray points out that in the urban areas, problems are not alleviated with technological advancement. Rather, as technology advances, social ills reinforce human suffering and worsen communities. For this reason, Ray is convinced that ministers must redouble their efforts to teach and evangelize the culture and not succumb to self-deceit:

> Jungles have instructive and disciplinary value . . . The curriculum of the jungle is an essential part of ministerial training. Moses, Elijah, and Jesus had the discipline of the desert . . . They found oases of hope and faith in the desert.[17]

Adding scriptural reinforcements, Ray draws into his creative storytelling other disciplined prophetic figures who took residence in backcountries where God had sent them. With this imagery he compels this gathering of

ministers to stand proverbially in "John's shoes," to realize the value of soli-
tude and to recognize that the wilderness is preparatory for fulfilling one's
ministry charge in places beyond it. He asserts, "You must not accept the
wilderness as your permanent home. You must have a sustained discontent
with the jungle."[18]

Hope's antithesis is clearly outlined as Ray pinpoints the social crises of
his times. But Ray's refusal to relinquish hope in the jungle is what defines
the sermon's theological thrust. The reality that Ray moves his listener
toward daringly speaks of an ever-present God who delivered the children
of Israel from their wilderness and required their obedient action en route
to the Promised Land. Similar to King's "Mountaintop" sermon, the Exodus motif is central here as well. Though there's no alternate route to the
Promised Land but to travel through the jungle, Ray claims:

> We have seen happy souls emerge from the jungle. When Israel panicked
> at the Red Sea, the multitude turned on Moses, criticizing him for leading
> them into what they thought was a death trap. The record says that Moses
> prayed to God for orders in the crisis. God advised him to "stand still"
> and watch God act. God sent a strong wind that divided the water and
> allowed them to walk through on dry land.[19]

As it was for Moses, Elijah, and Jesus, the "curriculum of the jungle"
(a notable beauty mark), says Ray, is not only instructive but is essential for
ministry. These persons, Ray adds, "found oases of hope and faith in [their]
deserts." Finally, there is the Christocentric turn:

> Our Lord entered this jungle on a redemptive mission. The animals of
> jealousy, envy, hatred, and arrogance made their attacks on him . . . the
> pressures were so great that he talked to his father about another way
> out of this terrifying jungle (notice the subtle flashback to John and his
> father's strange relationship). In this sermon, the cross and the resurrec-
> tion testify to the triumph of his pilgrimage through the jungle.[20]

Doctrinally speaking, in the end, *Journeying through a Jungle*, is a prophetic message that invites ministers to examine the nature of their call and
grapple with the twin realities of divine providence and divine deliverance.

BENJAMIN ELIJAH MAYS

Why Dives Went to Hell, 1980[21]

Dr. Benjamin E. Mays served as president of Morehouse College from 1940 to 1967, following a six-year term as dean of the Howard University School of Religion (later renamed Howard University School of Divinity). With his long tenure as president of Morehouse, Mays' legacy of mentoring numerous African American scholars and religious leaders from Howard Thurman to Martin L. King Jr. to Robert Michael Franklin is unparalleled.

Benjamin Mays was a Christian intellectual "race man" with a broad global and ecumenical vision for justice. Beyond his title "school master," at bottom, like King, Mays was a Black Baptist preacher" concerned about the fate and faith of the Christian church. In his 1954 address at the conference in New England on the "The Life of the Church," Mays sought to detail the common core essentials of Christianity as practiced by Roman Catholics, Eastern Orthodox, and various enclaves of Protestantism. According to Mays, five fundamental beliefs epitomize the core of Christian faith. The first belief is that humanity's origin is in God as parent of all—a universal God for all people, every nation and clan. Correspondingly, God sustains and judges the world and, thus, the world is to be essentially moral and ethical.[22]

Second, the conviction exists to say that Jesus Christ is the clearest revelation of what God is like and what God is; or simply put, Jesus is both God and Savior. The modern church's ministry, Mays maintains, may embrace all that science has to offer to nurture and improve the minds and living conditions of humans, but "no amount of science can make a man good."[23]

Third, the church is a creation of God and not the creation of humans, which means that the strength of the church is in Jesus Christ and though kingdoms of the world rise and fall, the church will never collapse or fail.[24]

His fourth conviction articulates that each human being is unique and of supreme worth and value to God, not in humanity's own right but through divine conferral.

Finally, fifth, all share the belief that the eternal destiny of humankind is in the hands of the Creator God. Though Christians share different views about the nature of life beyond death, Christians, contends Mays, believe that God sustains human life in the present and beyond death.[25]

From these core essentials, Mays concludes that it does make a difference what the church believes. He maintains, "We are what we do and what we believe. No one can live fully with a system of beliefs and convictions and no man can face the stern realities of life with confidence, poise and hope without an abiding faith of some kind."[26] The church is the institution that says that every person needs God and needs to be reborn. Whether preached in university chapels, to Black congregations in the metro Atlanta area, at national interreligious gatherings, or occasioned by death of some prominent figure, the sermons in Mays' homiletic corpus rest squarely on these five basic ecclesiological convictions.[27]

The central issue of "Why Dives Went to Hell" is economic justice, specifically the exploitation of the poor and marginalized. The sermon takes a problem-resolution course beginning with the task of demythologizing the meaning of hell. He says, "Hell is not where the fire burns and is seven times hotter than the fire we know." While this may evince fear in some individuals, Mays is not convinced that this is an apt deterrent for ending hostility among nations, racial hatred, or unethical activities of political officeholders. Impatient with the self-deceptive idolatry of racial chauvinism, he aesthetically adorns his critical remarks. Hell is also "no deterent [sic] to Blacks hating Whitey while they kill Blackey."[28] But not only this, for many, "Heaven is no motivation for goodness, justice and mercy. Christian nations are just as brutal and cruel as communist nations who deny the existence of God."[29] Having lived through the Cold War, beginning in the late 1940s and continuing through the 1980s and early 1990s (around the time he preaches this second composition of the "Dives" sermon), and operating from that historical construct, Mays names this reality in more explicit, definite terms. He continues, "In war, the United States, a Christian nation, is just as brutal and deceptive as Russia, a Communist nation."[30]

In Mays' first turn to the text, he explains that the rich man of Luke 16, often referred to as "Dives," a Latin adjective meaning "rich," is a carry-over from the fourteenth century. He operates from the straightforward claim of the text, which declares that Dives is hell-bound and Lazarus is heaven-bound. After this, he explains that his hermeneutical insights will spring from focusing on Dives' end: "I shall deal more specifically with Dives going to Hell than with Lazarus going [to] heaven."[31] Mays correctly sees that the text makes no mention that Dives was a bad man or that he "exploited the poor, that he was immoral, a drunkard, gambler, or an extortioner [sic].

It is conceivable that Dives was a decent, respected and respectable man in his community."[32] Characteristic of the prophetic mode and consistent with his own ecclesiological ethic regarding the supreme worth and value of every person, he reminds his listeners that there is no virtue in being poor: "Lazarus is not in Heaven because he was poor."[33] Following this comes a personal acknowledgment of his economically privileged status, a factual reality that is counterbalanced intertextually with another of Jesus' parables: the talents (Matt 25:14-30 and Luke 19:11-27). His proof-texting to make a case for wealth accrual as a Jesus-endorsed expression of good stewardship is clear and biblically defensible if one pairs these two parables. But in this sermon, perhaps regrettably so, Mays offers no critique of capitalism or capitalistic motivations. He says, "Some of the finest people I know are rich . . . Jesus himself complimented and rewarded the men who used their talents and condemned the man who hid his."[34]

Finally, he attempts an answer to the sermon's titular question, "Why then is Dives in Hell?" As parables lend themselves to teach one truth on the one hand or obscure it on the other, in this parable of Jesus, Mays stakes his claim on the former, giving no deference to other ways of reading this parable.[35] According to Mays, "Dives landed in Hell because he had no social conscience."[36] Mays' concrete naming and adorning urge captures most visibly the meaning in his explanation:

> Here is a man whom God had blessed. He fared sumptuously every day, dressed in purple and fine linen. In modern parlance, he had it made . . . he had houses and land, stocks and bonds, money galore in the bank. Let us say his house was in suburbia . . . away from the so-called common people . . . he had economic security, prestige [sic] and position and he was listed in the social register.[37]

Following this move, he then creatively adorns his message in vivid word pictures. He describes the scene in this way: "At the other extreme of the economic ladder sat Lazarus, a man whom life had licked [note the play on words] and beaten, sick, clinging to life, poor, and full of sores."[38] Finally, the sermon closes on a hopeful yet serious appeal to the consciences of his economically privileged hearers. He cautions, "Bear in mind, Dives could have been me. He could have been you. So let us be kind to Dives."[39]

SAMUEL DEWITT PROCTOR

The Bottom Line, 1984[40]

Religious historian Adam Bond characterizes Norfolk, Virginia, native and famed preacher Samuel D. Proctor as a "race man" true to his generation who "embraced the social consciousness of the black theological leaders of his day and held fast to the 'liberation theology' of his black social gospel rearing."[41] Bond carefully notes, however, that Proctor was not a liberation theologian of the manner of Black theology forefathers James H. Cone or J. Deotis Roberts. As Proctor saw it, says Bond, to attach race to theology as a lasting corrective to the theological parochialism of classical White theology could never be more than a "transient fix."[42] Nor could Proctor, adds Bond, be situated within the conservative wing of Black Evangelicalism alongside National Baptist ministers such as E. V. Hill, whose "Christ of faith, Just Jesus" theology would have left him theologically suspicious and intellectual wanting at best.[43] Proctor was a politically astute, civic-minded clergyman and mentor of Jesse Jackson. However, in terms of method, Jackson's political evangelism/rainbow theology and Black messianic understanding of the African American experience in many ways stood in contradiction to Proctor's Black Social "American" Gospel commitments. Bond surmises that while each of these expressions of Black public faith found common ground in the vocation of protesting White supremacist practices, Proctor is best understood as a bridge between these Black theological traditions. Essentially, "[Proctor's] understanding of the Christian gospel was a type of pragmatic middle ground of black public faith."[44]

Like Howard Thurman, J. Pius Barbour, Martin L. King Jr., and a few select other first- and second-wave Black intellectuals admitted to northern White institutions beginning in the mid-1920s, Proctor was exposed to theological liberalism, Personalism philosophy, and historical-critical approaches to the Bible espoused by his teachers at Crozer Seminary and Boston University School of Theology (where he earned a doctorate in theology). Proctor admired White liberal preachers such as New York Riverside Church's pastor Harry Emerson Fosdick, who had cross-cultural appeal. As Lewis Baldwin notes in his book *There Is a Balm in Gilead*, several misguided interpretations exist regarding White liberal preachers' influences on King's preaching, and the same care must be taken for such claims regarding White clerical effects for other Black preachers. Bond points out that although Proctor used some of the features of Fosdick's preaching method, it would be a rush to judgment to make a case that Proctor desired to imitate Fosdick or "borrow" his material for his own homiletic program.[45] Proctor's intellectual exposures, wedded to his rearing in a class-conscious, Black, middle-class Christian family, helped Proctor forge a unique Black Social Gospel tradition of public faith that affirmed the universality of human experience, appealed to the life and ethical teachings of a universal Christ, challenged notions of White superiority and Black inferiority, and unapologetically focused on social reform and ministry to society's "least of these."

Proctor's sermon "The Bottom Line," based on Matthew 25:31-46, synthesizes these principal strands in response to the sermon's focus on the basic requirements of Christian life. Looking retrospectively at Jesus' earthly ministry and reasoning dialectically, Proctor begins his lengthy sermon with an exposition of the passage, retelling, in brief, what led Jesus to give the parable of the sheep and the goats. With the crucifixion not far, says Proctor, Jesus' teaching on the subject of sheep and goats expresses Jesus' desire of a verdict from those who profess Christ. Announcing God's judgment on Christians who have performed actions in Jesus' name while failing to meet the basic requirements of Christian faith, Proctor chides:

> It is embarrassing to see how straightforward Jesus was in setting out the basic requirements of God for his people and how confusing and complicated we have made it. We have seen Europe soaked in blood over religious wars . . . burning scholars at the stake, beheading so-called heretics, imprisoning Bible translators . . . And yet Jesus, in simple clarity, gave us the bottom line: "I was an hungred and ye gave me meat; I was thirsty, and ye gave me drink . . . I was in prison, and ye came . . . That's the very bottom line."[46]

After stating the sermon's antithesis, Proctor continues to build his argument, discussing the deplorable realities that come with being marginalized and treated as social outcasts. He illustrates this by mentioning the "untouchables" crisis in India. In concrete language he further emphasizes his disgust with the mayor of New York's disregard of the homeless and criticizes Ronald Reagan's social policies that have overburdened churches with problems both the church and national programs should together address.

Chock-full of suspenseful and protracted personal illustrations, Proctor, known for his gift of storytelling, narrates an account about a "country orphan"—a student whom he had met while he served as a college president. The young man's money had run out, and he was in desperate need for someone to drive him fifty miles into the country to retrieve his personal items. Proctor recalls the temptation to brush off the young man and charge someone else to address the young man's situation. Proctor, soon after, reports in the sermon that he borrowed the school's pickup truck and took the student to gather his belongings. This changed my entire perspective on the gospel, he declares, regarding what it means to help the less fortunate. Adorning his story with color and culturally conditioned imagery, Proctor describes his encounter:

> The student and I had headed out for the country to get a country orphan's leavings. And the trip went fast because we sang and talked about the life of a country orphan all the way. That old truck seemed like the upper room where the Spirit descended or the temple where Isaiah saw the Lord. It was benchmarked for me, and brief moments like that have been spread over my years, and they have blessed me.[47]

And then turning to the text, he carefully inserts a refrain that biblically and theologically grounds the sermon and propounds the sermon's major claim: "Lord, when saw we thee a stranger, or naked, or hungry . . . 'In as much as you did it to the least of these my brethren, ye did it unto me.' The bottom line."[48] Proctor's interpretation of the gospel's justice agenda through an intertextual insert of the Last Supper motif followed by the prophet Isaiah's vision of God in the temple makes the spiritual connection. These images connect the speech-act with praxis by communicating the sacred significance of acts of kindness and mercy as godly requirements:

> One wonders what was said around the Lord's table when the decision was made to do such a thing, even in the 1950s. How did this action relate to the Christ whose praises the church members sang with zest? Of course, many Christians have a strange view of their religion; they think that it only prepares them for death and heaven and that concern for the hungry, the hurt, the dispossessed, the alienated is some kind of liberalism or social gospel. By giving it such a label, they think they have gotten rid of the concern. But it was no "liberal" or "social gospel" propagandist who said, "Inasmuch as you did it not unto the least, ye did it not to me . . . go away into everlasting punishment."[49]

In summary, Proctor demonstrates the pragmatic side of prophetic proc-lamation by offering a final word of criticism chastened by hope. "Good reli-gion," preaches Proctor, "meets life right where it is and deals with it. And I fear that the Christian faith will have to get closer to the real issues of life before it can become relevant to these times."[50]

Post-Civil Rights Sermons[51]

KATIE GENEVA CANNON

Prophets for a New Day, 1998[52]

Womanist scholar Dr. Katie Cannon teaches theological ethics at Union Presbyterian Seminary of Richmond. Cannon advocates for the inclusion of African American women's voices in theology and ethics fields as a nec-essary corrective to theological conversations that privilege the voices of White European Americans, both male and female, and African American male theologians. The first African American woman ordained in ministry by the Presbyterian Church (U.S.A.), Cannon's distinct theological perspec-tive not only names injustices perpetrated against women but also does so while wrestling with the question, "How does the Christian commu-nity move closer to genuine community?" where representatives from all groups have a place at the table. Cannon draws on Black women literary figures such as Zora Neale Hurston and other seldom-considered persons of color as theological sources. While Cannon focuses on the intersection of race, gender, and class concerns as it relates to creating theological space for Black women, it would be wrong to restrict her religious and scholarly views to this intersection.

The sermon featured here, for example, makes no explicit reference to what might be considered a particular matter of womanist theological concern per se. Here, Cannon simply calls for any and all prophetic voices to rise up obediently in pursuit of God's will for the lives of people and pro-phetically to address matters of educational disparity that negatively stunt the professional development of young persons of color. The sermon is based on 1 Kings 13:29-30 (NIV), a text that details the mordant duel between an unnamed prophet of Judah who prophesied doom and destruction against idol worshippers, and King Jeroboam, the empire-protecting, shrine-builder who, according to Scripture, practiced evil in high places. Marshaling metaphor, Cannon begins with a question, "Who are the Jeroboams in our national public arenas burning incense at the altar who are causing the people to fall into apostasy, to bow down and worship idol gods?" Taking poetic license, she admonishes her listeners to cut the bait from leaders who look for openings to lobby and lure their victims into deceitful acts that dishonor God and perpetuate human suffering.

> Sisters and brothers, just like the prophet from Judah, we have a tendency to yield, time and time again, to temptation whenever we are baited by persons who purport to be just like us. We hear things like "Why, we were born under the same zodiac sign." "We have the same alma mater." "We do the same kind of work." "Our children were born in the same hospital." And the biggest bait of all: "We are all Christians, and we serve the same God." The problem with being pulled hook, line, and sinker by this so-called sameness is that far too often we end up easing the true and living God out of our lives.

After this sermonic set up, Cannon's sermon unfolds in a predetermined traditional three-point pattern that moves from problem to hopeful resolution.[53] She asks, "How do we become prophets for a new day?" and she recommends three things: (1) we commit ourselves to spiritual introspection; (2) we remain obedient to God's will; and, (3) in our prophetic assignments, we give praise to a sovereign God.

Cannon begins by calling her listeners to self-critical examination. "First, we need to take a spiritual inventory. Each of us needs to get away from the hustle and bustle of daily life and discover exactly what it is that God is calling us to do."[54] The second thing that must take place in order for one to become a prophet relevant for today's challenges is simply to obey the will of God. Accordingly, "obedience for us may mean engaging in strategic action and reflection about the social crisis around us involving our children and teenagers." Forging a connection between prophetic speech and concrete prescription, she also highlights the crisis of educational preparation for disadvantaged Black and Brown youth who languish in low-performing public schools that are under-resourced and poorly administered. Then, moving beyond the confines of the biblical text in unambiguous prose, Cannon removes the rose-tinted glasses of her captive crowd by iterating the optics of neglect and recites lines extracted from Jonathan Kozol's book *Savage Inequalities: Children in America's Schools.*

> There are public schools (primarily populated by African American and Hispanic children) where teachers are forced to set up classes in coatrooms. Some classes are held in storage bins and bathrooms . . . Obedience in the face of this gross systemic neglect and abuse may mean making the conscious connections between children in public schools and those youth and adults in the church and community who are added to the illiterate population at the rate of 2.3 million every year.[55]

The third and final thing required in order to become prophets for a new day is to give praise and honor to almighty God in a hope-filled manner.

_____

OTIS MOSS JR.

A Prophetic Witness in an Anti-Prophetic Age, 2004[56]

Otis Moss Jr.'s commitment to the work of social justice and prophetic criticism is well documented. A Civil Rights/post–Civil Rights era leader and former senior pastor of Olivet Institutional Baptist Church in Cleveland, Ohio (a congregation built on the institutional church model discussed in the second chapter), Moss holds the distinction of having served alongside Martin Luther King Sr. as copastor at Ebenezer Baptist Church and with Dr. Martin L. King Jr. in the Southern Christian Leadership Conference (SCLC). Addressing a predominantly African American group of conferees at the 2004 Samuel DeWitt Proctor Conference, Moss' sermon "A Prophetic Witness in an Anti-Prophetic Age" speaks to the decline of prophetic preaching in an age of conspicuous consumption, materialism, and milquetoast preaching. Drawing comparison between postsermon responses to contemporary preaching and those Jesus received following his trial sermon in Nazareth, Moss details the nature and high costs of preaching prophetically:

> There is no danger in the sermons we preach, no challenge, and no threat to anybody in particular . . . But Jesus almost got killed on his first sermon—perhaps, his first public sermon. And let me say, we ought to remember that the community, the world does not like prophets, and

neither does the church. The world does not like prophets. Prophets override our creeds and our half-truths. Prophets expose our injustice and our contradictions and put to shame our mediocrity. The world does not like prophets and the church often refuses to celebrate them.[57]

For Moss, no one embodied the spirit of Jesus' prophetic vision more than Dr. Martin Luther King Jr. The sermon is eulogistic in tone. Moss gives firsthand accounting of the price King paid for speaking out on the Vietnam War. He recollects the staunch opposition King faced from African Americans in his hometown of Atlanta, King's ousting from the National Baptist Convention during the movement and the attempts of leaders of the newly formed Progressive National Baptist Convention to silence him from speaking out against the Vietnam War. In this respect, King's prophetic witness harmonized with Isaiah's prophecy, which casts him as a twentieth-century type of Christ or messianic figure in America's freedom struggle.

Moss surmises that, more than anything, the adversary that ministers must confront is personal fear. Ideally, if one's ministry has been guided by Jesus' inaugural vision, one would see that prophetic ministry is fourpronged. Moss maintains that to be prophetic in an antiprophetic age requires that preachers have a firm grasp of the theological, economical, educational, and sociological elements of interpreting the gospel with an eye toward justice and an antioppression commitment. A captivating poet, he declares that if he had time to unpack his message over the course of the week, he would spell out the particulars of Jesus' vision in turn:

> Now, if I was going to be here for a week, I would deal with this whole text; but time is running out. If you go down—"The Spirit of the Lord is upon me . . . God has anointed me"—that has to be theological. "To proclaim good news to the poor"—I believe that's economics. "God told me to get release to the captives"—that must be political. To "recover the sight of the blind"—that's educational and sociological. "To let the oppressed go free"—that's liberation theology. And then, "to proclaim the year of Jubilee; to proclaim the acceptable year of the Lord"—that's theological.[58]

Speaking in the indicative in the breakdown that immediately follows the aforementioned segment, Moss employs poetic devices to establish the sermon's melodic rhythm and to transport his hearers beyond the church sanctuary into the public realm where crucial life decisions are formed and made:

So, at the top of the text is theology. And in between is economics, politics, and sociology. In between it's all of the social public policy. And then at the bottom it's theology. At the top—theology—and all the rest in between. So, if you are preaching a gospel that has nothing about politics, nothing about economics, nothing about sociology, it's empty gospel with a cap and some shoes and no body to it. It might be popular, but it's not powerful. It might be expedient, but it's not saving.[59]

For Moss, a necessary condition for authenticating the gospel comes in the recognition that prophetic preaching carries a political mandate. Devoid of the preacher's holistic interpretation of the gospel as an emancipatory tool that speaks truth to power, what is proclaimed is inconsequential. Capturing imaginatively the gravity and serious nature of the prophetic proclamation, Moss chides preachers who spout what "itching ears want to hear" and empty the gospel's ethical and moral demands. The impression left with his hearers not only declares that preaching matters, but also that to preach prophetic hope in the service of God and God's church requires that preachers begin to reclaim their prophetic voice—one so easily muted and compromised in our times.

MARVIN A. MCMICKLE

How Much of Leviticus Do You Really Want? 2012[60]

In his early ministry, Reverend Dr. Marvin McMickle served as a ministry intern at the Abyssinian Baptist Church in Harlem under the tutelage of Samuel Proctor. From there he pastored churches in Montclair, New Jersey and, more recently, the Antioch Baptist Church in Cleveland, Ohio. In addition to his pastoral profile, McMickle has served as professor of preaching at Ashland Seminary in Ohio. In 2011, following his twenty-year pastorate in Cleveland, McMickle became the second African American president of Colgate-Rochester Crozer Divinity School (CRCD) in Rochester, New York. CRCD is a school formed from the merger of two theological institutions: one, the oldest Baptist seminary in America, where its most famous faculty member, Walter Rauschenbusch, launched the Social Gospel Movement in the late nineteenth century, and the other, the alma mater of prominent Black preachers King and Proctor.

Beyond establishing a job training program, hunger center, and credit union while serving at Antioch, McMickle led his congregation in instituting a first-of-its-kind ministry for people infected with or affected by HIV/AIDS. In "How Much of Leviticus Do You Really Want?" delivered before a group of veteran and aspirant Black clergy and predominantly African American college students, McMickle fielded questions relating to human sexuality in general and homosexuality specifically, touchy if not delicate topics for African American pastors and their congregations. In this lecture sermon, Marvin McMickle simply asks ministers to refrain from "cherry picking" biblical texts and, as biblical exegetes, be more sober and self-critical. This means that preachers of the gospel should think more deeply about controversial issues and wrestle with the whole counsel of Scripture before applying it and speaking on God's behalf.

In the excerpted clip from the transcript, McMickle speaks to the predicament of human suffering:

> Lives are being ruined. We don't discuss that here. Infections are being transferred. We don't discuss that here. Maybe the reason we don't discuss HIV is because we are afraid to discuss sex. Or maybe it's because our very strange use of exegetical practices has limited the particular sexual act we will discuss and leave all the rest out. If I hear one more preacher tell me about Leviticus 18:22, by itself, I will just scream. I know what Leviticus 18:22 says. "It is an abomination to lie with a man as with a woman." Yeah, I know all about Leviticus 18:22. The question is: If you are going to take Leviticus 18:22, are you going to take the rest of Leviticus? How much of Leviticus do you really want? Some people just take out the text that confirms what they already prejudicially believe, and leave out what is personally uncomfortable. You can't just take one verse from Leviticus. You've got to take all or none.[61]

McMickle's lengthy diatribe produces two noteworthy matters. First, he is clearly aware that he is in the buckle of America's Bible Belt, Nashville, Tennessee, where the theological dividing lines on the issue are much more defined than in the northern United States. He engages his listeners skillfully and moves from fervent, direct address about reinvigorating concern about HIV and then shifts to speculative argumentation, pointing out the contradictions and ironies of how ministers use certain texts to marginalize others. Second, by raising the question using suppositional language, he prompts his listeners to engage the topic intellectually and come to some resolute commitment to abandon faulty exegetical practices: "If you're going to take Leviticus 18:22, are you going to take the rest of Leviticus?" This is not a rhetorical question. McMickle seeks the listeners' unquestioned conversion regarding this. Intent on unsettling his listeners, later in the sermon, he further propounds the issue as he marches toward a more careful historical reading of the Levitical holiness codes. To better contextualize the sermon and drive home his point, he points to Leviticus 11 before shifting the listeners' focus back to Leviticus 18.

> Leviticus 11 says, "Thou shalt not eat rabbit, pork, shrimp." If you are going to follow Leviticus, you can't eat meat that's got blood in it . . . If you are going to follow Leviticus 18, you cannot have sex with your wife during or seven days after her menstrual cycle . . . that's in Leviticus.[62]

Following this move, McMickle further develops the message. Not only does he explain that it is out of bounds to engage in irresponsible proof-texting and seize on one issue while disregarding important others, but also he seeks to tie the matter of human sexuality to another emancipatory concern. He pivots to Leviticus 25 where the matter of debt forgiveness is central. McMickle explains that when Jubilee is observed, "All debts are forgiven. All prisoners shall be released."[63] By interpreting the gospel in regard to multiple justice concerns, his theological expansion aligns well with Martin Luther King's claim, "Injustice anywhere is a threat to justice everywhere."

Near the closing, McMickle connects the speech-act with concrete practice, illustrating the personal story of his former church secretary who contracted HIV/AIDS at no fault of her own. McMickle's storytelling candor is a rhetorical mark of beauty. In this sense he knows well that certain sermon delivery style adjustments must take into consideration the cultural vernacular of the listener. Even if viewed indecorous in other contexts, speech candor is often the best way to arrest and sustain the attention of a lively, "talk back," African American audience. Note his use of synecdoche, for example, where the leper in Luke 5 represents all socially ostracized HIV victims, and also his creative use of repartee to challenge pastors to exercise greater empathy for those who suffer.

> What did Vivian Smith do? My church secretary. Vivian Smith. What did she do to get HIV/AIDS, to be HIV positive? She married a man who

either was unfaithful to her or had been infected before they got married. Either way, she was guilty of the sin of monogamy! She got HIV in her marital bed. And when she announced that she was HIV positive you would have thought she was like the leper in Luke chapter 5. Had to walk through life saying about himself . . . unclean. Not guilty. Unclean. Don't touch her. Unclean. What did she do? She laid down with her husband and she woke up with AIDS. She gave birth to two sons. Because she was HIV positive, they were HIV positive. What did they do?[64]

Finally, standing in opposition to clergy malaise and ecclesial practices that further injure HIV sufferers and their families, McMickle continues the story about Vivian Smith, offering the ministerial gathering a direct appeal injected with measured humor:

I know preachers. I hope there are none here who will not do funeral services for someone who has died of the disease because they cannot get pass the issue of how they contracted it. Did you get this disease in some immoral sexual act? No. Did you get this disease because you were sharing an IV needle? No. Well, how did you get it? I laid down with my husband! Papa was a rolling stone, and wherever it was he laid his hat he brought this home with him.

To summarize, in this sermon McMickle calls for empathy from his hearers—to be merciful and mindful of those who suffer from diseases, especially ones who suffer at no fault of their own.

———

CHERYL J. SANDERS

What Does God Require of Us? 2014[65]

Harvard Divinity School alumna Dr. Cheryl Sanders is professor of Christian ethics at the Howard University School of Divinity and senior pastor of Third Street Church of God in Washington, D.C. Her distinguished bivocational ministerial career has earned her numerous citations and has afforded her opportunities to lecture and preach the gospel in congregational and academic contexts locally and nationally.

In her sermon "What Does God Require of Us?" delivered on the weekend of Dr. Martin Luther King Jr.'s eighty-fifth birthday, Sanders calls her congregation to a renewed commitment to justice. Elaborating on the words of Micah 6:6-8, *"With what shall I come before the Lord . . . ? He has told you, O mortal, what is good; and what does the Lord require of you but to do justice, and love kindness, and to walk humbly with your God?"* she lays out the particulars of divine summoning. The prophet beckons the nation of Israel to repent of their apostasy, to remember their heritage as defenders of justice and mercy, and to live self-introspectively.

Sanders does not complicate her message. In sync with the tripartite structure of the scripture verse, her sermon focuses the listener's attention on a nonnegotiable triadic mandate, which should characterize the moral and ethical life of the Christian. The critical imperative of the divine request is "doing justice by undoing injustice"; lovingkindness or mercy "by refusing to turn a deaf ear and a blind eye to the lament of suffering people"; and walking with God in prayer and contemplative reflection. As she summarizes, "Incorporated into these three moral mandates are social ethics, compassionate ministry, and personal piety." Theological parochial shortsightedness, she contends, upends "the implementation of . . . [the] integrity ethics of justice, compassion and piety."

According to Sanders, the abandoning of Micah's prophecy and Martin L. King's modern embodiment of Micah's prescription is part of the reason faith communities have devolved into irrelevance and seldom progress beyond their own religious interests and restrictive views.

Congregations today remain in their denominational camps and protect their theological turf. While the church suffers, society's most vulnerable citizens are left without their spiritual and basic physical needs met. She diagnoses the problem:

> For some reason, throughout the history of Christianity as far as I can tell, people have chosen to emphasize one of these three mandates as characteristic of their tradition while excluding or ignoring the others. Some liberal traditions emphasize social justice in their liturgies, policies and resolutions, with or without corresponding social action. Some conservative traditions practice compassionate ministries—feeding the hungry, doing mission projects in poor communities—while consciously or unconsciously exempting themselves from directly addressing the political policies and economic practices that sustain poverty and privilege. Yet another group of Christians historically identify strongly with personal piety, getting saved, refraining from sinful practices, going to heaven . . . as if their entire world of ethical accountability is contained within their

chosen sanctuary or prayer closet—as is the position of some of *us* in the holiness camp.[66]

Pairing her reading of Micah 6 with Matthew 23:23, Sanders continues, "Jesus warns against exclusive notions of ethical practice and concern when He chastises the religious intelligentsia of His time [when He says]: *Woe to you, scribes and Pharisees, hypocrites! For you tithe mint, dill, and cumin, and have neglected the weightier matters of the law: justice and mercy and faith. It is these you ought to have practiced without neglecting the others.*" Asking her listeners to name their reality, Sanders concludes in an anaphoric refrain, leaving a charge with her twenty-first-century communicants:

> So what shall we do? What does God require of us Christians 50 years after the Civil Rights Movement and 45 years after King was felled by the assassin's bullet? Yes, we should continue with our liturgies and litanies and resolutions. Yes, we should reach out to the poor at home and abroad with acts of charity and gifts of compassion. Yes, we should nurture spiritual disciplines of prayer and fasting and Bible study. The challenge we face, however, is to do all of the above with the understanding that to do one in exclusion of the others is to fall short of God's requirement.[67]

With the multivalent challenges facing African Americans, a few courageous Black clerics of interwar-period America did become the architects of hope for later generations. Connecting authoritative prophetic speech to a focus on correcting social and ecclesial imbalances in the greater society, preachers in the Civil Rights and post–Civil Rights eras also sought to inspire the homiletic imaginations of their hearers. What is evident in their prophetic sermons is a turning to the performances of their forebears as a homiletic and spiritual resource, but also clearly apparent in these more contemporary sermons are forward-looking glances at a world picture of genuine and hopeful community not saddled by nostalgia and undue deference to past players. The true mark of their homiletic innovations centers on their ability to call persons in their times to form "coalitions of conscience," to use Dr. Otis Moss Jr.'s words, in order to confront the horrific experiences faced during the freedom marches and sit-ins in the 1950s and 1960s and also to challenge the troubling picture of hypercapitalism that would explode on the scene in the late 1980s and 1990s. Their methods of genius involved their ability to give their auditors a spiritual and linguistic capacity to confront despair and redefine the portrait of their reality.

CONCLUSION

Petitionary Truth Telling
The Moral Challenge for America

If prophetic preaching is to be restored to a vibrant place in the pulpits of America, it will be necessary for preachers to operate with a twenty-first century understanding of the message they are being called upon to declare. It is still our task to call people back from the worship of Baal and other idols, but we will need to attach twenty-first century identities to those false gods.

—Marvin A. McMickle[1]

Somebody ought to take a stand. I'm about to make a commitment to a cause greater than myself.

—Frederick D. Haynes III[2]

The Continuing Relevance of the Prophetic Black Preaching Paradigm

For years the prophetic Word has been decisive speech in America's Black pulpits in crisis times, amid a range of congregational and secular community expectations. But today, the once typically asset-rich Black pulpit is in deep crisis because it has become confused about its mission to the African American community. More than a few Black preachers, even some of the most revered, have confused the biblical prophet's message of divine intentionality with both pious God-talk and their own preoccupations with preaching the gospel of health and wealth on the one hand and their embrace of impious living in blatant disregard for holiness and righteousness on the other. Prophetic preaching is diametrically opposed to the prosperity message; its agenda shuns manipulation tactics and names self-serving, self-deceiving ideological practices sin.

A myriad of issues having negative impact on Black life in America have contributed to the blunting of the African American church's prophetic message. But the prosperity movement seems to be the ideological root cause of many of the distorted views about health and material success, which have long been a preoccupation of historically disenfranchised Black people. The prosperity gospel often veils itself as priestly in nature; it speaks concern about spiritual renewal and faith formation, but its message empties the cross of its meaning.

Prosperity preachers use the language of "prophecy" to motivate people to support materialistic agendas that little serve the faithful. According to the prosperity message, the "blessed life" is the divine right of every Christian, the believer's reward for her or his unshakable faith and positive thinking. Although the mortgage crisis in the United States affected virtually all American citizens, it dealt a particularly crushing blow to Black communities, where the rate of foreclosure, credit card debt, unscrupulous payday lending practices, violent crime, and underemployment have become too difficult to ignore. By promoting the worldview that gave us this economic crisis, prosperity theologians are partly to blame. Whether luring congregants to spacious amphitheater or storefront start-ups, messages centered on obtaining wealth based on one's positive confession and faith have had great appeal to Blacks of every class, especially given the rapid proliferation of Black megachurches in the last three decades.[3]

The prophetic Word delivered as an expression of the Black communal rhetorical tradition is an absurd declaration about justice overcoming forces of injustice. To communities in crisis, it is a Word of life in the place of death—a daring dispatch of hope in the predicament of human suffering. African American prophetic preaching proclaims a speaking God who helps preachers and congregations to negotiate faithful possibilities for struggling against concrete forms of oppression, naming in concrete terms the places and processes that call for deeper commitment and higher participation for the flourishing of human community.

Exemplary African American preaching can be found, but too much of what passes for good preaching in Black Christianity today is not only contemptible but also veils a deeper anemia, a more chronic malady—*vocational quietism*. Vocational quietism takes a narrow view of obligation toward finding ways—in the emerging postmodern ethos—to honor biblical faith, community concern, and the holistic character of human existence. This condition involves, but is not limited to, preachers ritually organizing conferences, church effectiveness seminars, and church growth campaigns at exorbitant costs to attendees with only slight regard for the community's psychosocially dead and spiritually wounded citizens. Vocational quietism vigorously upends justice and mars human personhood whenever God is brought in to baptize plans God has never endorsed. The prophetic Word, to the contrary, is contextually conscious, divinely directed speech, naming concretely God at work in the world. The prophetic sermon is always a summoned word. Therefore, prophetic proclamation begins with an inquiry after God. The genesis and terminus of proclamation rests in God. Preaching as proclamation illustrates theologically authorized speech (rhetoric) having concern about what is fitting to its receptor's context.[4] Consequently, the preacher must have a prophetic Word that not only takes a critical stance against the social ills of the community but also offers rebuke to the false religion of the church.[5]

Facing the Hour: The Loss of Centers and Anchor Institutions

Dramatic changes to patterns of family structure, loss of civic and social centers, educational inequality, expansion of the prison industry, shifts in the broader economy, and high rates of joblessness and underemployment among African Americans are leading, interrelated factors contributing to the distressing realities that plague African American communities today. Harvard sociologist William Julius Wilson argued nearly two decades ago that when work prospects for inner-city Blacks cease to exist in the absence of strong revisions to current public policy, family and community deterioration and unrest are inevitable unless both the public and private sectors address the social inequities in American society. If the problem of shrinking revenue and inadequate social services for Black urbanites is left unresolved, the poor will remain persistently poor and the social and economic hemorrhaging of communities will not be abated.[6] Just as mass production jobs infused hope in the psychological imaginations of Black southern migrants who made their way to industry hubs like Detroit and Chicago during the early twentieth century, disillusionment and disappointment have met their descendants with crippling force as decent paying jobs have left the inner city. This American portrait exposes an ever-increasing divide between the "haves and the have-nots."

Exploiting the metaphoric adage of the African proverb, "It takes a village to raise a child," Robert Michael Franklin argues that the place to begin the social transformation and needed restoration of hope is with the "anchor" or "mediating" institutions of the village—Black families, Black churches, and Black colleges.[7] Little has changed since the publication of Tavis Smiley's edited volume *The Covenant with Black America* (2006), where he reports a range of distressing statistics of exigent issues within African American communities in the United States, from HIV infections to mass incarceration.[8] But statistics provide a glimpse at only a few important concerns that militate against the health of African American villages. As Richard Lischer rightly suggests, "The multiple traumas of the twentieth and now the twenty-first centuries have produced a sense of futility among those with a vocation in language . . . making a mockery of [the preacher's] words."[9]

But who will speak legitimately on behalf of the village's weak and most vulnerable citizens if not the leaders within Black churches? Who will fight for social and policy reform and the reconstruction of human community? What will be the communal strategy to halt the rapidly expanding prison industry, that which Michelle Alexander calls America's new "racial caste system"?[10] So what then is the answer? What must be the contemporary Black preacher's rejoinder on the community's behalf? The answer lies in bringing these issues to a local and national level of consciousness where they can be dealt with. As Martin Luther King Jr. once advised those fighting for freedom and justice during the Civil Rights era, all must name these crisis issues as finite disappointment even as all adhere to infinite hope. King once preached that the answer to the blighting of hope is to confront one's shattered dreams and to ask oneself, "How may I transform this liability into an asset . . . transform this dungeon of shame into a haven of redemptive suffering?"[11]

Because of infinite hope, King could attest in the grueling era of seg-regation that "almost anything that happens to us may be woven into the purposes of God." According to King, for Blacks to suffer in a righteous cause, two important ends are accomplished: they achieve their humani-ty's full stature—that is, guarding themselves against bitterness so that their vision transcends present ordeals—and they seize the opportunity to trans-figure themselves and American society.[12] Adherence to infinite hope is not the bitter acceptance of fatalism nor is it palliative hope, which renders individuals passive and incapable to speak out for change. Adherence to infinite hope clings to realistic hope and speaks truth to power, which is the only viable upshot to community flourishing. But adherence to hope is not enough. Prophetically conscious discourse must extend beyond naming the crises in the village; it must also reframe the naming process itself. Refram-ing the conversation pushes individuals to be self-critical and confront their biases. Differences must be seen and appreciated because the pursuit of colorblindness dehumanizes—repressing the full expression of minoritized voices—and promotes false perceptions about the other.

Inherent in prophetic preaching resides a creative and constructive agenda. Communicatively, prophetic speech consists in tactical inversion. Counterintuitive approaches start with declarations about what is right in our society. As a present-future–oriented discourse, prophetic preaching doles out criticism but eschews the spirit of incessant carping and replays of the full range of Black distress data that promotes compassion fatigue; for, in the final analysis, its disruptive mandate points to a merciful, promise-bearing, divine interventionist at work in the world. African American pro-phetic preaching carries an impulse for beauty in its use of language and culture to the end of making unseen hope seen.

In our culture of fear, contemporary Black preachers are commissioned to the work of their Great Migration predecessors to name God and voice God's enduring concern about human suffering and despair and not to overlook what God has done in the person of Jesus Christ, who personi-fied prophetic fulfillment. In the same way that the biblical prophet had to have great concern about the integrity of the spoken Word, African Ameri-can preachers would do well to gain critical knowledge about the prophet's social world and bold task to interpret God's instruction in human speech. For this reason prophetic sermons must resist the political moralizing temptation. Instead, they must sound of thorough engagement with the Word of scripture and, with an eye and ear to the culture, discern biblical intentionality. Only then can African American preaching become the kind of proclamation that Brueggemann contends emerges from contexts where exists a long available memory of pain and suffering and people actively practicing hope.[13]

From the Reconstruction period to the present, a call has gone out for prophetic preaching in African American churches and communities. The call persists because there continue to be rhetorical situations that need and invite it, and because the majority of African Americans still remain victims of America's broken promise of justice, African American prophetic preaching in the last analysis is speech about humanization. Those committed to the work of transforming the world order through proclamation of the gospel of Jesus Christ understand that the pursuit of authentic freedom and justice is to, in the words of Paulo Freire, recognize the seemingly inescapable problems of dehumanization and believe that concern for the process of humanization leads to a solution not only as an ontological possibility but also as a historical reality.[14] This means that prophetic preaching is a costly enterprise because, fundamentally, it is about telling the truth. Though preachers who take seriously the work of the prophet often inhabit a lonely position, happy are they who have found the all-sufficiency of Christ at work in them while laboring prophetically. For those who dare to preach lovingly and radically discover the sanctuary of God and usher others into it.

APPENDIX A

Chapter 4 Sermons

REVERDY CASSIUS RANSOM

Message: *"Heralds and Prophets of a Changed Order and a New Day"*

Scripture: John 1:23

Date: n.d., but mostly likely written in the early 1920s.

Context: Sermon originally published in *A.M.E. Church Review.* Reproduced by permission of Ransom biographer Annetta Gomez-Jefferson.

"The voice of one crying in the wilderness, make straight the way of the Lord."

—John 1:23

An atmosphere of bewilderment and frustration hangs over Americans of African descent. It pervades their political, economic, social, educational and even their religious life. Their greatest need is not wealth, legislation, schools and churches. There is no deliverance in these things unless the spirit and the voice of the herald and prophet lie within them.

The Jewish race has survived for more than three thousand years, not through military force and power of its arms, not through commerce and wealth, not by superior science and learning, or even by the boundary lines of a national domain. The strength of the Jews has always lain in the message and spirit of their prophets and heralds. Moses stood before Pharaoh and delivered a race of slaves out of the mire of the brickyards of Egypt. Elijah came out of the Gilead forests to point his people back to the paths of their high destiny; Isaiah brought them golden visions and dreams to kindle their aspirations and keep alive their hopes. When aspiration faded and hope had well nigh fled, then John, of the Jordan valley and the wilderness came proclaiming the approach of a changing order and the advent of a new day. Across the centuries, nations and peoples have been delivered and set forward on the paths of survival and progress by the deep convictions of the free spirits who have pointed to paths of freedom and power beyond the reach of fire and sword, or lure of gold.

The strength and vitality of a message resides in its carrying power. The ether waves are still vibrant with the voice of Abraham across the distance of thirty centuries; St. Paul is still vocal from his broadcasting stations, in Philippi, Athens and Rome; Savonarola [sic] rises from his incinerated dust in the streets of Florence to condemn the lynchers of freedom and the dupes of tyranny; Martin Luther and Richard Allen still blaze the path for religious liberty and the freedom of the mind; the cry and call of Daniel A. Payne for an educated ministry, ring louder today than they did when his race made their first stand outside the prison house of slavery. But what shall we say of Garrison and Sumner, Emerson and Beecher, Phillips and Frederick Douglass and all these prophets and saints combined, then, that the world has advanced no faster and no farther than men in like manner have freed their own spirits to become servants and prophets of the day and age? Where the beacon is burning, there the eyes of the watchers turn.

In this place today, are looking bewildered youths, strongly [ ], faintly hoping for the cry [ ] ringing voice that will point to [ ] for adventurous action.

Our people, with a sense of frustration bordering upon discouragement, if not despair, have listened and are listening now, for a voice proclaiming how and where they can find a door of escape. We have our education, politics and wealth, the churches, emphasizing chiefly [ ] and freedom in a world after [ ]. We do not want to live and leave our children to struggle there in the generations to come. We want some of our paradise now. Each one of us holds the solution within his own [ ]. We confess our inadequacy and hopelessness while the deliverance we seek lies within our own minds and spirits.

We have surrendered the dignity and freedom of our own minds and spirits to economic pressure, to political and social barriers, and to religious forms whose withered leaves neither inspire nor perish.

I am here to declare redemption, salvation and deliverance, to come of old. We must pass through our own Gethsemane and bear our own cross. We must cast off the yoke and break the chains which for centuries have made us but mere [ ] and echoes of the white man in social, political, economic and religious affairs. We should take the world that lies behind the barriers to which our race has been confined and make it an empire of triumphant freedom and power.

The Negro Spirituals are the only wings which here the human spirit has forged; they are the only child to which the human soul has given birth on American soil. They will go on living when Bunker Hill has become a plain and Washington's Monument has crumbled into dust. They are the visions and dreams, ideals, aspirations and desires; they are intuitions of the soul clothed with that poetic insight which gives the spirit power to rise above its prison house and enter into the enjoyment of things to come as though they were present realities. It is intuition, communion with one's own soul, obedience to our higher instincts, which creates for us a world that cannot be conquered by the sword and lies beyond the price and power of gold.

How with our present attitude in matters of education can we produce masters of the spirit to blaze for us the path of social and intellectual freedom? Our youth schooled in the white colleges and universities of the north are transformed by having their rich racial inheritance conformed to the cold rigid angles of the white man's outlook and vision.

In thought, culture and ideals they are cast in his mould and feel themselves educated only in the degree to which they conform to his intellectual image and his social and spiritual outlines. The schools financed for Negroes by white people are of the same spirit. But behold the Negro college! It rates its standing and wields its influence in proportion as it is an echo, or copy of the intellectual outlook, social and ethical ideals, and academic goal of the white college.

I am voicing no tirade against that body of classified knowledge which is the intellectual inheritance of the world enlarged and enriched from one generation to another, and to which all countries and races have contributed. I simply proclaim the freedom of our own souls from slavish devotion and bondage to the spirit and ideals of another race or people.

Why should an opinion or idea carry more weight with us because a white man voiced it? I reject it or enlarge it, as I perceive its defects or narrowness. But on the other hand, if the voice of truth comes from Mount Sinai or the Acropolis, from Galilee or Mecca, or from the heart of Africa or Asia, I will follow it to the ends of the earth. The book of nature is open to everyone who has eyes to read its message in the various languages it speaks. Music should strike its sweetest chords through me, true to the individual note I sing. Shall I crave the wings of Dante, Milton, or Shakespeare, when my own spirit may forge wings to ascend the heights of vision and sing in meters of its own, the inspirations of my soul? The future deductions of philosophy, and discoveries of science await the hours when black men shall join the honorable company of Plato, Galileo, Bacon and Edison. Phidias and Michel Angelo [sic], Rubens and Rembrandt shall hail our creations of brush and chisel when, true to our own artistic instincts, we paint and carve new forms of beauty, love and awe to be the praise and rapture of future generations.

But it is in the realm of religion that our own people wait, on the verge of perishing, for heralds and prophets to appear with a bold authoritative message. Our African inheritance has richly endowed us with a deep-rooted emotional nature, and a religious instinct which makes us one of the most spiritually minded people in the world. Here in America for three hundred years, we have adopted every form of religious doctrine and policy that the country offered, save Mormonism, and only avoided this because its Ecclesiastical doors, fortunately, have been closed securely and locked against our admission to its fold.

In our spiritual quest for expression, we have tried to bind the sunlight and chain the wind to the cold and cheerless forms of Calvinism. We have caged the lark from the skies and staked the soaring eagle to the earth in the spiritual straightjacket of Puritanism, and the bloodless rationalizing of Unitarianism. Since the Methodists and Baptists offered the most congenial atmosphere for spiritual expression and religious enthusiasm, we have flowed into these churches in largest numbers. But since these are becoming cold and formal, we are turning increasingly to the "Holiness Church," to the Apostolic Church of God, and similar organizations that bind less weight to our spiritual and emotional wings.

In the matter of religion our fathers fared better than we. They grafted on to such faiths as they found here, old tribal dances and customs that gave an outlet for freer expression of the emotions awakened by religion. They furnished their household of faith with the most available material they could find to supply their spiritual needs.

But for us a new age has dawned, a new generation is upon the field of action. You had just as well attempt to bind the stars as to chain the youth of today to the religious forms and modes of spiritual expression and social diversion that belonged to the days of their fathers' fathers.

I do not blame the Negro youth of today for turning away from what most of the churches offer in the name of religion. The ashes of the dead past, the dry husks of doctrines and creeds, the empty sermons have no bearing upon the political, social, economic and moral problems of today, certainly possess no attraction for its tens of thousands of our youths who graduate annually from our various schools and colleges.

To have vitality, dignity and power, a people, like an individual, must be self-formed and not crushed into the mould of another mind or spirit. And here is where the spiritual call comes to the Negro youth of today. The pulpit of the Negro church offers them a stronger throne and the widest range of influence, service and power that can be commanded by any other field of endeavor. It also offers higher honors and greater rewards, for it will be coming to the rescue of a people who are the last hope for the social and spiritual salvation of our decadent and tottering American democracy.

They can give us a gospel that flames with light upon the problems of today that articulates our aspirations, instincts and institutions. They can wield the whip of cords and drive out the moneychangers from the temple of our faith. They can shatter the vengeful and ruthless gods who, under the cloak of divinity, invade our freedom and impede our progress. They can take up the challenge of the political, economic and social Goliaths who confront us and with the weapons of an invincible spirit armed with truth, go forth to meet them in open combat.

They will discard outgrown customs. The Class Leader will be chosen, not for his fluency in speech and song, to act in the capacity of official goodness and piety, but because of his intelligent comprehension and capacity for leadership in social and economic affairs, as well as things of the spirit. Then people will throng the classroom, not to give testimony about their hopes and prospects, but to confer together concerning relief of suffering poverty and distress, to talk of their social and economic problems, to find fellowship in the appreciation of music, art, beauty, and the joy of service.

They will requisite all the musical talent of the community, of singing voices, wind instruments, and instruments of strings, together with piano and organ and let them express the rhythm, poetry, emotions, and aspirations that sigh and sob, and moan and weep, and dance and shout through this glorious medium of expression the very heart and spirit of our race.

The great foundation stones upon which our nation is based are Democracy and Christianity. Is our American Democracy to become an instrument of corruption and oppression, or a fortress of freedom, and justice, of civic righteousness and peace? Is our American Christianity to be voiceless for peace when faced by war, silently acquiescent when challenged by social, economic injustice and oppression and political corruption and tyranny? Or will it stand as the defense and champion of Equality, Justice, Freedom, Righteousness and Peace?

Whom shall we send? Who will go? Who will lift up his voice and cry aloud? Is the spirit of the race still bound in fetters? Is its soul imprisoned in a dungeon of [ ] and despair? Arouse [ ] receive in your souls and bring [ ] children who shall bear the [ ] Truth, be filled with the [ ] able spirit of freedom, and [ ]ing conquered their own souls be forever invincible. Springing from the loins of the mind a [ ] of the race, we must produce men and women who will be the embodiment, the ambassadors [ ] heralds and prophets of the [ ] of Brotherhood, Justice, Righteousness and Peace.

Against France under N[ ] Toussaint L'Overture threw off the yoke of oppression and won the freedom of Haiti. But that freedom and independence have been largely because there was no succession of prophets to nourish and guide the spirit of the Haitian people. Frederick Douglass did more than the abolitionists, statesmen, writers and [ ] to make the world believe the Negro was fit for freedom. Upon the mire of the slave-pen, he [ ] as the living refutation of lie [ ] the irrefutable evidence of the [ ] and latent power of his race [ ] there have been civic and political retrogression since his day, it is because we have failed to nourish and keep alive that spirit willing to [ ] under protest, but never cringe, [ ] promise, or surrender in the face of any social or political opposition. Within the Church Richard Allen [ ] a protest against injustice, proclaiming the banner of liberty and equality at the altars of religion. Men were not to surrender their common humanity and manhood, or dishonor God, by accepting a secondary or inferior place in any religious fold bearing the name of Christ. It was not a question of money, of personal ambition, or of peace at any price, but one of freedom, of equality, the dignity of man and the honor of God. Is this body willing to dedicate itself to this heritage of ecclesiastical freedom, support it, defend it, and vindicate it before the world?

Intelligent and self-respecting Negroes cannot accept the precepts of our American democracy and respect its constitution and honor its flag, if they must be subjected to social degradation, industrial oppression, legal injustice and be politically outlawed and oppressed. Yet survive they must, both politically and economically. Who, but our prophets and redeemers shall teach them that not through the doors of Socialism or Communism lie their escape, but that the key to deliverance and the scepter of power, lie in the strength of their own minds and spirits. When they honor their own personality and believe in themselves with all the exalted fervor with which a saint believes in his God, sacrifice, suffering, martyrdom and loss shall be a willing tribute to pay to the final triumphs of a people whose spirit is victorious against every weapon that may be formed against it.

[entire line] ing youth cannot be led to follow Christ as he is openly portrayed in the spirit and practice of religious denominations. Who cares to invite the cold look of rejection, or segregation that waits in the aisles and altars of his church? Who would meekly countenance the looks of contempt and scorn he wears in refusing to yield the enjoyment of the ordinary conveniences and necessities of travel? These silent partners of lynchers and of mobs, these plunderers and oppressors of the weak and poor, these Herods who seek out the Negro youth to slay his ideals and aspirations, on the threshold of the most inviting opportunities. Who would clasp the cruel hands or follow the brutal feet that daily lead us to some new Gethsemane of suffering and pain? Who wants to follow a Christ that stands for American Christianity? Or what black person cares to strive for a heaven if they must associate with such people forever more?

Not upon the banks of the Galilean lake or in the wilderness of the valley of Jordan, but in the streets of Chicago, Atlanta and New York we wait for men to expose and vanish hypocrisy and lies. Men who shall restore for us confidence in God and faith in Jesus Christ. Today in the streets, Christ is fainting under the weight of his cross as he goes to his Calvary to be crucified afresh. Who will take up the cross and be crucified with Christ—revealed [missing line] . . . the divine life made manifest, going in and out before us? If Christianity is not true, it is the most stupendous delusion ever imposed upon human credulity. You may preach it with eloquence and learning, or set it to music, or dress it up in fine churches and lofty cathedrals, but if the fire of divine love does not burn within it, faith dies on the threshold of the hollow mockery.

While the white man's world is busy making war, or preparing for war, immersed in commerce, finance and trade, intent upon science and invention, and carrying exploitation and oppression to the ends of the Earth, the spirit of a heavy hearted world yearns for the appearance of the prophet of the reign of God in the life of men. But no herald can communicate that, which he has not received. He must bear valid credentials from the Most High God with the seal of Christ upon them. This commission is given in the depths of his own soul where the inner life of his spirit holds intercourse with the Divine. May sons of thunder, men of the spirit, sons of God, through this race of ours, visit this earth again pointing its weary feet to paths of peace, and setting its heart in tune to Brotherhood and love through Jesus Christ.

Whose voice shall raise the Cry? Whose hand shall strike the blow? Whose feet shall take the thorny path out of our spiritual and social wilderness? The bondage of our spirits is more galling than the tyrants' chain. We stand at the conflux of despair and hope where destiny bids us choose— Christ or Chaos.

> If Jesus Christ were a man,
> And only a man, I say,
> That of all mankind, I would cleave
> To Him
> And to Him I would cleave always.
> If Jesus Christ were a god,
> And only a god, I declare
> I would follow Him through heaven and
> Hell,
> The Earth, the Sea and the Air.

ADAM CLAYTON POWELL SR.

Message: *"The Colored Man's Contribution to Christianity and When It Will Be Made"*

Scripture: Psalm 68:31

Date: 1919

Context: Abyssinian Baptist Church and delivered in other settings

Ethiopia shall soon stretch out her hands unto God.

—Psalm 68:31 (KJV)

The word soon in this prediction is a stone of stumbling to many Bible readers. Some of them unhesitatingly say that the prophecy is discredited and annulled because it was uttered three thousand years ago. At that time it was proclaimed that Ethiopia would soon reach out after God, and these puzzled readers argue that, since thirty centuries have elapsed without witnessing any united movement of the colored people of the earth toward God, the prophecy has become obsolete or, in the language of the lawyer, has expired by the statute of limitation. These readers forget that our puny methods of reckoning time are vastly different from God's calendar. It is believed by some of the best biblical and scientific students that the seven days mentioned in Genesis represent at least seven thousand years. This opinion is in harmony with the teachings of both the Old and New Testaments which declare that a thousand years with the Lord are but as yesterday. In God's eye-view, then, it was only three days ago when it was said, "Ethiopia shall soon stretch out her *hands* unto God."

An extended hand signifies at least two things. First, a desire for a better acquaintance and more cordial relationship. When an honest man extends to you his hand he expresses a wish for a closer contact, a better understanding and more intimate fellowship. Now, it is prophesied by the Psalmist that "Ethiopia shall soon stretch out her *hands* unto God." This she will do, in the first place, as a manifestation of her desire to know God better and to be on closer terms of intimacy with Him. It is not without tremendous significance that the plural is used instead of the singular, for, mark you, the prophecy reads that Ethiopia is to stretch forth her *hands*, not her hand. The fulfillment of nearly all God's promises depends upon human conditions. God is ready to bless Ethiopia and to make Ethiopia a channel of blessing to others when she stretches both hands to Him. A man or a race cannot expect to be used of God as long as one hand reaches after Him and the other after things which are out of harmony with His plans and purposes. After years of travel, observation and study, I cannot escape the conclusion that God has an important mission for the colored people of the world to perform. I am forced to this conclusion first, because of their numerical strength. For every one white person on this planet there are at least three colored persons. Abraham Lincoln used to say that God must love the colored people because He made so many of them. God not only made them to love them but to serve some great purpose in this world.

Secondly, I am encouraged in the belief that colored people will yet make a valuable contribution to religion by the fact that all the white races which have come in contact with the religion of our one Lord have made contributions to it. The Jews made two contributions to religion before passing it on to the Gentiles. We are indebted to the Jews for the idea of the oneness of the Godhead. The prophets of this sturdy race were the first to preach monotheism. All other races, including the mighty Romans, worshiped gods innumerable. The Greeks, despite their superior intelligence, created a god for every condition, and fearing they had not met all conditions they erected a monument TO THE UNKNOWN GOD. The non-Christian nations like India, China, Japan and Africa, have gods by the tens of thousands. Missionaries returning from Africa bring back their trunks full of gods—little gods, big gods, all kinds of gods. We are not burdened and cursed today by a multiplicity of gods because the old Hebrew people, from whom we inherited our religion, stood up three thousand five hundred years ago and declared that "the Lord our God is one Lord and we will have no other gods before Him; we will not bow down to them nor serve them."

The Jews also taught us that a nation as well as an individual may serve God. This was not only expressed in the dictum of their outstanding prophet "Righteousness exalteth a nation but sin is a reproach to any people," but it was exemplified by their national life. Old Thomas Carlyle says, "David's life was a succession of falls," which is equal to saying it was a succession of get ups. This may be applied with equal truth to the life of the nation. For centuries, the pendulum of Hebrew national life swung between righteousness and sin. When they served God as a nation oceans fled before their presence, rivers rolled back, the wheels in the timepiece of creation stood still, and no power in the universe could resist their onward march. When they wandered away from God, they were treated more scurvily than the dogs that ate the crumbs from the tables of heathen tyrants. While there is not a Christian nation on earth today, the fact remains that the Jews have taught us that a nation can be and should be Christian in all of its political, diplomatic, social and economic relations.

The Jews nationalized religion.

Rome was noted for its genius of organization. The morning the angels sang at Bethlehem the civilized world was under the organized power of Rome. When Christianity reached Rome a few years later, the old Romans, true to their disposition to organize everything with which they came in contact, proceeded to form a worldwide Christian organization. The Roman Catholic Church is the oldest, most powerful and perfect organization in the civilized world of today. All organized governments are weak compared to it and no other ecclesiastical organization can approach it in perfection. It is the only organization in Christendom that can say to its members, "Come," and they will come; "Go," and they will go. The Pope sits in the Vatican on the Tiber and issues orders which are obeyed with mathematical exactness not only by the humblest priest in the farthest nook of the earth, but by bishops and cardinals. The unpardonable sin in the Catholic Church is for a member to disobey his priest.

The Romans organized religion.

The Greeks were the most intellectual people that have yet appeared on the globe. They tried to furnish an ultimate, rational explanation for all things and they came very nearly succeeding. Their philosophy is still studied in our schools and in many respects it seems to be the last word in scientific thinking. Our philosophy of religion as taught in the theological seminaries today came from the Greeks. Their system of thinking has taught us that it is a reasonable thing to trust God and to present our bodies to Him as a living sacrifice.

The Greeks philosophized religion.

It remained for the Anglo-Saxon to individualize religion. When the Pilgrim Fathers landed at Plymouth Rock, they threw off the power of popes, priests and potentates and declared that every man has a right to worship God according to his own conscience and under his own vine and fig tree without anyone to molest him or make him afraid. Whatever may be said to the discredit of the American people, the world is eternally indebted to these early seekers after freedom of conscience for the religious liberty enjoyed today.

To summarize: The Jews nationalized religion; the Romans organized religion; the Greeks philosophized religion; the Anglo-Saxons individualized religion.

Now, what contribution will the colored man make to religion, and when?

I believe that the colored people are going to emotionalize religion. They possess enough emotion to move the world when it is properly confined and directed. The serious religious thinker criticizes colored people not because they are emotional but because of the way they express their emotions. Electricity is the most powerful and useful thing yet discovered. When it leaps from its scabbard in the skies, splits trees, burns up houses and knocks people down, we are startled and frightened and declare that it is a bad thing, but the scientific thinker knows that we are mistaken. Confine it to batteries, dynamos and wires, and this wild, frightful something runs our trains, drives our automobiles, propels our ships and flying machines, makes our cities and homes look like noonday at midnight, annihilates time and space and brings New York and Hong Kong within whispering distance of each other.

When you see colored people leaping and jumping, running and shouting, in the midst of some great religious service, the thing which moves them is not to be either crushed or criticized. Wait until they are properly refined, cultured and directed, and that thing which makes them go wild and knock people down who happen to be in their way will yet make the Christian church throb with power and vibrate with progress. Those who decry the emotionalism of the colored man are not serious students of psychology, philosophy or religion. Sympathy and love are the greatest of the emotions and these are the outstanding features of the colored man's psychology. He is the most sympathetic and loving being on earth. He represents the only race that has enough love to love its enemies. I can never be moved from the opinion that the colored man was placed in America by the providence of God to teach the white man the meaning of genuine Christian love and sympathy. In this particular the colored man has shown his superiority to the white man, for the one who loves is always superior to the one who hates. What the white man's Christianity needs is not organization, not money, not more adherents, not knowledge, but the whole system needs to be fired and energized by that deep and inexpressible emotion called love. Benjamin Kidd, in that remarkable book, "The Science of Power," declares that emotion, instead of knowledge, reason and physical force, is the greatest power in the world. This power is conspicuous by its absence in the overwhelming majority of Christian churches. Visit one hundred churches on the American continent and you will return home with the feeling that ninety-eight of them need that dynamic power which Paul tried to coin into these words—"The Love of Christ constraineth me."

It is not thought that moves but thought set on fire. In the last analysis it is not organization and men and knowledge that turn the wheels of industry but the mysterious electric current. What the current is to the machinery the emotions are to religion. The colored man—allow me to repeat—has enough emotional power to vitalize our dead churches and he is going to make this contribution to Christianity when he stretches forth both *hands* to God.

In the extended hands of the prophecy we have a picture of utter helplessness. This picture most fittingly represents the condition of the twelve million colored people in America at the present hour. Reaching after God is our one hope. At this time there is a wonderful lesson for us in Peter's experience on Galilee. It is as dark as pitch. Jesus is in the mountain praying. The ship on which the disciples ride is hopelessly tossed on the storm-driven billows. They can make no harbor because of the furious contrary winds. At the fourth watch of the night Jesus comes trudging over the billows, exclaiming, "It is I; be not afraid." The impulsive Peter prays for the privilege of meeting his Lord. As the maddening waves growl and froth and gnash their teeth beneath his trembling feet, Peter begins to sink. It requires no stretch of the imagination to see him reaching out both hands to God amid the engulfing waves as he cries, "Lord, save me! Lord, save me!"

The colored people, like Peter, are walking on a rough sea. The billows of prejudice, hatred and injustices of every kind threaten to swallow us up. God is waiting for us to stretch forth both hands, crying, "Save, Lord, or we perish!" The stretching of both *hands* to God is an acknowledgment that earthly things cannot supply the needed help.

"Father, I stretch my hands to Thee,
No other help I know;
If Thou withdraw Thyself from me,
Ah, whither shall I go?"

As a race we have sung this hymn for fifty years but we have never put it into practice. In fact, in our distress we have stretched our hands to everybody and everything but God. Our leaders told us to get education and property and other people would respect us and treat us as men and American citizens. Following their leadership, we reached after property and education. Our bitterest enemies, including Congressman Byrne, publicly acknowledge that no group of people has ever made greater intellectual and material progress. Instead of hatred and injustice diminishing in proportion to our progress, their rapid increase threatens the very foundations of our democratic government. I am second to no one in my desire to see my race accumulate property and acquire an education, but the most stupid observer of the signs of the times is forced to admit that the solution of the race problem does not lie along the lines of advance.

Another group of leaders is saying now with fiery vehemence, "The only way for the colored man to save himself is to arm and defend himself." I have absolutely no apology to make to any man for the vigorous and successful way colored people defended themselves against the mobs in Washington, Chicago and other places, and I do not advise them not to resort to similar defense under similar circumstances. The fact remains, however, that colored people can never save themselves by physical force. Such a course can only end in the extinction of the race in this country. There are about twelve million colored people in the United States and ninety million whites. Suppose the same number should be killed on both sides in the slaughter. There would be seventy-eight million white people left doing business after the colored people were all annihilated.

Every department of the government, including the machinery of destruction, is in the hands of white men, except a few razors and pistols. The men who are advising colored people to arm and fight are either fools or they are deliberately preparing the race to commit suicide. Nowhere in the world is the colored man prepared to fight the white man. Even if we were prepared to fight, this method would not assure us racial permanency. This is not the method proclaimed by the text. It is not taught anywhere in the Bible or even in experience, that a race will be blessed and made a blessing by carrying carnal weapons in its hands, but by stretching its *hands* to God.

None of the things that constitute our idea of civilization, such as wealth, education, armaments, have ever yet saved a nation or race. Egypt, Babylon, Rome, Carthage and Greece possessed all of these in a marked degree. Only a few pyramids tell of the former greatness of Egypt, and a heap of civilized rubbish marks the location of the once great Babylon which made the power-intoxicated Nebuchadnezzar exclaim, "Is not this great Babylon, that I have built for the house of the kingdom, by the might of my power, and for the honor of my majesty?" The tramping Roman legions that shook the earth and conquered the civilized world have completely disappeared, and Athens inhabited two thousand years ago by the mental giants of the world is today a marble wilderness.

But it is not necessary to hark back to the musty ancients to prove that intellectual attainments, material prosperity and organized material force are no guarantee of racial permanency. Just a few years ago the Germans were regarded as the best educated and most highly civilized people of modern times. Students from the universities of every land went to Germany to finish their education. The world so utterly depended upon Germany that civilization was to a great degree thrown out of gear when her exports were cut off. Germans had the most perfect and powerful military machinery ever constructed by science and the most efficient army that ever obeyed the command, "Forward, march!" In her great rush for power and conquest she turned away from the Bible that made her great at the beginning of her history, substituted human rationalism for supernatural authority, and the colossal house of the Hohenzollerns tumbled down with a thunder crash that will echo and re-echo around the world until the tall archangel shall blow out the last breath of time. The continued decline of the German race will be sure and swift unless it goes back to the Bible of Martin Luther. The signing of the armistice on the 11th day of November 1918, served notice on humanity that mentality, money and munitions of war can never save a race. Let the colored people learn this lesson and be saved from the graves of the ancients and be used to help save the moderns. White and colored people were deluded into the belief that the war would make the world "a fit place in which to live." On the other hand, it has made the world a more unfit place in which to live by stirring up all the latent evil forces. There never were such manifestations of hatred and wickedness as now. President

Nicholas Murray Butler of Columbia University in an address delivered October 14, 1919, said, "From numberless openings in the crust of the political and economic world there are coming constant signs, explosions more numerous and louder, which mark the presence of hidden and heated forces of destruction that may one day burst forth and destroy civilization."

No group has been so sorely disappointed in the after effects of the war as the colored race in America. We bought liberty bonds and stamps for bread and we have been given stones from the rioters in return. We sacrificed and died on battlefields for an egg and on our return home we are whipped to death with scorpions in the hands of the mob. But all these horrible experiences will be richly rewarded if we will learn that the only thing that can save any race or individual is to repent of sin and to seek the kingdom of God and his righteousness. If the weapons of persecution in the hands of white men will but force us to stretch out our hands unto God, we will yet live to see the day when we shall rejoice in these awful tribulations. Had I a stentorian voice touched with Pentecostal fire, I would burn the words Paul uttered on Mars Hill into the heart of every member of my race, "And hath made of one blood all nations of men, for to dwell on all the face of the earth and hath determined the times before appointed, and the bounds of their habitation. That they should seek the Lord if haply they might feel after him, and find him, though he be not far from every one of us."

The thought to be stressed here is not "of one blood all nations," but "feeling after God and finding Him." The race which feels after God always finds Him a very present help in the time of trouble. If my race would seriously read the book of Esther and translate its teachings into action, a marvelous deliverance would come and come quickly. A conspiracy was formed to put to death every Jew living in the one hundred and twenty-seven provinces of the Medo-Persian Empire during the twelfth month of the year. The conspiracy was not only sanctioned by the government, but a huge sum of money was appropriated from the national treasury to meet the expense of the slaughter. Mordecai apprised Queen Esther of the impending doom and the following proclamation was issued by her: "Go, gather together all the Jews that are present in Shushan, and fast ye for me, and neither eat nor drink for three days or nights: I also and my maidens will fast likewise; and so will I go in unto the king, which is not according to the law; and if I perish, I perish."

These days of praying and fasting wrought a veritable revolution in the empire. Haman, the leader of the conspiracy, was hanged on the gallows prepared for the execution of Mordecai, the entire race was completely delivered from its enemy, and the "Jews had light and gladness, and joy, and honour," while Mordecai in position and influence stood next to the king.

The colored people of America are in a similar situation. The present policy of the white Hamans is to either reduce them to the status of a plantation mule or completely annihilate them with the gun, rope and torch. This policy has the silent sanction of the United States government. While this country is lifting its hands in holy horror and shedding crocodile tears over the oppressed peoples of Europe and Asia, colored men and boys are dragged through the streets in open daylight, shot, hanged and burned, and mothers are ripped open and their unborn children murdered, without even so much as creating a ripple in the Department of Justice. The only remedy left is for Ethiopia to stretch forth her helpless *hands* to God. The God who delivered the Jews in the Medo-Persian Empire two thousand five hundred years ago is not dead. "Behold, the Lord's hand is not shortened that it cannot save, neither His ear heavy that it cannot hear." He is the same yesterday, today and forever to those who feel after Him with both *hands*.

Why should not the colored people of America begin the fulfillment of the prophecy of the text and hasten on the day when Ethiopia shall everywhere stretch forth her *hands* to God? If I were the Pope of my people I would issue a proclamation calling every colored man, woman and child to prayer and fasting on a certain day. The proclamation would not only forbid them to eat or drink or enter any place of amusement on that day, but to abstain from all work and to keep off the street corners. Every colored man and woman away from work and from the streets, shut up in their homes, laying insults, indignities, injustices and all the unspeakable outrages heaped upon their race before God, would be the most powerful and effective protest that ever went to Heaven from any continent. It is just as certain that God cannot tell a lie. In spite of all the appeals and protests made to the government, the situation for us is growing more serious and tense. Everything else under the sun has been tried; let the race now try God. When the Supreme Court of the United States declared that no black man had a single right that any white man was bound to respect and the master was fulfilling his boast by calling the roll of his runaway slaves at the foot of Bunker Hill, some white people asked a good old Christian woman what her people thought of the Dred Scott decision. She replied, "We are going to take an appeal." "Appeal to what?" asked her interrogators. "Don't you know there is no appeal from the Supreme Court of the United States?" "But," said she, "honeys, we are going to appeal to the Supreme Court of Glory." On their humble knees they did appeal to Almighty God. Up from the blue grass hills of Kentucky, up from the cane-brakes of Louisiana, up from the rice swamps of Mississippi, up from the orange groves of Florida, up from the cotton fields of Georgia and Alabama, up from the turpentine hills of North and South Carolina, up from the tobacco patches of Virginia, up from the corn fields of Maryland, up from the coal fields of Ohio and Pennsylvania, up from sand-enshrouded New Jersey, up from the busy marts of New York, up from the rock-ribbed hills of New England, went the agonizing appeal to the Lord God which caused the Supreme Court of Glory to reverse the decision of the Supreme Court of the United States and it was declared in the midst of the awful roar of cannon and the terrible flow of blood that the black man had some rights which the white man was bound to respect.

Let us try this appeal again. We have appealed to legislators and they will not hear us; we have appealed to governors and they will not hear us; we have appealed to every session of Congress for twenty-five years and they will not hear us; and we have appealed to all of the Presidents, Democrats and Republicans, and they will not hear us; we have appealed to members of the League of Nations and they will not hear us; we have appealed to the white pulpits and churches and they will not hear us. I ask you now, I beseech you, I beg you, I implore you, my people everywhere, to carry our protest to the Supreme Court of Glory and with outstretched *hands* let us make our appeal at the Great White Throne of God, and we will be heard, for the Judge of all the earth has not only promised to do right, but He has said, "Call upon me in the day of trouble and I will deliver thee." If the race heeds this call, it will not only save itself as surely as the God of the Bible lives, but it will become a savior of other races and will add a lasting contribution to the Christian religion.

APPENDIX B

Chapter 5 Sermons

KATIE CANNON

Message: *"Prophets of a New Day"*

Scripture: 1 Kings 13:29-30 (NIV)

Date: 1998

Context: Sermon preached in multiple settings; earliest version
at Presbyterian Church of the Ascension in New York City

²⁹*So the prophet picked up the body of the man of God, laid it on a donkey, and
brought it back to his own city to mourn for him and bury him.* ³⁰*Then he laid the
body in his own tomb, and they mourned over him and said, "Oh, my brother!"*

One day King Jeroboam, the king of Israel, went to the city of Bethel
to prepare for a special feast. The king wanted to make things ready
for a high and holy day so that he could celebrate his kingdom in
all of its splendor and all its wonder. Just when King Jeroboam started to
burn the incense on the altar, one of God's prophets from Judah arrived on
the scene. The prophet from Judah was a man of God who had entered into
a covenant with God the Creator and Sustainer, the same kind of covenant
that God-fearing women and men, and girls and boys, have made down
through the ages. The prophet of Judah wanted to be obedient to the word

of God wherein God called the prophet to go forth and prophesy against the sacrificial altars and idol worship of King Jeroboam. The prophet predicted desecration, pronounced doom, and declared death and destruction because King Jeroboam was causing the people to turn away from following the true and living God. Doers of justice today need to ask ourselves the question, Who are the Jeroboams in our churches and our communities who embody spiritual wickedness in high places? Who are the Jeroboams in our national public arenas burning incense at the altar who are causing the people to fall into apostasy, to bow down and worship idol gods?

Sisters and brothers, just like the prophet from Judah, we have a tendency to yield, time and time again, to temptation whenever we are baited by persons who purport to be just like us. We hear things like "Why, we were born under the same zodiac sign." "We have the same alma mater." "We do the same kind of work." "Our children were born in the same hospital." And the biggest bait of all: "We are all Christians, and we serve the same God." The problem with being pulled hook, line, and sinker by this so-called sameness is that far too often we end up easing the true and living God out of our lives. More than ever before we need true prophets, prophetic women and prophetic men, prophetic youth and prophetic adults, who will be God's people—and no other's . . . We need prophets who will not be baited by the attraction of sameness and compromise.

How do we become prophets for a new day? First, we need to take a spiritual inventory. Each of us needs to get away from the hustle and bustle of daily life and discover exactly what it is that God is calling us to do.

The second thing that we need to do in order to become prophets for a new day is obey the will of God. This means, among other things, that we must accept the findings of our spiritual inventory. The spiritual inventory may mean that God is calling us to be more loving in our homes . . . We may need to stop fighting and nagging. We may need to eliminate the pouting and mood swings. We may need to seek recovery from all kind of substance abuse and addictive behavior that make our homes feel more like war zones instead of places where peace, love, and justice begin.

Obedience for us may mean engaging in strategic action and reflection about the social crisis around us involving our children and teenagers. As Jonathan Kozol documents in his book, *Savage Inequalities: Children in America's Schools* (New York: Crown, 1991) there are public schools (primarily populated by African American and Hispanic children) where teachers are forced to set up classes in coatrooms. Some classes are held in storage bins and bathrooms . . . Obedience in the face of this gross systemic neglect and abuse may mean making conscious connections between children in public schools and those youth and adults in the church and community who are added to the illiterate population at the rate of 2.3 million every year.

The third and final thing we need to do in order to become prophets for a new day is give praise and honor to almighty God. In the story, the old man gains entry to the prophet from Judah through the latter's idle moment . . . he is sitting under a tree doing nothing when the tempter comes . . . I interpret the prophet's nothing, not just in terms of laxity toward the word of God as revealed to the prophet, but in terms of worship of God as required of us all.

Needed: Prophets who will take a spiritual inventory, prophets who will obey God's will, and prophets who will display an attitude of gratitude to the ends of both the praise and power of God.

———

OTIS MOSS JR.

Message: *"A Prophetic Witness in an Anti-Prophetic Age"*

Scripture: Isaiah 61:1 (KJV)

Date: February 2004

Context: Samuel DeWitt Proctor Conference

[1]*The Spirit of the Lord is upon me; because the Lord hath anointed me to preach good tidings unto the meek; He hath sent me to bind up the brokenhearted, to proclaim liberty to the captives, and the opening of the prison to them that are bound.*

It is amazing that Jesus, after being protected in Africa among people who looked like him, came back to Nazareth, and decided to go to a normal gathering, an ordinary gathering, and brought to it an extraordinary, unexpected prophetic word. They simply gave him a document. The King James translation version says, "They gave him a book," but we know that's not true. They gave him a scroll out of the prophetic tradition, what we now call the sixty-first chapter of Isaiah and told him to read it. He started reading it and then preached a sermon shorter than the text. "This day is this scripture fulfilled in your hearing" (Luke 4:21, KJV). And the record said he sat down. What a sermon! Have you ever preached a sermon shorter than your text? And then they engaged in a brief dialogue. I think it was after the sermon. And he started talking about some things. And before the dialogue was over, we would call it a fellowship, he almost got killed just talking about the sermon.

How often have our lives, as representatives of the gospel of Jesus Christ, been threatened for having dialogue about the sermon we had just delivered? We are not in particular danger because we have too often adjusted to this anti-prophetic age. There is no danger in the sermons we preach, no challenge, and no threat to anybody in particular.

But Jesus almost got killed on his first sermon—perhaps, his first public sermon. And let me say, we ought to remember that the community, the world, does not like prophets, and neither does the church. The world does not like prophets. Prophets disturb us. They shake us out of our dogmatic slumber. So we prefer comfort to commitment. The world does not like prophets. Prophets override our contradictions and put to shame our mediocrity. The world does not like prophets and the church often refuses to celebrate them.

We all have Dr. King's photograph on our walls. But I was there when his own denomination excommunicated him and, in the words of Gardner Taylor, denied him a home address. In his own denomination, he was vice president of the National Baptist Sunday School and BTU Congress, now the Christian Education Congress. But by tyrannical acts of a few people, he was removed without a vote from that position and made unwelcome. I stood after that with tears in my eyes, and I heard not a member of the Ku Klux Klan, but I heard a brother who looks like us say: "He's got everything; on the cover page of *Time* magazine. Every time I open the newspaper he's in it. Every time I turn on the television he's on it. Give us something." And that was the size and depth and the height and the width of his ministry.

We don't like prophets. Let me tell you something you might not have heard before. Dr. King gave his final message to the Progressive National Baptist Convention against the war in Vietnam. In less than a year he would be assassinated. I was a regional representative of the Southern Christian Leadership Conference and Dr. Abernathy called me and said: "Otis, here's what we want you to do. Go out and get five thousand leaflets printed and put on it the time that Dr. King is going to speak to the Convention and give the subject: *The War in Vietnam and the Christian Conscience.*" Put that on the leaflet and distribute that throughout the Convention and the Cincinnati community. I said, "Yes," but before I could get to the printer I got a telephone call that I did not return because the Spirit told me that it was a call that I wanted to get afterwards.

So I had all of the leaflets printed up and got some young people from our congregation to help distribute them and then I took the call. The call came from a high official in our convention—I'm talking about the Progressive National Convention—called me and said: "You have a relationship with Dr. King. Please tell him not to speak on Vietnam." Some of the brethren won't like it. Well, by that time I had already sent out the leaflets. I said: "Well, I'll tell you, I can't talk to him because I don't know where he is. He's on his way here and the leaflets are already out. Why don't we just pray?"

On that occasion Dr. King spoke, and the Progressive National Baptist Convention after he spoke unanimously endorsed and adopted a resolution that we had written in his hotel room against the war in Vietnam. It was the last time he spoke to the Progressive National Baptist Convention, but there were a handful of ministers who left before he spoke. He was not wanted in Atlanta.

Now listen to me carefully. I was here when the announcement went out that Martin Luther King, Jr. was moving from Montgomery, Alabama, to Atlanta, Georgia. The governor of Georgia, whose name at that time was Ernest Vandiver, called a press conference in the state capitol and said that Martin Luther King, Jr. is not welcome in Georgia. Now he [King] was born here. And then a black reporter from *Atlanta Daily World*, a black newspaper, went throughout the community interviewing—not white folk—but black folk. He said: "What do you think about King's coming to Atlanta?" Leader number one: "No comment." Scholar number two: "I don't want to get into that controversy." Leader number three: "We've already got enough leaders in Atlanta." He was not wanted in his own hometown. So, bombed in Montgomery; jailed in Birmingham, Albany, and St. Augustine; stoned in Chicago; invited out of town in Cleveland; and unwanted in Atlanta.

But the Spirit of the Lord was upon him. And, if I could rephrase it I would say, he was wounded for his nation's transgressions, bruised for America's iniquities, and the burdens of black people and white people and all people were upon his shoulders. And because he was a prophet, everybody here, and those who are not here can stand a little taller; walk the earth with a little more dignity. He gave teachers more to teach and preachers more to preach. He made newspapers worth reading, and televisions worth watching. Why? Because the Spirit of the Lord was upon him. God told him to proclaim the good news.

Now, if I was going to be here for a week, I would deal with this whole text; but time is running out. If you go down—"The Spirit of the Lord is upon me . . . God has anointed me"—that has to be theological. "To proclaim good news to the poor"—I believe that's economics. "God told me to get release to the captives"—that must be political. To "recover the sight of the blind"—that's educational and sociological. "To let the oppressed go free"—that's liberation theology. And then, "to proclaim the year of Jubilee; to proclaim the acceptable year of the Lord"—that's theological (see Isa 61:1).

So, at the top of the text is theology. And in between is economics, politics, and sociology. In between it's all of the social public policy. And then at the bottom it's theology. At the top—theology—and all the rest in between. So, if you are preaching a gospel that has nothing about politics, nothing about economics, nothing about sociology, it's empty gospel with a cap and some shoes and no body to it. It might be popular, but it's not powerful. It might be expedient, but it's not saving. Let me put it another way: it might be safe, but it's not saving. God told me to tell you that we need prophets in this age where prophets are not liked. We need prophets of peace—I didn't say peaceful prophets. Prophets of peace understand why we could have taken medicine to Iraq and not bombs.

Now let me back up just a moment and say that the church has allowed generals of the army to become more prophetic than we are. That's a bold statement. Let me defend myself. After World War I, Field Marshal Haig said: "It is the business of the church to make my business as a soldier impossible." I'm quoting not Amos and Hosea and Micah, now. I'm quoting generals of the army. General H. H. Arnold said: "We won the last war"—talking about World War II—"and it is the last war we will ever win. For in a nuclear age victory is no longer possible. War itself is defeat." General Omar Bradley, who was not even a registered voter, said: "We have too many men of science and too few men of God. We know more about killing than we know about living. We know more about making war than we know about making peace. We live in an age of nuclear giants and ethical infants." I'm still quoting the generals. I haven't gotten to the prophet yet. And, General Douglas MacArthur, who was perhaps at the bottom of his being a racist, said: "War should be outlawed." General Sherman is reported to have said—we're not sure that he said it—but allegedly said: "War is hell." And it is.

And the prophet said they shall beat their swords into ploughshares and spears into pruning hooks. Nation shall lift up sword against nation. Neither shall they learn war anymore. We need prophets of peace. Let me tell you I know where the weapons of mass destruction are. I know where they are and you know where they are! According to statistics, AIDS is a weapon of mass destruction. Mis-education and no education are weapons of mass destruction. Children with good minds and no money to go to school are weapons of mass destruction. People who have done no wrong living outdoors and under bridges this morning are weapons of mass destruction. And the prophet said, "Come unto me all ye that labor and are heavy laden and I will give you rest" (Matt 11:28, KJV).

Let me close with a country illustration. You can see something and hear something and feel something and say something and do something that appears to be strange to other folks because if you have a mountain moving faith and a mountain climbing faith and a mountain claiming faith—you can develop that, too.

I came from the country and I have country illustrations. There was a young woman who was working in a restaurant and one day when she went to work they were expecting a large turnout because it was a day before a holiday. They cooked an extraordinary supply of chicken, but the expected company and customer base didn't come. So, towards the end of the day when she had already worked overtime, the proprietor of the restaurant told her to take some of the chicken home. But by this time she had missed her last bus and had to walk home in the dark, somebody moved out of the dark alley and put a choke hold around her neck and dragged here down the alley. And she said a strange thing: "While the attacker was dragging me, I heard a voice that said, take out a piece of chicken and eat it." And strangely enough she obeyed the voice and while she was taking out the chicken, there were two hungry alley dogs down the alley fighting a garbage can. But when she pulled up the chicken out of the bag, the aroma got caught up on the wings of angels and moved down the alley and captured the attention and appetite of the hungry dogs. They came charging down the alley, growling and ready to fight and the attacker turned her loose and ran away. And she gave a little chicken to the dogs. And then for the rest of her journey as she walked home, she would take a little piece of the chicken out of the bag and give it to these alley dogs.

You know the Lord is my shepherd (see Ps 23). Yeah though I walk through the valley, but drop the "v" and say; yeah though I walk through the alley of the shadow of death, I will fear no evil because God can take alley dogs and make them guardian angels. For God's prophet, proclaim the year of jubilee!

———

MARVIN A. MCMICKLE

Message: *"How Much of Leviticus Do You Really Want?"*

Date: April 2012

Scripture: Leviticus 18:22

Context: American Baptist College's 2012 Garnett-Nabrit Lecture, Nashville, Tennessee

[22]*You shall not lie with a male as with a woman; it is an abomination.*

Lives are being ruined. We don't discuss that here. Infections are being transferred. We don't discuss that here. Maybe the reason we don't discuss HIV is because we are afraid to discuss sex. Or maybe it's because our very strange use of exegetical practices has limited the particular sexual act we will discuss and leave all the rest out.

If I hear one more preacher tell me about Leviticus 18:22, by itself, I will just scream. I know what Leviticus 18:22 says. "It is an abomination to lie with a man as with a woman." Yeah, I know all about Leviticus 18:22. The question is: If you are going to take Leviticus 18:22, are you going to take the rest of Leviticus? How much of Leviticus do you really want? Some people just take out the text that which confirms what they already prejudicially believe, and leave out what is personally uncomfortable. You can't just take one verse from Leviticus, you've got to take all or none. Leviticus 11 says, "Thou shalt not eat rabbit, pork, shrimp." If you are going to follow Leviticus, you cannot eat meat that's got blood in it. Therefore, rare or medium steak cannot be engaged in. If you are going to follow Leviticus 18, you cannot have sex with your wife during or seven days after her menstrual cycle . . . that's in Leviticus.

If you're going to take Leviticus, you're going to have to take all of Leviticus. You've got to take Leviticus 25 that says, that every 50 years is a Sabbath or Jubilee to the Lord. All debts are forgiven. All prisoners shall be released. What might happen in America if we took Jubilee into account? Oh my God. All debts are forgiven and all prisoners are set free. No bank I know observed Leviticus. No judge I know observed Leviticus. But here we are scrawling around on Leviticus 18:22, "Thou shalt not lie with a man as with a woman, it is an abomination to the Lord." Yes, so is everything else in Leviticus to be observed literally and practically? How much of Leviticus do you really want before you realize that I have to ask myself the question, "Are these practices which probably made some logical sense in the 8th century B.C. . . . but if I'm not going to observe all of them I ought not invoke one of them unless I'm just trying to find the one sexual act of which I am not guilty?"

So I skip around the ones of which I am guilty. But I can be outspoken on the ones . . . O, I don't like homosexuals, say some people. Well, they might not like you either. But do you love adulterers? Does an adulterer have the right to condemn a homosexual? Do people who molest children have anything to say about same-sex activity? When did that become a more severe sin than any other? I'm not trying to approve, condone, or authorize anything. I'm trying to stop bad exegesis. I am trying to keep preachers from using the Bible to condone prejudices, which if they kept reading might eventually judge them as well. You can't stand outside of the Bible and read it from the point of view of which you are not guilty. Just keep reading. Or read Romans chapter one. So God gave them over to a perverse spirit. And because they were given over to a perverse spirit they became engaged in same-sex activities. I do not doubt what it says. Just keep reading. Because if you don't feel condemned by Romans 1:25-26, just keep reading. Two verses later, what do you have? A malicious spirit, envy, gossiping, backbiting, pride, arrogance, anger, and jealousy.

Come on. Are there no preachers guilty of pride, envy? Nobody here who wishes they could do what Dr. Watson just did? None of you? Nobody will take what he just said and rework it and put your twist on it? And not mention his name, and act as if you are the beneficiary of some divine revelation? Just keep reading and sooner or later everything that we are falls under the same condemnation. Why do we not engage on this issue? Perhaps because we don't discuss sex. Perhaps because we don't know how to read the Bible properly. Or perhaps it is because we are too judgmental. Leviticus is where Jesus was writing in the ground . . . they brought to him a woman who was taken in adultery. A woman. The text in Leviticus says, if you catch a man and a woman in adultery, bring them both, that they both may be stoned . . . that the abomination may be taken out from Israel.

Now, you know, I'm just exegetically exploring. When Jesus was writing in the ground after they brought the woman who was taken in adultery, I think what he was writing in the ground was, "Where is the man?" How can you catch her in adultery and not catch him? It does at some level take two to tango. He was not dancing by himself. That would not have been adultery. Where is the man? We are judgmental. We are. We are. We are quick to say who is good and who is bad. Who is right and who is wrong. Who is redeemable and who is not. Is it possible that the Church does not engage on the issue of AIDS because the Church is judgmental?

We who ought to be the instruments of God's grace, proponents of redemption, advocates of a second chance . . . or, is there nobody here who is the beneficiary of grace? Nobody here? Conscious of who you were and who you are? Nobody here who could say, I once was lost but now I'm found. I was blind but now I see. Nobody? How can forgiven people be so unforgiving? How can folk that God has given a second chance be so quick to condemn those, if in fact what they have done is a sin. Because they have done something. We hold them in contempt because of something they've done. Well, what did they do?

What did Vivian Smith do? My church secretary. Vivian Smith. What did she do to get HIV/AIDS, to be HIV positive? She married a man who either was unfaithful to her or had been infected before they got married. Either way, she was guilty of the sin of monogamy! She got HIV in her marital bed. And when she announced that she was HIV positive you would have thought she was like the leper in Luke chapter 5. Had to walk through life saying about himself . . . unclean. Not guilty. Unclean. Don't touch her. Unclean. What did she do? She laid down with her husband and she woke up with AIDS. She gave birth to two sons. Because she was HIV positive, they were HIV positive. What did they do? I know preachers. I hope there are none here who will not do funeral services for someone who has died of the disease because they cannot get pass the issue of how they contracted it. Did you get this disease in some immoral sexual act? No. Did you get this disease because you were sharing an IV needle? No. Well, how did you get it? I laid down with my husband! Papa was a rolling stone, and wherever it was he laid his hat he brought this home with him.

Judgmental. Unforgiving. Harsh. Critical. Condemning of some sins. I give you two verses to ponder. The first is Luke chapter 5 and the second is Romans 12. Luke 5 is the story of a leper. Leprosy was a socially distancing, highly contagious, physically impactful disease. It ate at your body. It didn't kill you in a day, it killed you over days. It drove away your family. It drove off your friends. The only companions you would have are those who were similarly infected and impacted. And one day a leper hears that Jesus is passing by and takes a chance on the Lord. He did not say, unclean, but will you give me a chance. He just said, "you could make me whole if you would." He had ears. He had eyes. He had memory. He had seen what Jesus had done for blind people . . . maybe it will work for a leper? He had seen what it had done for lame people . . . "you could make me whole if you would." Now, Jesus does two things. Before he heals him. He touches him.

In Luke 10, Jesus healed lepers from a long distance. So we know that Jesus doesn't have to touch you to heal you. He could have said to this man, "Go. Show yourself to the priest. You are already clean. I can do it long distance if I want to . . ." [recording ends].

———

CHERYL J. SANDERS

Message: "What Does God Require of Us?"

Scripture: Micah 6:6-8

Date: January 9, 2014

Context: Third Street Church of God, Washington, D.C.

6With what shall I come before the Lord, and bow myself before God on high? Shall I come before him with burnt offerings, with calves a year old? 7Will the Lord be pleased with thousands of rams, with ten thousands of rivers of oil? Shall I give my firstborn for my transgression, the fruit of my body for the sin of my soul? 8He has told you, O mortal, what is good; and what does the Lord require of you but to do justice, and to love kindness, and to walk humbly with your God?

This weekend as we observe the 85th birthday of Dr. Martin Luther King, Jr., we have before us the prophecy of Micah, a clear and strong summary of the ethics of the Bible. The Lord requires of us three things that are non-negotiable, irreducible, not subject to contextual interpretation, individual preferences or cultural conditions: (1) do justice; (2) love kindness, or mercy; (3) walk humbly in a relationship with God. Incorporated into these three moral mandates are social ethics, compassionate ministry, and personal piety.

For some reason, throughout the history of Christianity, as far as I can tell, people have chosen to emphasize one of these three mandates as characteristic of their tradition while excluding or ignoring the others. Some liberal traditions emphasize social justice in their liturgies, policies and resolutions, with or without corresponding social action. Some conservative traditions practice compassionate ministries—feeding the hungry, doing mission projects in poor communities—while consciously or unconsciously exempting themselves from directly addressing the political policies and economic practices that sustain poverty and privilege. Yet another group of Christians historically identify strongly with personal piety, getting saved, refraining from sinful practices, going to heaven . . . as if their entire world of ethical accountability is contained within their chosen sanctuary or prayer closet—as is the position of some of *us* in the holiness camp.

Jesus warns against exclusive notions of ethical practice and concern when He chastises the religious intelligentsia of His own time in Matthew 23:23: *Woe to you, scribes and Pharisees, hypocrites! For you tithe mint, dill, and cumin, and have neglected the weightier matters of the law: justice and mercy and faith. It is these you ought to have practiced without neglecting the others.* Micah's proclamation takes away the excuse of ignorance: God has told you, declared to you, shown you what is good. How and when did God show us?

Dr. King showed us what is good on Micah's terms. First, to do justice by undoing injustice. Second, to love mercy, to embrace kindness by refusing to turn a deaf ear and a blind eye to the lament of suffering people, in other words, by rejecting the apathy that keeps justice and hope in check. Thirdly, Dr. King showed us the good by his walk with God, the prayer, the reflection, contemplation and other disciplines of head and heart that characterized his intellectual pilgrimage to nonviolence as described in his first book, *Stride Toward Freedom.*

So what shall we do? What does God require of us Christians 50 years after the Civil Rights Movement and 45 years after King was felled by the assassin's bullet? Yes, we should continue with our liturgies and litanies and resolutions. Yes, we should reach out to the poor at home and abroad with acts of charity and gifts of compassion. Yes, we should nurture spiritual disciplines of prayer and fasting and Bible study. The challenge we face, however, is to do all of the above with the understanding that to do one in exclusion of the others is to fall short of God's requirement. Why pray, if you don't care? Why write up a resolution without seeking revolution? Why perform acts of compassionate ministry on your own terms, with first asking your needy neighbors how they want to be helped?

Can we do it all? Can we do justice, love kindness and walk humbly with God? I believe the last one is the key to the implementation of this integrity ethics of justice, compassion and piety. To walk humbly with God is to learn how to be led by God, to allow God to give us direction and correction as we engage in the work of social change and personal transformation.

To walk humbly with God is to let God be the caring parent and let me be the toddler. This view of our walk with God as a parent does not encourage childish dependency, but rather a depth of humility where we fully acknowledge what we don't know and can't do, but are willing to be taught and told and led, step-by-step, as God takes us by the hand and empowers us to participate in the fulfillment of God's purpose in the world—to do justice, to respond to suffering with kindness and compassion, and to never let go God's hands.

> Time is filled with swift transition,
> Naught on earth unmoved can stand,
> Build your hopes on things eternal,
> Hold to God's unchanging hand.

NOTES

Introduction

1   The terms *prophetic Black preaching, African American prophetic preaching,* and *Exodus preaching* are used interchangeably in this book. However, my intent with the use of the term *Exodus preaching* is to give particular accent to the fact that though this proposal is intentionally context specific, my ultimate goal is to urge all justice and hope seekers, irrespective of race, ethnicity, or subcommunity, toward a unified vision of "beloved community." Inviting others to name their own storied realities as they seek a better life in a socially fragmented and increasingly pluralistic world honors our historical particularities and common share in the larger society. Virtually every label applied to human beings has its limitations since humans continue to construct identity in fluid communities. No racial or ethnic group can claim a monopoly on human suffering and victimization.

   Finally, my decision to capitalize the term *Black* is in recognition of the fact that many scholars are moving away from the term *black* in lowercase, which primarily suggests an ontological description of identity formation solely based on race. Also, my decision to use the term *Black,* which is frequently used as an alternate expression to the term *African American,* indicates a certain respect I have for the politics of the fluid and intergenerational usage of the term *Black* in the vernacular of persons in communities of African descent. Cf. Ronald Walters and Robert C. Smith, *African American Leadership* (New York: SUNY Press, 1999), 21; Nancy Lynn Westfield, ed., *Being Black, Teaching Black* (Nashville: Abingdon, 2008), xvi–xvii.

2   The Great Migration signaled a crucial turning point in African American history. Scholars have interpreted the migration symbolically and historically to describe the overall mass movement of American Blacks from the South to the North as well

as the westward drive that began in 1873. The Great Migration, however, refers to the period between 1916 and 1940 when more than 1.5 million southern Blacks relocated to northern communities. It occurred between two distinguishable major social events—the onset of World War I and the eve of World War II. I use the term *Great Migration* interchangeably with *migration, interwar period*, and *mass exodus*.

3   Rhondda Robinson Thomas' excellent work demonstrates how Blacks as early as the late eighteenth century had appropriated the Exodus narrative in their own literary productions. Portraying themselves as protagonists in their own liberation struggle, Blacks deliberately shifted the traditional Exodus narrative to counterbalance illegitimate interpretations of it, which were espoused by some Euro-Americans who used the Bible either to reinforce White supremacy and racial hierarchy or to abolish slavery, though never to the extent of ensuring racial equality. Rhondda Robinson Thomas, *Claiming Exodus: A Cultural History of Afro-Atlantic Identity, 1774–1903* (Waco, Tex.: Baylor University Press, 2013), 5.

4   Absalom Jones, *A Thanksgiving Sermon* (Philadelphia: Fry and Kammerer, 1808), 17–18, preached at St. Thomas' African Episcopal, January 1, 1808.

5   Jones, *Thanksgiving Sermon*, 18.

6   Gardner C. Taylor, "Parting Words," in *The Words of Gardner Taylor*, vol. 4, *Special Occasion and Expository Sermons* (Valley Forge, Pa.: Judson, 2001), 109–13.

7   Lloyd F. Bitzer defines this term as a complex of persons, events, objects, and relations presenting an actual or potential *exigence* (an imperfection marked by urgency; a problem, something waiting to be done), which can be completely or partially removed in discourse. When introduced into the situation, it can so constrain human decision and action as to bring about the significant modification of the *exigence*. In the way that audience, speaker, subject, occasion, and speech are standard constitutive elements of rhetorical discourse, the situation, maintains Bitzer, is likewise indispensable since it seeks to know the nature of those contexts in which speakers create discourse. See Lloyd D. Bitzer, "The Rhetorical Situation," *Philosophy and Rhetoric* 1, no. 1 (1968): 1, 4–6. Reprinted in *Contemporary Rhetorical Theory: A Reader*, ed. John Louis Lucaites, Celeste Michelle Condit, and Sally Caudill (New York: Guilford Press, 1999), 217, 220.

8   Other homiletic scholars have made inquiries into the nature of African American preaching as a form of sociopolitical and sociocultural discourse. Cleo LaRue Jr.'s *The Heart of Black Preaching* (Louisville, Ky.: Westminster John Knox, 2000), for example, deals with a particular hermeneutic that he believes is central to Black preaching in general. He lists five domains into which and out of which Black preaching is spoken. None of his domains, however, specifically address prophetic Black preaching. And though LaRue concerns himself with social justice and corporate concerns, he does not specifically address an understanding of "prophetic preaching" as a distinctive homiletic preaching mode. James Henry Harris' *Preaching Liberation* (Minneapolis: Augsburg Fortress, 1995) raises critical questions about the causal appropriation of the effectiveness of praxis as a theological method in a Black context, yet his proposal never analyzes prophetic preaching within the discrete context of social change.

In *Practical Theology for Black Churches: Bridging Black Theology and African American Folk Religion* (Louisville, Ky.: Westminster John Knox, 2002), Dale Andrews broaches the subject of prophetic witness by interpreting the estrangement of Black theology from early and contemporary modes of African American folk religion. His ecclesiological analysis of preaching and pastoral care in Black churches and the construction of what he terms "Prophetic Black Theology in Covenant" is an invaluable resource. However, his methodological reliance upon hearer-response criticism (associated with reader-response criticism) gives limited consideration to historical embedding and conditioning of textual realities that are so important to our revelatory encounter with them.

Marvin McMickle's texts, one marginally addressing prophetic preaching and the other giving more exclusive engagement on the subject, deserve mention. In *Preaching to the Black Middle Class* (Valley Forge, Pa.: Judson, 2000), he evaluates the impact of class on preaching in Black churches and emphasizes the importance of a homiletic sensitivity to changing social demographics. But in view of some of McMickle's prescriptions in *Preaching to the Black Middle Class*, absent is any serious attention to prophetic preaching. It is important to note, however, that McMickle's more recent book *Where Have All the Prophets Gone? Reclaiming Prophetic Preaching* (Cleveland: Pilgrim Press, 2006) addresses this matter. In this latter work, he squarely centers his argument on the need for America's churches to hold fast to the biblical principles of justice and righteousness, which give clout to prophetic preaching. Still, while McMickle picks up various justice themes and relates them to Black church worship and Black life in America in general, he does not attempt to define prophetic preaching and its principal characteristics within the bounds of the African American rhetorical tradition. In *Exploring Prosperity Preaching* (Valley Forge, Pa.: Judson Press, 2012), Debra Mumford helpfully tracks the theology of preachers linked to the "Word of Faith" movement, surveying the movement's origins and theorhetorical constructs. And Luke Powery's pneumatological approach in *Dem Dry Bones: Preaching, Death, and Hope* (Minneapolis: Fortress, 2012) seeks to understand the deep contours of death and hope in the African American spirituals. Though Powery provides a thoughtful critique of theologically light prosperity-preaching texts, both Mumford and Powery give little to no sustained attention to prophetic preaching proper.

European American homileticians such as J. Philip Wogaman (*Speaking the Truth in Love: Prophetic Preaching to a Broken World* [Louisville, Ky.: Westminster John Knox, 1998]) and Lenora Tubbs Tisdale (*Prophetic Preaching: A Pastoral Approach* [Louisville, Ky.: Westminster John Knox, 2010]) have refocused attention on prophetic preaching as central to the pastor's vocational identity; however, in sum and substance, their works only address this subject matter in a generalized way. Still, other scholars have investigated preachers whose sermons address various justice-related themes within the purview of Black church worship and Black life in America in general, but none attempt to define African American prophetic preaching and its principal characteristics. These works are largely synthetic and foundationalist on the subject. They provide more cultural criticism than offer new theoretical ground with regard to the distinctive characteristics of prophetic preaching I have noticed in African American church contexts. Therefore, as I see it, this book's perspective on the subject respects the postmodern reader in a way other homiletic proposals have not.

Chapter 1

1 Carter G. Woodson, *A Century of Negro Migration* (Washington, D.C.: Association of Negro Life and History, 1918; repr., Mineola, N.Y.: Dover, 2002), 121. Citations refer to the Dover edition.

2 Thomas Watson Harvey, interview by Giles R. Wright, April 30, 1976, transcript, New Jersey Multi-Ethnic Oral History Project, Trenton, N.J.

3 Harvey, interview by Wright, 6.

4 Harvey, interview by Wright, 6. S. P. Fullinwider corroborates Harvey's recollection of Walker's notoriety in "Racial Christianity," in *African American Religious Thought: An Anthology*, ed. Cornel West and Eddie Glaude Jr. (Louisville, Ky.: Westminster John Knox, 2003). Fullinwider notes that Walker achieved fame in the 1880s, and gained the reputation as the "Black Spurgeon" in a way reminiscent of Booker T. Washington (481). Ironically, by 1901 Walker had been named pastor of two prominent congregations in the North and South—Tabernacle Baptist in Augusta and Mt. Olivet Baptist in New York. Cf. Silas X. Floyd, *The Life of Charles T. Walker, D.D.: "The Black Spurgeon," Pastor of Mt. Olivet Baptist Church, New York City* (New York: Negro Universities Press, 1969), a biography with sermon extracts published before the migration tide (115–23).

5 Milton C. Sernett, *Bound for the Promised Land: African American Religion and the Great Migration* (Durham, N.C.: Duke University Press, 1997), 43.

6 See Jason Berry, *The Spirit of Black Hawk: A Mystery of Africans and Indians* (Jackson: University Press of Mississippi, 1995).

7 Harvey, interview by Wright, 4.

8 James A. Geschwender, *Racial Stratification in America* (Dubuque, Iowa: WC Brown, 1978), 172.

9 Blyden Jackson, "Introduction: A Street of Dreams," in *Black Exodus: The Great Migration from the American South*, ed. Alferdeen Harrison (Jackson: University of Mississippi Press, 1991), xvii.

10 James Grossman, *Land of Hope: Chicago, Black Southerners, and the Great Migration* (Chicago: University of Chicago Press, 1989), 110–13. Carol Marks complicates Grossman's five steps thesis a bit in her work *Farewell—We're Good and Gone: The Great Migration* (Bloomington: Indiana University Press, 1989). Marks contends that the majority of migrants were not the agrarian types as commonly projected in most migration literature but relatively skilled southern urbanites who went northward when refused upward mobility due to racism. See Mark A. Huddle, "Exodus from the South," in *A Companion to African American History*, ed. Alton Hornsby Jr. (Malden, Mass.: Blackwell, 2005). Huddle's essay appears as the best literature review of the Great Black Migration to date. For the southern expression of the migration and migrants, see Isabel Wilkerson, *The Warmth of Other Suns: The Epic Story of America's*

Great Migration (New York: Vintage Books, 2010), winner of the National Book Critics Circle Award.

11 Sernett, *Bound for the Promised Land*, 45.

12 Sernett, *Bound for the Promised Land*, 22, 55.

13 According to Brundage, roughly 34 percent of Georgia's and 40 percent of Virginia's lynchings committed by Whites were of this type. See W. Fitzhugh Brundage, *Lynching in the New South: Georgia and Virginia, 1880-1930* (Urbana: University of Illinois Press, 1993), 58; Orlando Patterson, *Rituals of Blood: Consequences of Slavery in Two American Centuries* (Washington, D.C.: Civitas Counterpoint, 1998), 173-79.

14 Woodson, *Century of Negro Migration*, 169-70.

15 Woodson, *Century of Negro Migration*, 171.

16 Nell Irvin Painter, *Exodusters: Black Migration to Kansas after Reconstruction* (New York: Alfred A. Knopf, 1977), 109, 113, 115-17.

17 See Sernett, *Bound for the Promised Land*, 17; and E. Franklin Frazier, *The Negro Church in America* (1964; repr., New York: Schocken Books, 1974), 52. See also Dernoral Davis, "Toward a Socio-Historical and Demographic Portrait," in Harrison, *Black Exodus*, 7. According to Davis' stats, Carol Marks' claim is all the more controversial. Out of the 90 percent of Blacks who remained in the South, as Davis claims, only 5 percent lived in urban southern cities in the first decade of the twentieth century.

18 See C. Vann Woodward, *The Strange Career of Jim Crow* (Oxford: Oxford University Press, 2002). This book was originally published in 1955.

19 Sernett, *Bound for the Promised Land*, 15.

20 Woodward, *Strange Career of Jim Crow*, 6.

21 Sernett, *Bound for the Promised Land*, 15-16.

22 Kimberly L. Phillips, *AlabamaNorth: African-American Migrants, Community, and Working Class Activism in Cleveland, 1915-45* (Urbana: University of Illinois Press, 1999), 5.

23 Sernett, *Bound for the Promised Land*, 60-64.

24 Sernett, *Bound for the Promised Land*, 3, 61.

25 Albert Raboteau, "The Black Experience in American Evangelicalism: The Meaning of Slavery," in *The Evangelical Tradition in America*, ed. Leonard Sweet (Macon, Ga.: Mercer University Press, 1984), 195-97.

26 Spencer R. Crew, *Field to Factory: Afro-American Migration, 1915-1940* (Washington, D.C.: Smithsonian Institution, 1987), 34, 55.

27 Allen H. Spear, *Black Chicago: The Making of a Negro Ghetto, 1890-1920* (Chicago: University of Chicago Press, 1967), 177.

28 Sernett, *Bound for the Promised Land*, 4. Milton Sernett's focus on historic African American Protestant denominations examines the internal dynamics that sustained various aspects of the religious rituals within these established churches (e.g., preaching, singing, and praying).

29 James Manheim, "Austin, Junius C., Rev. 1887-1968," in *Contemporary Black Biography* (2004), *Encyclopedia.com*, accessed February 8, 2016, http://www.encyclopedia.com/doc/1G2-3431000009.html.

30 These dominant perspectives and their limitations will be demonstrated later. Despite the similar aims of progressives or instrumentalist Black pastors, the specific mode of preaching I am investigating cannot be constrained by Sernett's categories. Sernett, *Bound for the Promised Land*, 243.

31 Van Gelder describes "operational missiologies" within the postmodern context. But inasmuch as they signify the multiplication of competing paradigms or mission approaches defining the relationship of the gospel to culture, the term is theoretically constructive for any previous era or contextual setting. For Van Gelder, operational missiologies include anything from church-effectiveness campaigns that seek to rapidly acculturate church newcomers to denomination building to church renewal and church growth efforts. Similar approaches were noticeable in the Great Migration. Craig Van Gelder, "Defining the Center—Finding the Boundaries: The Challenge of Re-visioning the Church in North America for the Twenty-First Century," in *The Church between Gospel and Culture: The Emerging Mission in North America*, ed. George R. Hunsberger and Craig Van Gelder (Grand Rapids: Eerdmans, 1996), 27.

32 Sernett, *Bound for the Promised Land*, 184.

33 Sernett, *Bound for the Promised Land*, 148.

34 Sernett, *Bound for the Promised Land*, 163.

35 Sernett, *Bound for the Promised Land*, 124.

36 Sernett, *Bound for the Promised Land*, 245.

37 Albert J. Raboteau, *Canaan Land: A Religious History of African Americans* (New York: Oxford University Press, 2001), 85.

38 Raboteau, *Canaan Land*, 153.

39 Wallace D. Best, *Passionately Human, No Less Divine: Religion and Culture in Black Chicago, 1915–1952* (Princeton: Princeton University Press, 2005), 3–8. To arrive at a precise definition of the term Black church or African American church that would satisfy all is near impossible. However, Raphael G. Warnock offers a brief and yet thoughtful description that captures the essence and secures the intended meaning of the term. According to Warnock, the term refers to "varied ecclesial groupings of Christians of African descent, inside and outside black and white denominations, imbued with the memory of a suffering Jesus and informed by the legacy of slavery and segregation in America." See *The Divided Mind of the Black Church: Theology, Piety, and Public Witness* (New York: New York University Press, 2014), 9.

40 Sernett, *Bound for the Promised Land*, 120.

41 Hans A. Baer and Merrill Singer, *African-American Religion in the Twentieth Century: Varieties of Protest and Accommodation* (Knoxville: University of Tennessee Press, 1992), 44.

42 Baer and Singer, *African-American Religion in the Twentieth Century* (1st ed.), 242.

43 Reverdy C. Ransom, *The Pilgrimage of Harriet Ransom's Son* (Nashville: A.M.E. Sunday School, 1949), 37.

44 Thomas H. Jackson was a member of the first graduating class of Wilberforce University in 1870.

45 But despite his difference of opinion with Jackson's pedagogical scheme, Jackson had later licensed him as a local preacher, secured his first appointment, and united

him and Emma in marriage. In conversation with AME bishops Daniel Alexander Payne and Benjamin W. Arnett, an older Ransom affectionately declared, "More than any other man, [Jackson] met me at the decisive turning points of my early career." Annetta Gomez-Jefferson, *The Sage of Tawawa: Reverdy Cassius Ransom, 1861–1959* (Kent, Ohio: Kent State University Press, 2002), 21.

46 Instead of constructing truth claims about faith that rely on Cartesian objectivism, Ricoeur's stance is that we cannot clear ourselves from the responsibility and risk of interpretation. Paul Ricoeur, *Lectures on Ideology and Utopia*, ed. George H. Taylor (New York: Columbia University Press, 1981), 312. See Dan R. Stiver, *Theology after Ricoeur: New Directions in Hermeneutical Theology* (Louisville, Ky.: Westminster John Knox, 2001), 150-57.

47 Ric Roberts, "Old Man Eloquent: Bishop Ransom, 95, Last of First Generation," *Pittsburgh Courier*, February 18, 1956, city edition. The age reported in this newspaper is incorrect. Ransom in fact died on April 22, 1959, at the age of ninety-eight.

48 LaRue, *Heart of Black Preaching*, 66.

49 David Wills, "Reverdy C. Ransom: The Making of an A.M.E. Bishop," in *Black Apostles: Afro-American Clergy Confront the Twentieth Century*, ed. Richard Newman and Randall K. Burkett (Boston: G. K. Hall, 1978), 194.

50 Gomez-Jefferson, *Sage of Tawawa*, 73.

51 More than three hundred such outlines are collected from his ministry at both Bethel and Institutional in Chicago, Bethel in New York, and Charles Street in Boston. Gomez-Jefferson, *Sage of Tawawa*, 73.

52 Reverdy C. Ransom, *The Disadvantages and Opportunities of the Colored Youth* (Cleveland: Thomas & Mattill, 1894), 3.

53 Gomez-Jefferson, *Sage of Tawawa*, 73.

54 Gomez-Jefferson, *Sage of Tawawa*, 73-74.

55 Ransom's pastoral career could be divided into four phases: (1) *1886–1890*: he is assigned to a string of small African Methodist churches in western Pennsylvania—Altoona, Tyrone, and Manchester mission in North Pittsburgh. (2) *1890–1896*: he rises to regional prominence; Bishop Daniel Alexander Payne assigns Ransom to North Street in Springfield, Ohio (1890-1893), followed by St. John's Church, Cleveland, Ohio (1893-1896). (3) *1896–1907*: he develops a national reputation as a preacher; he is assigned to Bethel Church in Chicago (1896-1900) but resigns to organize Institutional Church and Social Settlement (1900-1904) a few blocks away. He pastors in Massachusetts—New Bedford (1904-1905) and Charles Street AME in Boston (1905-1907). (4) *1907–1924*: his national footing is solidified; he is appointed to Bethel Church in New York City (1907-1912); he establishes and pastors Church of Simon of Cyrene in New York City (1913) with wife Emma while concurrently serving as editor of *A.M.E. Church Review* until elected the forty-eighth bishop of the AME Church.

56 Gomez-Jefferson, *Sage of Tawawa*, 54.

57 Ransom, *Pilgrimage*, 82-83.

58 Ransom, *Pilgrimage*, 83.

59 Donald A. Drewett, "Ransom on Race and Racism: The Racial and Social Thought of Reverdy Cassius Ransom—Preacher, Editor and Bishop in the African Methodist Episcopal Church, 1861–1959" (Ph.D. diss., Drew University, 1988), 273.

60 The AME Zion church, like Richard Allen and Daniel Coker's AMEs, was formed following acts of racial discrimination experienced from their White Methodist counterparts.

61 "Randolph, Florence Spearing, Biographical Note," New Jersey Historical Society, accessed July 8, 2015, http://www.jerseyhistory.org/findingaid.php?aid=1321.

62 Betty Robison, "Florence Spearing Randolph," *Charisma Magazine*, January 31, 2004, accessed August 8, 2013, http://www.charismamag.com/site-archives/24-uncate gorised/9848-florence-spearing-randolph.

63 According to scholars, "link migration" begins when a relative or even a religious leader pioneers the way up north and invites others later to settle. One might reasonably consider Harriet Tubman's escape on the Underground Railroad later to free others in the antebellum period as its historical precursor.

64 Bettye Collier-Thomas, "Minister and Feminist Reformer: The Life of Florence Spearing Randolph," in *This Far by Faith: Readings in African American Women's Religious Biography*, ed. Judith Weisenfeld and Richard Newman (New York: Routledge, 1996), 178.

65 Bettye Collier-Thomas, *Daughters of Thunder: Black Women Preachers and Their Sermons, 1850–1979* (San Francisco: Jossey-Bass, 1997), 103.

66 Cheryl Townsend Gilkes, "There Is a Work for Each One of Us," in *"How Long This Road": Race, Religion, and the Legacy of C. Eric Lincoln*, ed. Alton B. Pollard III and Love Henry Whelchel Jr. (New York: Palgrave Macmillan, 2003), 133.

67 Collier-Thomas, "Minister and Feminist Reformer," 180.

68 Cited in Collier-Thomas' *Daughters of Thunder*, 106.

69 Gilkes, "There Is a Work," in Pollard and Whelchel, *"How Long This Road,"* 133.

70 Ben Richardson, *Great American Negroes*, rev. ed. (New York: Thomas Y. Crowell, 1945), 209.

71 Adam Clayton Powell Sr., *Against the Tide* (1938; repr., New York: Arno Press, 1980), 70. Citations are to the 1980 edition.

72 Powell, *Against the Tide*, 70.

73 Ralph G. Clingan, *Against Cheap Grace in a World Come of Age: An Intellectual Biography of Clayton Powell, 1865–1953*, Martin Luther King, Jr. Memorial Studies in Religion, Culture, and Social Development 9 (New York: Peter Lang, 2002), x–xi. Also see Reggie L. Williams' *Bonhoeffer's Black Jesus: Harlem Renaissance Theology and an Ethic of Resistance* (Waco, Tex.: Baylor University Press, 2014), which traces Bonhoeffer's work at the church and its model for him in his return to Nazi Germany.

74 Powell, *Against the Tide*, 299.

75 See John William Kinney's "Adam Clayton Powell, Sr. and Adam Clayton Powell, Jr.: A Historical Exposition and Theological Analysis" (Ph.D. diss., Columbia University, 1979).

76 Powell, *Against the Tide*, 209.

77 Powell, *Against the Tide*, 210–17.

78 Clingan, *Against Cheap Grace in a World Come of Age*, x.

79 Powell, *Against the Tide*, 221.

Chapter 2

1   Andrew J. Theising, *Made in the USA: East St. Louis, The Rise and Fall of an Industrial River Town* (St. Louis: Virginia Publishing, 2003), 146–47.

2   Sernett, *Bound for the Promised Land*, 124.

3   Marks, *Farewell–We're Good and Gone*, 32.

4   Sernett, *Bound for the Promised Land*, 34.

5   Sernett, *Bound for the Promised Land*, 99–100.

6   Acronyms for African Methodist Episcopal, African Methodist Episcopal Zion, and Colored Methodist Episcopal denominations.

7   Reverdy C. Ransom, "Quadrennial Sermon: The Church That Shall Survive," in George Singleton's *Romance of African Methodism: A Study of the African Methodist Episcopal Church* (New York: Exposition Press, 1952), 151.

8   Sernett, *Bound for the Promised Land*, 98, 110.

9   See C. Eric Lincoln and Lawrence H. Mamiya, *The Black Church in the African American Experience* (Durham, N.C.: Duke University Press, 1990), 25–28.

10 Sernett, *Bound for the Promised Land*, 110.

11 Sernett, *Bound for the Promised Land*, 111–12.

12 Sernett, *Bound for the Promised Land*, 116.

13 Anne H. Pinn and Anthony B. Pinn, *Fortress Introduction to Black Church History* (Minneapolis: Fortress, 2002), 114.

14 Terrell Dale Goddard's excellent article "The Black Social Gospel in Chicago, 1896–1906: The Ministries of Reverdy C. Ransom and Richard R. Wright, Jr." (*The Journal of Negro History* 84, no. 3 [1999]) provides a concise overview of the classic texts and major figures included in the historical record of the late nineteenth- and early twentieth-century Social Gospel Movement. Goddard analyzes the classical literature in light of recent scholarship, which brings challenge to the limited scope of the traditional understandings of the Social Gospel Movement. He cites the works of Ralph Luker, Susan Lindley, and Ronald C. White as counterproposals to the traditional assumption that the SGM was a focused response from the Protestant liberal pulpits of Rauschenbusch, Gladden, and others. Goddard analyzes the merits of the recent debate. From recent scholarship he recognizes how the activity and stories of Black leaders like Nannie Helen Burroughs, Reverdy Ransom, and Richard Wright Jr. suggest that the Social Gospel was more pervasive than the historical record evidences. Though the category of race was largely factored out in favor of class in the early scholarship, and though these recent scholars differ on certain matters relating to causation and consequence in reference to the SGM, importantly, they all contend that the Social Gospel theory and method was "employed by a more diverse group in a broad variety of social justice efforts" (227–28, 231). Cf. Ralph Luker, *The Social Gospel in Black and White: American Racial Reform, 1885–1912* (Chapel Hill: University of North Carolina Press, 1991); Susan Lindley, " 'Neglected Voices' and

Praxis in the Social Gospel," *Journal of Religious Ethics* 18, no. 1 (1990), 75–102; Ronald C. White Jr., *Liberty and Justice for All: Racial Reform and the Social Gospel, 1877–1925* (San Francisco: Harper & Row, 1990). Sernett, *Bound for the Promised Land,* 116, 130–31.

15 Fullinwider, "Racial Christianity," in West and Glaude, *African American Religious Thought,* 477.

16 Darryl M. Trimiew, "The Social Gospel and the Question of Race," in *The Social Gospel Today,* ed. Christopher H. Evans (Louisville, Ky.: Westminster John Knox, 2001), 27–29.

17 Trimiew, "Social Gospel and the Question of Race," in Evans, *Social Gospel Today,* 27–29.

18 Sernett, *Bound for the Promised Land,* 116, 119.

19 Trimiew, "Social Gospel and the Question of Race," in Evans, *Social Gospel Today,* 32.

20 Lincoln and Mamiya, *Black Church in the African American Experience,* 116. Given this historical legacy, Black ministers are still expected to play an important role in all affairs concerning Black life. The authors cite August Meier and Elliot Rudwick's study, *From Plantation to Ghetto,* 3rd ed. (New York: Hill & Wang, 1976), on this point.

21 Luker, *Social Gospel in Black and White,* 178.

22 Luker, *Social Gospel in Black and White,* 2. Cf. Rayford W. Logan, *The Betrayal of the Negro: From Rutherford B. Hayes to Woodrow Wilson* (New York: Collier Press, 1965), 11, 171–73, 183, 273–75. Luker acknowledges that although the criticism of these key propagators of the social gospel is widely shared, alternate opinions by those such as William A. Clebsch, who argued that Abbott and Strong's theological thrusts were the first to challenge racial superiority in American Protestantism, must not be disregarded. What this implies for Luker is that neither point of view in a comprehensive way adequately portrays American social Christianity's record on race relations.

23 Luker, *Social Gospel in Black and White,* 2.

24 David L. Lewis, *King: A Critical Biography* (Baltimore: Penguin Books, 1970), 29–30.

25 *Tertium quid* is a Latin phrase meaning "a third something." According to Wilmore, the most significant characteristics of Black religion have emerged as a result of religious fusion. Gayraud S. Wilmore, *Black Religion and Black Radicalism: An Interpretation of the Religious History of African Americans,* 3rd ed. (Maryknoll, N.Y.: Orbis Books, 1998), 24–25, 36.

26 Reverdy C. Ransom, *First Quadrennial Report of the Pastor and Warden of the Institutional Church and Social Settlement to the Twenty-Second Session of the General Conference and to the Connectional Trustees of the African Methodist Episcopal Church* (Chicago: Quinn Chapel, 1904).

27 W. E. B. Du Bois, *The Negro Church* (Atlanta: Atlanta University Press, 1903), 85.

28 Luker, *Social Gospel in Black and White,* 174.

29 Ransom, *Pilgrimage of Harriet Ransom's Son,* 117.

30 Gomez-Jefferson, *Sage of Tawawa,* 111.

31 Sernett, *Bound for the Promised Land,* 117. With the rise of other secular social service agencies in Chicago and dwindling financial support for Ransom's ICSS, by the end

of WWI, the congregation went into sharp decline. Baer and Singer, *African American Religion* (2nd ed.), 47.

32   Luker, *Social Gospel in Black and White*, 176–77.

33   Luker, *Social Gospel in Black and White*, 177.

34   Thurmon Garner and Carolyn Calloway-Thomas, "African American Orality: Expanding Rhetoric," in *Understanding African American Rhetoric: Classical Origins to Contemporary Innovations*, ed. Ronald L. Jackson II and Elaine B. Richardson (New York: Routledge, 2003), 46–48.

35   "Proctor, Henry Hugh (1868-1933)," *BlackPast.org*, accessed July 8, 2015, http://www.blackpast.org/aah/proctor-henry-hugh-1868-1933.

36   Harvey, interview by Wright, 6.

37   Harvey, interview by Wright, 6–7.

38   Marcus Garvey, "Liberty Hall Speech," delivered on August 21, 1921, and included in *Negro World* 11, no. 2 (1921): 2. Reprinted in Randall K. Burkett, *Black Redemption: Churchmen Speak for the Garvey Movement* (Philadelphia: Temple University Press, 1978), 27.

39   Garvey, "Liberty Hall Speech," in Burkett, *Black Redemption*, 28–29.

40   Cf. Tony Martin, *Race First: The Ideological and Organizational Struggles of Marcus Garvey and the Universal Negro Improvement Association* (Dover, Mass.: Majority, 1986). Statistical data is quoted in Akinyele Umoja's "Searching for a Place: Nationalism, Separatism, and Pan-Africanism," in Hornsby, *Companion to African American History*, 535. Burkett, *Black Redemption*, 4.

41   Cf. Wilson Jeremiah Moses, *The Golden Age of Black Nationalism, 1850–1925* (Oxford: Oxford University Press, 1978), 15–16. Umoja, "Searching for a Place," in Hornsby, *Companion to African American History*, 535.

42   Conversionist-Renewalist church traditions are often grouped under the label Spiritualist/Holiness/Pentecostal traditions. Baer and Singer refer to these church traditions as conversionist and thaumaturgical sects. Robert Franklin calls individuals who act within these religious frameworks grassroots revivalists and prosperity positivists. In recent Pew Studies on Pentecostalism, the term "renewal" is used to cover many related groups (Holiness, Pentecostals, Apostolic, Charismatic, Neo-Pentecostal, Word of Faith, etc.). I use the terminology Conversionist-Renewalists as a covering term for the Spiritualist, Holiness, and Pentecostal traditions. Common to these traditions is a religiomagical approach to social problems. These church traditions tend to either reject "the world" or develop alternative ways where some type of spiritual/magical practice is performed. Also common to these church traditions is the perception of their mission as that of renewing (recovering or bettering) Christian faith and practice.

   "Holiness" churches are defined as those sects that require a testimony of conversion, sanctification (leading a pure life), and spirit possession (filled with the Holy Spirit) before an individual is recognized as being "saved" and offered membership. Cf. Arthur H. Fauset, *Black Gods of the Metropolis: Negro Religious Cults of the Urban North* (Philadelphia: University of Pennsylvania Press, 1970), 8.

43 Though the term "storefront" is often associated with religious groups outside of mainstream Black denominations, because a substantial number of Black Baptist and Black Methodist congregations began as storefronts, it is important to view the term as a physical trait shared among several groups instead of a sociological category. Cf. Baer and Singer, *African American Religion* (2nd ed.), 49.

44 Spear, *Black Chicago*, 176–77.

45 Hans A. Baer, *The Black Spiritual Movement: A Religious Response to Racism* (Knoxville: University of Tennessee Press, 1984), 18. Cf. Spear, *Black Chicago*, 96, 176–77. Different from their White counterparts, many African Americans adapted Spiritualism to fit their own unique thaumaturgical orientation, incorporating ritual content from a range of religious sources in the Black community. Cf. Baer and Singer, *African American Religion* (2nd ed.), 184.

46 Raboteau, *Canaan Land*, 86.

47 In addition to his descriptive analysis of five cults, Fauset helpfully provides an alternative interpretation to E. Franklin Frazier and Melville Hertzkovits' classic debate claims. Regarding Frazier's view that the Christian religion formed a new basis of social cohesion for African Americans as African religions were obliterated during American slavery, Fauset's study of the unorthodox and African traditional religions arguably disproves Frazier's claim. Still Fauset is careful not to affirm uncritically Hertzkovits' notion that there is an "instinctive religious 'bent' or 'temperament,'" which sets apart Blacks from other Americans." See Fauset's *Black Gods of the Metropolis*, 101–3. Cf. Frazier's *Negro Church in America*, 14.

Chapter 3

1 Quote taken from Benjamin Mays' eulogy of Dr. Martin Luther King Jr. See full sermon manuscript in his work *Born to Rebel: An Autobiography* (1971; repr., Athens: University of Georgia Press, 2003), 357.

2 Horst Dietrich Preuss, *Old Testament Theology*, vol. 2 (Louisville, Ky.: Westminster John Knox, 1996), 68.

3 Preuss, *Old Testament Theology*, 68–69.

4 Preuss, *Old Testament Theology*, 93–94.

5 Wogaman, *Speaking the Truth in Love*, 7.

6 Gene Tucker, "Prophetic Speech," in *Interpreting the Prophets*, ed. James L. Mays and Paul Achtemeier (Philadelphia: Fortress, 1987), 39.

7 Tucker, "Prophetic Speech," 424.

8 Tucker, "Prophetic Speech," 424.

9 Tucker, "Prophetic Speech," 430–31.

10 Michael Walzer, *In God's Shadow: Politics in the Hebrew Bible* (New Haven: Yale University Press, 2012), 67.

11 Walzer, *In God's Shadow*, 431.

12 Patrick D. Miller, *The Religion of Ancient Israel* (Louisville, Ky.: Westminster John Knox, 2000), 186.

13 Cf. 1 Samuel 3, Isaiah 6, and Jeremiah 1.

14   Abraham J. Heschel, *The Prophets* (New York: Harper & Row, 1962), 2:10.

15   Brueggemann's time-honored classic *The Prophetic Imagination*, first published in 1978, "remains one of the most perceptive uncoverings of the prophetic voice in contemporary Old Testament study." Patrick D. Miller, ed., foreword to *Texts That Linger, Words That Explode: Listening to Prophetic Voices*, by Walter Brueggemann (Minneapolis: Augsburg Fortress, 2000), vii. The second, revised edition of *The Prophetic Imagination*, published in 2001, is updated based on three significant changes. First, Brueggemann's scholarship has adopted affinities with the new methods of social-scientific criticism and rhetorical criticism, where focus is placed upon seeing texts as ideological statements evoking specific forms of social action and policy. Written or spoken, texts have generative power, and the meaning of prophetic texts is never separable from its relation to the real social processes in which it is imbedded. His scholarship on the prophets is profoundly endowed by the hermeneutics of Paul Ricoeur. A second alteration to the 1978 text makes a deeper commitment to connect his liberation hermeneutics more evidently to the core tenets of liberation theology. A third and final change rests in his acknowledgment that since the book's first publication, the church community's voice in its "mainline" expressions has increasingly become less authoritative.

16   Brueggemann, *The Prophetic Imagination*, rev. ed. (Minneapolis: Fortress, 2001), 63–64.

17   Brueggemann, *Prophetic Imagination*, 71, 75, 63–65.

18   Brueggemann, *The Practice of Prophetic Imagination: Preaching an Emancipating Word* (Minneapolis: Fortress, 2012), 27.

19   Elizabeth Achtemeier, *Preaching from the Old Testament* (Louisville, Ky.: Westminster John Knox, 1989), 110.

20   Preuss, *Old Testament Theology*, 80.

21   Robin Lovin, "Justice," in *A New Handbook of Christian Theology*, ed. Donald W. Musser and Joseph L. Price, 266–67 (Nashville: Abingdon, 1992). In the modern sense of the term, however, Glen Tinder argues that the pursuit of perfect or equal justice in a society governed by fallen people inevitably leads to inequities. Whether determined a free market system or welfare state, if the practical aims of society are military and economic efficiency, infringements on justice are ineluctable. Glen Tinder, *The Political Meaning of Christianity: An Interpretation* (Baton Rouge: Louisiana State Press, 1989), 62–63.

22   James F. Kay, *Preaching and Theology* (St. Louis: Chalice Press, 2007), 26.

23   Bitzer, "Rhetorical Situation," in Lucaites, Condit, and Caudill, *Contemporary Rhetorical Theory*, 220.

24   Brueggemann, "Prophetic Word of God and History," in Miller, *Texts That Linger*, 44.

25   Paulo Freire, *Pedagogy of the Oppressed*, trans. Myra Bergman Ramos (New York: Continuum, 1993), 17–18. Daniel S. Schipani, *Conscientization and Creativity: Paulo Freire and Christian Education* (Lanham, Md.: University Press of America, 1984), 10.

26   Freire, *Pedagogy of the Oppressed*, 17–18; Schipani, *Conscientization and Creativity*, 10.

27   Schipani, *Conscientization and Creativity*, 10.

28   Donald McKim, *The Bible in Theology and Preaching* (Nashville: Abingdon, 1985), 150.

29 Freire, *Pedagogy of the Oppressed*, 33.

30 Richard Schall, quoted in Freire, *Pedagogy of the Oppressed*, 13–14.

31 Quoted in Freire, *Pedagogy of the Oppressed*, 13–14.

32 Freire, *Pedagogy of the Oppressed*, 68–73.

33 Quoted in Freire, *Pedagogy of the Oppressed*, 69.

34 Freire, *Pedagogy of the Oppressed*, 69.

35 Freire, *Pedagogy of the Oppressed*, 69–70.

36 Freire, *Pedagogy of the Oppressed*, 95.

37 Ngugi wa Thiong'o, *Something Torn and New: An African Renaissance* (New York: Basic Civitas Books, 2009), 20.

38 Gloria Albrecht, *The Character of Our Communities: Toward an Ethic of Liberation for the Church* (Nashville: Abingdon, 1995), 68. Albrecht's feminist ethics of emancipation seeks to upend two basic internal contradictions she sees in postliberal theologian Stanley Hauerwas' theory of human subjectivity and his problem with social justice and liberation. She claims that his work to reject liberal theory for its uncritical embrace of reason, individualism, and the autonomous self in favor of leaning on a view of the church that does not adequately question its own narrative and authority constructs exposes a failure in the postliberal project. Though theologically communitarian as she, according to her, he does not see the difference that historical particularity makes within the church and its narrative. Differences of social location, she claims, by necessity lead to differing themes about the human condition, and about how dominant groups use political power to teach theology and shape the Christian narrative, which invariably works to suit the self-interest of the dominant group.

39 Walter Brueggemann, *Finally Comes the Poet: Daring Speech for Proclamation* (Minneapolis: Fortress, 1989), 4.

40 John W. de Gruchy, *Christianity, Art and Transformation: Theological Aesthetics in the Struggle for Justice* (Cambridge: Cambridge University Press, 2003), 171.

41 Willie James Jennings, "The Aesthetic Struggle and Ecclesial Vision," in *Black Practical Theology*, ed. Dale P. Andrews and Robert London Smith Jr. (Waco, Tex.: Baylor University Press, 2015), 163.

42 Jennings, "Aesthetic Struggle and Ecclesial Vision," in Andrews and Smith, *Black Practical Theology*, 174.

43 Cf. Paul Scott Wilson, *Imagination of the Heart: New Understandings in Preaching* (Nashville: Abingdon, 1988), 32–39; Wilson, "Imagination," in *Concise Encyclopedia of Preaching*, ed. William H. Willimon and Richard Lischer (Louisville, Ky.: Westminster John Knox, 1995), 266–67.

44 Zora Neale Hurston, *The Sanctified Church* (Berkeley: Turtle Island, 1983), 51.

45 Hurston, *Sanctified Church*, 54.

46 Hurston, *Sanctified Church*, 53.

47 Hurston, *Sanctified Church*, 54.

48 Lynda Marion Hill, *Social Rituals and the Verbal Art of Zora Neale Hurston* (Washington, D.C.: Howard University Press, 1996), 9. Hill contends that Hurston's essentialist point of view is intentional. Establishing herself as a spokesperson and authority, her ethnographic work avoided the more popular acculturation and assimilation

views and descriptive appraisal of Black life in early twentieth-century America. Instead, race consciousness and retaining notions of cultural distinction defined her work.

49 Hill, *Social Rituals*, 9.

50 The value of these controls allows the implications of prophetic preaching in a considerably broader way that the "constitutive" characteristics do not allow.

51 Brueggemann, "Prophetic Word of God and History," in Miller, *Texts That Linger*, 36.

52 Brueggemann, "Prophetic Word of God and History," in Miller, *Texts That Linger*, 36. Cf. Brueggemann, *Practice of Prophetic Imagination*.

53 Dolan Hubbard, *The Sermon and the African American Literary Imagination* (Columbia: University of Missouri Press, 1994), 7. The Black sermon signifies a communal voice that is raised in opposition to the realities of injustice and racism perpetuated by the dominant culture. Then the ostracized community's quest for closure begins in the social and material realm, and then action moves toward the spiritual and sacred. Finally, because the preacher's message carries cosmological weight that possesses a power to speak to the listener's core being, at that juncture, the preacher's initiation in the speech-act releases people from physical and psychological strongholds.

54 Cf. Brueggemann, "Prophetic Word of God and History," in Miller, *Texts That Linger*, 36.

55 Wogaman, *Speaking the Truth in Love*, 7.

Chapter 4

1 Quote taken from Howard Thurman's *Meditations of the Heart* (1953; repr., Boston: Beacon, 1981), 104.

2 The basis for selecting these preachers was their diversity of background and earned social status, national and local significance ecclesiastically and politically, observable evidence of commitment to Christian praxis in sermonic materials, and ampleness of documented materials (e.g., autobiographical sources, sermons and writings).

3 Historians such as Albert J. Raboteau and Eugene Genovese have argued that visible strands of a prophetic Black preaching mode existed as early as the stirrings of the "Invisible Church" in the antebellum South.

4 Reverdy C. Ransom, "The Industrial and Social Conditions of the Negro: A Thanksgiving Sermon" (sermon preached at Bethel AME Church in Chicago, November 26, 1896). Reverdy C. Ransom Collection, Payne Theological Seminary at Wilberforce University, Wilberforce, Ohio, box 15, folder 12.

5 Ransom, "Industrial and Social Conditions of the Negro," 7–8.

6 Ransom, "Industrial and Social Conditions of the Negro," 9.

7 Ransom, "Industrial and Social Conditions of the Negro," 12.

8 Ransom, "Industrial and Social Conditions of the Negro," 12.

9 Reverdy C. Ransom, "Thanksgiving Sermon: The American Tower of Babel; or, The Confusion of Tongues" (sermon delivered at Bethel AME Church, New York, November 25, 1909). Available in Reverdy C. Ransom, *The Spirit of Freedom and Justice: Orations and Speeches* (Philadelphia: A.M.E. Sunday School Union, 1926), 62–70.

Reprinted in Anthony B. Pinn, ed., *Making the Gospel Plain: The Writings of Bishop Reverdy C. Ransom* (Harrisburg: Trinity International, 1999), 102–11.

10 Ransom, "Thanksgiving Sermon," in *Spirit of Freedom and Justice*, 63.

11 Ransom, "Thanksgiving Sermon," in *Spirit of Freedom and Justice*, 65.

12 Ransom, "Thanksgiving Sermon," in *Spirit of Freedom ankd Justice*, 66.

13 Ransom, "Thanksgiving Sermon," in *Spirit of Freedom and Justice*, 69.

14 Ransom, "Thanksgiving Sermon," in *Spirit of Freedom and Justice*, 70.

15 Ransom, "Thanksgiving Sermon," in *Spirit of Freedom and Justice*, 69 (emphasis added).

16 Ransom, "Thanksgiving Sermon," in *Spirit of Freedom and Justice*, 69.

17 Florence S. Randolph, "Hope" (sermon preached before the National Association of Colored Women in 1898). Included in Collier-Thomas, *Daughters of Thunder*, 119–20.

18 Randolph, "Hope," in Collier-Thomas, *Daughters of Thunder*, 119.

19 Randolph, "Hope," in Collier-Thomas, *Daughters of Thunder*, 119.

20 Randolph, "Hope," in Collier-Thomas, *Daughters of Thunder*, 119.

21 Randolph, "Hope," in Collier-Thomas, *Daughters of Thunder*, 121.

22 Randolph, "Hope," in Collier-Thomas, *Daughters of Thunder*, 119.

23 Randolph, "Hope," in Collier-Thomas, *Daughters of Thunder*, 122.

24 Randolph, "Hope," in Collier-Thomas, *Daughters of Thunder*, 120.

25 Adam Clayton Powell Sr., "A Graceless Church" (sermon delivered at Abyssinian Baptist Church, Harlem, New York). Published in part in *New York Age*, September 21, 1911.

26 Powell, "Graceless Church."

27 Powell, "Graceless Church."

28 Powell, "Graceless Church."

29 Heschel, *Prophets*, 2:40–44.

30 Pinn, *Making the Gospel Plain*, 2.

31 Cf. the complete sermon manuscript of "The Church That Shall Survive," in Pinn, *Making the Gospel Plain*, 152–61.

32 Ransom, "Church That Shall Survive," in Pinn, *Making the Gospel Plain*, 153.

33 Ransom, "Church That Shall Survive," in Pinn, *Making the Gospel Plain*, 155.

34 As Ransom reasons, the quadrennial sermon intends to be a thoughtful recounting of both the past four years of the church's stated missional commitment and future prospects relating to its opportunities, duties, and tasks.

35 Singleton, *Romance of African Methodism*, 146.

36 Ransom, "Church That Shall Survive," in Pinn, *Making the Gospel Plain*, 155.

37 Ransom, "Church That Shall Survive," in Pinn, *Making the Gospel Plain*, 155.

38 Ransom, "Church That Shall Survive," in Pinn, *Making the Gospel Plain*, 156.

39 Ransom, "Church That Shall Survive," in Pinn, *Making the Gospel Plain*, 160.

40 Ransom, "Church That Shall Survive," in Pinn, *Making the Gospel Plain*, 160.

41 Ransom, "Church That Shall Survive," in Pinn, *Making the Gospel Plain*, 159.

42 Reverdy C. Ransom, "Heralds and Prophets of a Changed Order and a New Day." The sermon was originally published in *A.M.E. Church Review*, n.d., but most likely written in the early 1920s. Annetta Gomez-Jefferson Collection, Wooster, Ohio.

Copied by permission of Ransom biographer Annetta Gomez-Jefferson. See the full manuscript in appendix C of Kenyatta R. Gilbert's "A Time to Preach, a Time to Cry: An Investigation into the Nature of Prophetic Preaching in Black Churches during the Great Migration Period 1916–1940" (Ph.D. diss., Princeton Theological Seminary, 2007). Quotes correspond with pages of appendix.

43 Ransom, "Heralds and Prophets," in Gilbert, "Time to Preach," 216.

44 Ransom, "Heralds and Prophets," in Gilbert, "Time to Preach," 217.

45 Ransom, "Heralds and Prophets," in Gilbert, "Time to Preach," 216.

46 Ransom, "Heralds and Prophets," in Gilbert, "Time to Preach," 219.

47 Ransom, "Heralds and Prophets," in Gilbert, "Time to Preach," 217

48 Ransom, "Heralds and Prophets," in Gilbert, "Time to Preach," 219.

49 Ransom, "Heralds and Prophets," in Gilbert, "Time to Preach," 219.

50 Ransom, "Heralds and Prophets," in Gilbert, "Time to Preach," 221.

51 Ransom, "Heralds and Prophets," in Gilbert, "Time to Preach," 221.

52 Ransom, "Heralds and Prophets," in Gilbert, "Time to Preach," 221.

53 Ransom, "Heralds and Prophets," in Gilbert, "Time to Preach," 219.

54 Ransom, "Heralds and Prophets," in Gilbert, "Time to Preach," 216.

55 Randolph, "Antipathy to Women Preachers," in Collier-Thomas, *Daughters of Thunder*, 110 (emphasis original).

56 Randolph, "Antipathy to Women Preachers," in Collier-Thomas, *Daughters of Thunder*, 10.

57 Randolph, "Antipathy to Women Preachers," in Collier-Thomas, *Daughters of Thunder*, 110.

58 Randolph, "Antipathy to Women Preachers," in Collier-Thomas, *Daughters of Thunder*, 127.

59 Randolph, "Antipathy to Women Preachers," in Collier-Thomas, *Daughters of Thunder*, 128.

60 Randolph, "Antipathy to Women Preachers," in Collier-Thomas, *Daughters of Thunder*, 128.

61 Randolph, "Antipathy to Women Preachers," in Collier-Thomas, *Daughters of Thunder*, 128.

62 Randolph, "Antipathy to Women Preachers," in Collier-Thomas, *Daughters of Thunder*, 128.

63 Randolph, "Antipathy to Women Preachers," in Collier-Thomas, *Daughters of Thunder*, 128.

64 Randolph, "Antipathy to Women Preachers," in Collier-Thomas, *Daughters of Thunder*, 128.

65 Randolph, "Antipathy to Women Preachers," in Collier-Thomas, *Daughters of Thunder*, 129.

66 Randolph, "Antipathy to Women Preachers," in Collier-Thomas, *Daughters of Thunder*, 129.

67 Adam Clayton Powell Sr., "The Model Church," in *Palestine and Saints in Caesar's Household* (New York: Richard R. Smith, 1939), 129.

68 Powell, "Model Church," in *Palestine and Saints in Caesar's Household*, 129.

69 Powell, "Model Church," in *Palestine and Saints in Caesar's Household*, 129.

70 Powell, "Model Church," in *Palestine and Saints in Caesar's Household*, 133.

71 Powell, "Model Church," in *Palestine and Saints in Caesar's Household*, 129.

72 Powell, "Model Church," in *Palestine and Saints in Caesar's Household*, 136.

73 Powell, "Model Church," in *Palestine and Saints in Caesar's Household*, 137.

74 Powell, "Model Church," in *Palestine and Saints in Caesar's Household*, 134.

75 Adam Clayton Powell Sr., "The Colored Man's Contribution to Christianity and When It Will Be Made, 1919" (sermon delivered at Abyssinian Baptist Church and in other settings, housed in Schomburg Center for Research in Black Culture, New York).

76 Powell, "Colored Man's Contribution to Christianity," 3 (emphasis in original).

77 Clingan, *Against Cheap Grace in a World Come of Age*, 77.

78 Powell, "Colored Man's Contribution to Christianity," 3.

79 Powell, "Colored Man's Contribution to Christianity," 7.

80 Powell, "Colored Man's Contribution to Christianity," 9.

81 Powell, "Colored Man's Contribution to Christianity," 10.

82 Powell, "Colored Man's Contribution to Christianity," 10.

83 Powell, "Colored Man's Contribution to Christianity," 10.

84 Powell, "Colored Man's Contribution to Christianity," 8.

85 Powell, "Colored Man's Contribution to Christianity," 10–11.

86 Powell, "Colored Man's Contribution to Christianity," 11.

87 Powell, "Colored Man's Contribution to Christianity," 12.

88 Powell, "Colored Man's Contribution to Christianity," 13.

89 Powell, "Colored Man's Contribution to Christianity," 14.

90 Powell, "Colored Man's Contribution to Christianity," 14.

91 Powell, "Colored Man's Contribution to Christianity," 13.

92 James H. Evans Jr., *We Have Been Believers: An African American Systematic Theology* (Minneapolis: Fortress, 1992), 51.

93 Ransom, "Church That Shall Survive," in Pinn, *Making the Gospel Plain*, 153.

94 Ransom, "Heralds and Prophets," 216.

95 Ransom, "Heralds and Prophets," 220.

96 Wallace Best, "Passionately Human. No Less Divine: Racial Ideology and Religious Culture in the Black Churches of Chicago, 1915–1963" (Ph.D. diss., Northwestern University, 2000), 231.

97 Randolph, "Antipathy to Women Preachers," in Collier-Thomas, *Daughters of Thunder*, 126.

98 Powell, "Colored Man's Contribution to Christianity," 12.

99 Powell, "Colored Man's Contribution to Christianity," 10.

100 Powell, "Model Church," in *Palestine and Saints in Caesar's Household*, 132.

101 Powell, "Model Church," in *Palestine and Saints in Caesar's Household*, 132.

102 Peter J. Paris, *The Social Teaching of the Black Churches* (Philadelphia: Fortress, 1985), 9.

Chapter 5

1 Quoted in David Levering Lewis' *King: A Biography* (Champaign: University of Illinois Press, 1978), 380.

2 Martin Luther King Jr., "Letter from Birmingham City Jail," in *A Testament of Hope: The Essential Writings and Speeches of Martin Luther King, Jr.*, ed. James Melvin Washington (San Francisco: HarperSanFrancisco, 1986), 295.

3 King, Martin Luther, Jr. "I've Been to the Mountaintop, 1968." In *American Rhetoric Top 100 Speeches*. Accessed July 8, 2015. http://www.americanrhetoric .com/speeches/mlkivebeentothemountaintop.htm.. Martin Luther King Jr.'s "I've Been to the Mountaintop" sermon is commonly referred to as a speech rather than a sermon.

    Though King's sermon is primarily topical, its gospel features are undeniable—from its inductively narrated beginning to its three-point structured call to action. In terms of the scriptural texts and symbols King draws on to expand the Exodus motif (e.g., reference of Jeremiah's "fire in the bones" declaration; quasi-expository rendering of the Good Samaritan parable [Luke 10]; citation of Jesus' messianic announcement in Luke 4:18; the justice plea found in Amos 5:24; the ecclesial setting [Mason Temple of the Church of God in Christ]; and obvious theological content), it is fair to say that King's final message bears the classical marks of a Christian sermon. Whether a sermon's movement is inductive or deductive or some combination of the two or expository or topical, a Christian sermon, in the broadest sense, is an extended, biblically informed, theological conversation about what it means to speak of a promise-bearing God who addresses the real needs of real people. See Ronald J. Allen, ed., *Patterns of Preaching: A Sermon Sampler* (St. Louis: Chalice Press, 1998) for its description of the sermon.

4 "Memphis Sanitation Workers Strike (1968)," *King Encyclopedia* (online), The Martin Luther King, Jr. Research and Education Institute, Stanford University, accessed February 8, 2016, http://kingencyclopedia.stanford.edu/encyclopedia/encyclopedia/ enc_memphis_sanitation_workers_strike_1968/.

5 King, "I've Been to the Mountaintop," in Simmons and Thomas, *Preaching with Sacred Fire*, 516–17.

6 Before Moses dies he ascends to Mount Nebo and is permitted to view the land inheritance God promised to his ancestors Abraham, Isaac, and Jacob (Deut 34:1-4); Num 13:1-33 chronicles Moses' commissioning of twelve male representatives from each of Israel's tribes to scout the land of Canaan.

7 Lewis, *King: A Critical Biography*, 31.

8 King, "I've Been to the Mountaintop," 519.

9 Sermon excerpts taken from Sandy F. Ray's *Journeying through a Jungle* (Nashville: Broadman, 1979).

10 W. Franklin Richardson, "Introduction," in Ray, *Journeying through a Jungle*, 18–21.

11 Ray also delivered the eulogy at the funeral services of Alberta King, Martin Luther King Jr.'s slain mother. See "Ray, Sandy F. (1898–1979)," *King Encyclopedia* (online), The Martin Luther King, Jr. Research and Education Institute, Stanford University,

accessed July 8, 2014, http://kingencyclopedia.stanford.edu/encyclopedia/ency-clopedia/enc_ray_sandy_frederick_1898_1979/. Jared E. Alcántara, "Past Masters: Sandy Frederick Ray," *Preaching Magazine*, March 1, 2014, accessed July 8, 2015, http://www.preaching.com/resources/articles/11707471/.

12 Ray, *Journeying through a Jungle*, 24.

13 Ray, *Journeying through a Jungle*, 24.

14 Ray, *Journeying through a Jungle*, 24–25.

15 Ray, *Journeying through a Jungle*, 26.

16 Ray, *Journeying through a Jungle*, 25–26.

17 Ray, *Journeying through a Jungle*, 27.

18 Ray, *Journeying through a Jungle*, 28.

19 Ray, *Journeying through a Jungle*, 29.

20 Ray, *Journeying through a Jungle*, 29–30.

21 Benjamin Elijah Mays, "Why Dives Went to Hell." Typed manuscript. This ser-mon was delivered on September 21, 1980 at Hillside Chapel and Truth Center in Atlanta, Georgia, where Rev. Barbara King served as pastor. It was also delivered on August 17, 1980 at Second Baptist Church in Los Angeles, California. An early version was preached on August 21, 1955. Mays Collection, Moorland-Spingarn Research Center, Washington, D.C.

22 A note on the pamphlet reads, "this is a condensation of one of the main addresses at the Conference on 'The Life of the Church' of the New England SCM [Student Christian Movement] last spring." Benjamin E. Mays, "The Faith of the Church," *Intercollegian* 72, no. 4 (1954): 1–2.

23 Mays, "Faith of the Church," 2.

24 Mays, "Faith of the Church," 3.

25 Mays, "Faith of the Church," 4

26 Mays, "Faith of the Church," 4.

27 See sermon records from the archives of the Mays Collection at Moorland-Spingarn Research Center, Howard University, Washington, D.C.: April 1944, "The Inescap-able Christ," Brooklyn, N.Y. (typed manuscript on index cards and delivered mul-tiple times in various contexts), box 1; February 24, 1957, "The Meaning of 'Our Father,'" Chicago Sunday Evening Club, box 2; April 9, 1968, "Eulogy of Dr. Martin Luther King, Jr.," Atlanta, Ga., Box 5; 1969, eulogy of Rev. A. D. King, Atlanta, Ga., April 12, 1970, box 5; "What Man Lives by," Harvard University, Memorial Church, September 14, 1974, box 7; "Eulogy of Dr. Mordecai W. Johnson," Howard Univer-sity, Andrew Rankin Memorial Chapel, Washington, D.C., April 16, 1981, box 11; eulogy of Howard Thurman, May 16, 1982, box 11; "Man Shall Not Live by Bread Alone," Atlanta, Ga., box 11.

28 Mays, "Why Dives Went to Hell," 1.

29 Mays, "Why Dives Went to Hell," 1.

30 Mays, "Why Dives Went to Hell," 1.

31 Mays, "Why Dives Went to Hell," 2.

32 Mays, "Why Dives Went to Hell," 3.

33 Mays, "Why Dives Went to Hell," 2.

34   Mays, "Why Dives Went to Hell," 2.

35   Cf. Richard Lischer's *Reading the Parables in Interpretation: Resources for the Use of Scripture in the Church* (Louisville, Ky.: Westminster John Knox, 2014), where he lays out four theories for reading Jesus' parables.

36   Mays, "Why Dives Went to Hell," 3.

37   Mays, "Why Dives Went to Hell," 4.

38   Mays, "Why Dives Went to Hell," 5.

39   Mays, "Why Dives Went to Hell," 5.

40   Sermon excerpts from Samuel DeWitt Proctor's "The Bottom Line," taken from Samuel D. Proctor and William D. Watley's *Sermons from the Black Pulpit* (Valley Forge, Pa.: Judson Press, 1984).

41   Adam L. Bond, *The Imposing Preacher: Samuel DeWitt Proctor and Black Public Faith* (Minneapolis: Fortress, 2013), 9.

42   Bond, *Imposing Preacher*, 13.

43   Bond, *Imposing Preacher*, 13.

44   Bond, *Imposing Preacher*, 27.

45   Bond, *Imposing Preacher*, 69n15.

46   Proctor, "Bottom Line," in Proctor and Watley, *Sermons from the Black Pulpit*, 88.

47   Proctor, "Bottom Line," in Proctor and Watley, *Sermons from the Black Pulpit*, 91.

48   Proctor, "Bottom Line," in Proctor and Watley, *Sermons from the Black Pulpit*, 91.

49   Proctor, "Bottom Line," in Proctor and Watley, *Sermons from the Black Pulpit*, 92.

50   Proctor, "Bottom Line," in Proctor and Watley, *Sermons from the Black Pulpit*, 95.

51   See full manuscripts in appendix A. All published and unpublished sermons included in this volume are reprinted with the permission of the authors.

52   Katie Geneva Cannon, "Prophets for a New Day," in Simmons and Thomas, *Preaching with Sacred Fire*, 622–26. Earlier versions of this sermon were preached at Presbyterian Church of the Ascension in New York City, where Cannon served as Stated Supply Pastor (1975–77); First African Presbyterian Church in Philadelphia, Covenant United Presbyterian Church in Kannapolis, N.C.; and First United Presbyterian Church in Richmond, Va.

53   Although some contemporary homiletics scholars have questioned the usefulness of the traditional three-point sermon in an increasingly visually oriented society, Cannon, a student of the Interdenominational Theological Center's homiletics professor Isaac Rufus Clark, demonstrates that in the hands of some African American preachers, whether the sermon is expository or topical, the three-point tradition can be used to good effect. See Katie G. Cannon, *Teaching Preaching: Isaac Rufus Clark and Black Sacred Rhetoric* (New York: Continuum, 2007).

54   Cannon, "Prophets for a New Day," in Simmons and Thomas, *Preaching with Sacred Fire*, 624.

55   Cannon, "Prophets for a New Day," in Simmons and Thomas, *Preaching with Sacred Fire*, 624–25, discussing Jonathan Kozol's *Savage Inequalities: Children in America's Schools* (New York: Crown, 1991).

56 Otis Moss Jr., "A Prophetic Witness in an Anti-Prophetic Age," *The African American Pulpit* 7, no. 4 (2004): 68–72. Reprinted in Simmons and Thomas, *Preaching with Sacred Fire*, 777–82. Used by author's permission.

57 Moss, "Prophetic Witness," in Simmons and Thomas, *Preaching with Sacred Fire*, 778.

58 Moss, "Prophetic Witness," in Simmons and Thomas, *Preaching with Sacred Fire*, 779.

59 Moss, "Prophetic Witness," in Simmons and Thomas, *Preaching with Sacred Fire*, 780.

60 Marvin A. McMickle, "How Much of Leviticus Do You Really Want?" This didactic sermon was delivered extemporaneously before a lively "talk back" at a gathering of African American pastors, preachers, and students at the American Baptist College's 2012 Garnett-Nabrit Lecture in Nashville, Tennessee. See full sermon transcript in Appendix B.

61 McMickle, "How Much of Leviticus Do You Really Want?"

62 McMickle, "How Much of Leviticus Do You Really Want?"

63 McMickle, "How Much of Leviticus Do You Really Want?"

64 McMickle, "How Much of Leviticus Do You Really Want?"

65 Cheryl J. Sanders, "What Does God Require of Us?" (original, unpublished transcript of a sermon delivered on January 19, 2014, before her congregation, Third Street Church of God, Washington, D.C.). Used by permission of Cheryl J. Sanders. See full sermon transcript in Appendix B.

66 Sanders, "What Does God Require of Us?"

67 Sanders, "What Does God Require of Us?"

Conclusion

1 McMickle, *Where Have All the Prophets Gone?* 219.

2 Quoted in a message focused on the Supreme Court's deliberations in the *Shelby County v. Holder* case.

3 Although it would be inaccurate to claim that Black megachurches and prosperity theology go hand in hand since there are many progressive megachurches doing justice work and actively supporting community renewal initiatives, there are several megachurches, particularly in the South, who in divorce of denominational or connectional ties, in pursuit of enlarged memberships, have relaxed their commitment to prophetic ministry. See Tamelyn Tucker-Worgs, *The Black Megachurch: Theology, Gender, and the Politics of Public Engagement* (Waco, Tex.: Baylor University Press, 2011).

4 James F. Kay, "Reorientation: Homiletics as Theologically Authorized Rhetoric," *Princeton Seminary Bulletin* 24, no. 1 (2003): 33.

5 Russell Moldovan, *Martin Luther King, Jr.: An Oral History of His Religious Witness and His Life* (Lanham, Md.: International Scholars, 1999), 15.

6 William Julius Wilson, *When Work Disappears: The World of the New Urban Poor* (New York: Vintage Books, 1996), 218–19. Also see Wilson's groundbreaking studies *The Truly Disadvantaged: The Inner City, the Underclass, and Public Policy* (Chicago: University of Chicago Press, 1987) and, most recently, *More Than Race: Being Black and Poor in the Inner City* (New York: W. W. Norton, 2007).

7   Because this proverb communicates such an important message about the power of the collective in teaching children, presidential candidate Hillary Rodham Clinton adopted the phrase as the title for her book *It Takes a Village: And Other Lessons Children Teach Us* (New York: Simon & Schuster, 1996). Robert M. Franklin, *Crisis in the Village: Restoring Hope in African American Communities* (Minneapolis: Fortress: 2007), 3, 11–13.

8   African Americans are 13 percent of the nation's population and account for 56 percent annually of new HIV infections. A quarter of these new infections are among people under twenty-five years of age (K. Wright, "Time Is Now! The State of AIDS in Black America," Black AIDS Institute, Los Angeles, Calif., February 2005, 5, 8; quoted in Tavis Smiley, *The Covenant with Black America* [Chicago: Third World, 2006], 9). Nearly one-third—32 percent—of African Americans do not have a regular doctor. By contrast, only 20 percent of White Americans do not have a regular doctor ("2001 Health Care Quality Survey," The Commonwealth Fund, New York, N.Y., November 2001, chart 37; quoted in Smiley, *Covenant with Black America*, 9). One of every three Black males born today can expect to go to prison in his lifetime (Marc Mauer and Ryan Scott King, "Schools and Prisons: 50 Years After Brown vs. Board of Education," http://www.sentencingproject.org/pdfs/brownboard.pdf, The Sentencing Project; quoted in Smiley, *Covenant with Black America*, 53).

9   Richard Lischer, *The End of Words: The Language of Reconciliation in a Culture of Violence* (Grand Rapids: Eerdmans, 2005), 5.

10   See Michelle Alexander, *The New Jim Crow: Mass Incarceration in the Age of Colorblindness* (New York: New Press, 2012).

11   Martin Luther King Jr., *Strength to Love* (Philadelphia: Fortress, 1963), 91.

12   King, *Strength to Love*, 93.

13   Brueggemann, *Prophetic Imagination*, xvii.

14   Freire, *Pedagogy of the Oppressed*, 27.

BIBLIOGRAPHY

Achtemeier, Elizabeth. *Preaching from the Old Testament.* Louisville, Ky.: Westminster John Knox, 1989.

Albrecht, Gloria. *The Character of Our Communities: Toward an Ethic of Liberation for the Church.* Nashville: Abingdon, 1995.

Alcántara, Jared E. "Past Masters: Sandy Frederick Ray." *Preaching Magazine,* March 1, 2014. Accessed July 8, 2015. http://www.preaching.com/resources/articles/11707471/.

Alexander, Michelle. *The New Jim Crow: Mass Incarceration in the Age of Colorblindness.* New York: New Press, 2012.

Alkebulan, Adisa K. "The Spiritual Essence of African American Rhetoric." In *Understanding African American Rhetoric: Classical Origins to Contemporary Innovations,* edited by Ronald L. Jackson II and Elaine B. Richardson, 23–40. New York: Routledge, 2003.

Allen, Ronald J., ed. *Patterns of Preaching: A Sermon Sampler.* St. Louis: Chalice Press, 1998.

Andrews, Dale P. *Practical Theology for Black Churches: Bridging Black Theology and African American Folk Religion.* Louisville, Ky.: Westminster John Knox, 2002.

Arnesen, Eric. *Black Protest and the Great Migration: A Brief History with Documents.* New York: St. Martin's, 2002.

Asante, Molefi K. *The Afrocentric Idea.* Rev. ed. Philadelphia: Temple University Press, 1998.

Baer, Hans A. *The Black Spiritual Movement: A Religious Response to Racism.* Knoxville: University of Tennessee Press, 1984.

Baer, Hans A., and Merrill Singer. *African-American Religion in the Twentieth Century: Varieties of Protest and Accommodation*. Knoxville: University of Tennessee Press, 1992. Reprinted as *African American Religion: Varieties of Protest and Accommodation*. 2nd ed. Knoxville: University of Tennessee Press, 2002.

Bartow, Charles L. *God's Human Speech: A Practical Theology of Proclamation*. Grand Rapids: Eerdmans, 1997.

Berry, Jason. *The Spirit of Black Hawk: A Mystery of Africans and Indians*. Jackson: University Press of Mississippi, 1995.

Best, Wallace C. "Passionately Human. No Less Divine: Racial Ideology and Religious Culture in the Black Churches of Chicago, 1915-1963." Ph.D. diss., Northwestern University, 2000. Published as *Passionately Human, No Less Divine: Religion and Culture in Black Chicago, 1915-1952*. Princeton: Princeton University Press, 2005.

Bitzer, Lloyd. "The Rhetorical Situation." *Philosophy and Rhetoric* 1, no. 1 (1968): 1-14. Reprinted in *Contemporary Rhetorical Theory: A Reader*, edited by John Louis Lucaites, Celeste Michelle Condit, and Sally Caudill, 217-25. New York: Guilford Press, 1999.

Bond, Adam L. *The Imposing Preacher: Samuel DeWitt Proctor and Black Public Faith*. Minneapolis: Fortress, 2013.

Brueggemann, Walter. *A Commentary on Jeremiah: Exile and Homecoming*. Grand Rapids: Eerdmans, 1998.

———. *Finally Comes the Poet: Daring Speech for Proclamation*. Minneapolis: Fortress, 1989.

———. *The Practice of Prophetic Imagination: Preaching an Emancipating Word*. Minneapolis: Fortress, 2012.

———. *The Prophetic Imagination*. Rev. ed. Minneapolis: Fortress, 2001.

———. "The Prophetic Word of God and History." In Miller, *Texts That Linger*, 35-44.

———. "Prophets." In *Reverberations of Faith: A Theological Handbook of Old Testament Themes*, 158-61. Louisville, Ky.: Westminster John Knox, 2002.

Brundage, W. Fitzhugh. *Lynching in the New South: Georgia and Virginia, 1880-1930*. Urbana: University of Illinois Press, 1993.

Burkett, Randall K. *Black Redemption: Churchmen Speak for the Garvey Movement*. Philadelphia: Temple University Press, 1978.

Cahalan, Kathleen, and Gordon S. Mikoski, eds. *Opening the Field of Practical Theology: An Introduction*. Lanham, Md.: Rowman & Littlefield, 2014.

Campbell, Charles. *The Word Before the Powers: An Ethic of Preaching*. Louisville, Ky.: Westminster John Knox, 2002.

Cannon, Katie Geneva. "Prophets for a New Day." In Simmons and Thomas, *Preaching with Sacred Fire*, 621-26.

———. *Teaching Preaching: Isaac Rufus Clark and Black Sacred Rhetoric.* New York: Continuum, 2007.

Clingan, Ralph G. *Against Cheap Grace in a World Come of Age: An Intellectual Biography of Clayton Powell, 1865–1953.* Martin Luther King, Jr. Memorial Studies in Religion, Culture, and Social Development 9. New York: Peter Lang, 2002.

Collier-Thomas, Bettye. *Daughters of Thunder: Black Women Preachers and Their Sermons, 1850–1979.* San Francisco: Jossey-Bass, 1997.

———. "Minister and Feminist Reformer: The Life of Florence Spearing Randolph." In *This Far by Faith: Readings in African American Women's Religious Biography,* edited by Judith Weisenfeld and Richard Newman. New York: Routledge, 1996.

Cone, James H. *God of the Oppressed.* Rev. ed. Maryknoll, N.Y.: Orbis Books, 1997.

Crew, Spencer R. *Field to Factory: Afro-American Migration, 1915–1940.* Washington, D.C.: Smithsonian Institution, 1987.

Davis, Dernoral. "Toward a Socio-Historical and Demographic Portrait." In Harrison, *Black Exodus,* 1–19.

De Gruchy, John W. *Christianity, Art and Transformation: Theological Aesthetics in the Struggle for Justice.* Cambridge: Cambridge University Press, 2003.

Drewett, Donald A. "Ransom on Race and Racism: The Racial and Social Thought of Reverdy Cassius Ransom—Preacher, Editor and Bishop in the African Methodist Episcopal Church, 1861–1959." Ph.D. diss., Drew University, 1988.

Du Bois, W. E. B. *The Negro Church.* Atlanta: Atlanta University Press, 1903.

Ellison, Gregory C., II. *Cut Dead But Still Alive: Caring for African American Young Men.* Nashville: Abingdon, 2013.

Evans, James H., Jr. *We Have Been Believers: An African American Systematic Theology.* Minneapolis: Fortress, 1992.

Fauset, Arthur. *Black Gods of the Metropolis: Negro Religious Cults of the Urban North.* Philadelphia: University of Pennsylvania Press, 1970.

Floyd, Silas X. *Life of Charles T. Walker, D.D.: "The Black Spurgeon," Pastor of Mt. Olivet Baptist Church, New York City.* New York: Negro Universities Press, 1969. Reprint of *Life of Charles T. Walker, DD ("the Black Spurgeon"), Pastor Mt. Olivet Baptist Church, New York City.* New York: National Baptist Publishing Board, 1902.

Forbes, James A., Jr. *The Holy Spirit and Preaching.* Nashville: Abingdon, 1989.

Franklin, C. L. "Moses at the Red Sea." Sermon in *Give Me This Mountain,* edited by Jeff Todd Titon. Urbana: University of Illinois Press, 1989.

Franklin, Robert M. *Crisis in the Village: Restoring Hope in African American Communities.* Minneapolis: Fortress, 2007.

Frazier, E. Franklin. *The Negro Church in America.* 1964. Reprint, New York: Schocken Books, 1974.

Freire, Paulo. *Pedagogy of the Oppressed*. Translated by Myra Bergman Ramos. New York: Continuum, 1993.

Fullinwider, S. P. "Racial Christianity." In *African American Religious Thought*, edited by Cornel West and Eddie Glaude Jr., 477–84. Louisville, Ky.: Westminster John Knox, 2003.

Garner, Thurmon, and Carolyn Calloway-Thomas. "African American Orality: Expanding Rhetoric." In *Understanding African American Rhetoric: Classical Origins to Contemporary Innovations*, edited by Ronald L. Jackson II and Elaine B. Richardson, 43–55. New York: Routledge, 2003.

Garvey, Marcus. "Liberty Hall Speech," delivered on August 21, 1921 and included in *Negro World* 11, no. 2 (1921): 26–30. Reprinted in Burkett, *Black Redemption*.

Genovese, Eugene D. *Roll, Jordan, Roll: The World the Slaves Made*. New York: Vintage Books, 1976.

Geschwender, James A. *Racial Stratification in America*. Dubuque, Iowa: WC Brown, 1978.

Gilbert, Kenyatta R. *The Journey and Promise of African American Preaching*. Minneapolis: Fortress, 2011.

———. "The Prophetic and the Priestly: Reclaiming Preaching as Practical Theology." In *Koinonia XVI: The Princeton Seminary Graduate Forum* (2004): 124–39.

———. "A Time to Preach, a Time to Cry: An Investigation into the Nature of Prophetic Preaching in Black Churches during the Great Migration Period 1916–1940." Ph.D. diss., Princeton Theological Seminary, 2007.

Gilkes, Cheryl Townsend. "There Is a Work for Each One of Us." In *"How Long This Road": Race, Religion, and the Legacy of C. Eric Lincoln*, edited by Alton B. Pollard III and Love Henry Whelchel Jr., 131–40. New York: Palgrave Macmillan, 2003.

Glaude, Eddie, Jr. *Exodus! Religion, Race, and Nation in Early Nineteenth-Century Black America*. Chicago: University of Chicago Press, 2000.

Goddard, Terrell Dale. "The Black Social Gospel in Chicago, 1896–1906: The Ministries of Reverdy C. Ransom and Richard R. Wright, Jr." *Journal of Negro History* 84, no. 3 (1999): 227–46.

Gomez-Jefferson, Annetta. *The Sage of Tawawa: Reverdy Cassius Ransom, 1861–1959*. Kent, Ohio: Kent State University Press, 2002.

Gregg, Robert. *Sparks from the Anvil of Oppression: Philadelphia's African Methodists and Southern Migrants, 1890–1940*. Philadelphia: Temple University Press, 1993.

Grossman, James. *Land of Hope: Chicago, Black Southerners, and the Great Migration*. Chicago: University of Chicago Press, 1989.

Harris, James. *Preaching Liberation*. Minneapolis: Augsburg Fortress, 1995.

Harrison, Alferdeen, ed. *The Black Exodus: The Great Migration from the American South*. Jackson: University of Mississippi Press, 1991.

Harrison, Milmon F. *Righteous Riches: The Word of Faith Movement in Contemporary African American Religion*. Oxford: Oxford University Press, 2005.

Harvey, Thomas Watson. Interview by Giles R. Wright. Transcript. Trenton, N.J., April 30, 1976. *New Jersey Multi-Ethnic Oral History Project*.

Heschel, Abraham Joshua. *The Prophets*. 2 vols. New York: Harper & Row, 1962.

Hill, Lynda Marion. *Social Rituals and the Verbal Art of Zora Neale Hurston*. Washington, D.C.: Howard University Press, 1996.

Hornsby, Alton, Jr., ed. *A Companion to African American History*. Malden, Mass.: Blackwell, 2005.

Hubbard, Dolan. *The Sermon and the African American Literary Imagination*. Columbia: University of Missouri Press, 1994.

Huddle, Mark A. "Exodus from the South." In Hornsby, *Companion to African American History*, 449–62.

Hurston, Zora Neale. *The Sanctified Church*. Berkeley: Turtle Island, 1983.

Jackson, Blyden. "Introduction: A Street of Dreams." In Harrison, *Black Exodus*, xi–xv.

Jennings, Willie James. "The Aesthetic Struggle and Ecclesial Vision." In *Black Practical Theology*, edited by Dale P. Andrews and Robert London Smith Jr., 163–85. Waco, Tex.: Baylor University Press, 2015.

Jones, Absalom. *A Thanksgiving Sermon*. Philadelphia: Fry & Kammerer, 1808.

Kay, James F. *Preaching and Theology*. St. Louis: Chalice Press, 2007.

———. "Reorientation: Homiletics as Theologically Authorized Rhetoric." *Princeton Seminary Bulletin* 24, no. 1 (2003): 33–35.

King, Martin Luther, Jr. "I've Been to the Mountaintop, 1968." In *American Rhetoric Top 100 Speeches*. Accessed July 8, 2015. http://www.americanrhetoric.com/speeches/mlkivebeentothemountaintop.htm.

———. "Letter from Birmingham City Jail." In *A Testament of Hope: The Essential Writings and Speeches of Martin Luther King, Jr.*, edited by James Melvin Washington, 289–302. San Francisco: HarperSanFrancisco, 1986.

———. *Strength to Love*. Philadelphia: Fortress, 1963.

Kinney, John William. "Adam Clayton Powell, Sr. and Adam Clayton Powell, Jr.: A Historical Exposition and Theological Analysis." Ph.D. diss., Columbia University, 1979.

Kozol, Jonathan. *Savage Inequalities: Children in America's Schools*. New York: Crown, 1991.

Lamb, Matthew. *Solidarity with Victims: Toward a Theology of Social Transformation*. New York: Crossroads, 1982.

LaRue, Cleophus J., Jr. *The Heart of Black Preaching.* Louisville, Ky.: Westminster John Knox, 2000.

Leman, Nicholas. *The Promised Land: The Great Black Migration.* New York: Alfred A. Knopf, 1991.

Lewis, David Levering. *King: A Biography.* Champaign: University of Illinois Press, 1978.

———. *King: A Critical Biography.* Baltimore: Penguin Books, 1970.

Lincoln, C. Eric, and Lawrence H. Mamiya. *The Black Church in the African American Experience.* Durham, N.C.: Duke University Press, 1990.

Lindley, Susan. " 'Neglected Voices' and Praxis in the Social Gospel." *Journal of Religious Ethics* 18, no. 1 (1990): 75–102.

Lischer, Richard. *The End of Words: The Language of Reconciliation in a Culture of Violence.* Grand Rapids: Eerdmans, 2005.

———. *The Preacher King: Martin Luther King Jr. and the Word that Moved America.* Oxford: Oxford University Press, 1995.

———. *Reading the Parables in Interpretation: Resources for the Use of Scripture in the Church.* Louisville, Ky.: Westminster John Knox, 2014.

Logan, James S. *Good Punishment: Christian Moral Practice and Imprisonment.* Grand Rapids: Eerdmans, 2008.

Logan, Rayford W. *The Betrayal of the Negro: From Rutherford B. Hayes to Woodrow Wilson.* New York: Collier Press, 1965.

Long, D. Stephen. "Prophetic Preaching." In Willimon and Lischer, *Concise Encyclopedia of Preaching,* 387.

Lovin, Robin. "Justice." In *A New Handbook of Christian Theology,* edited by Donald W. Musser and Joseph L. Price, 266–71. Nashville: Abingdon, 1992.

Luker, Ralph. *The Social Gospel in Black and White: American Racial Reform, 1885–1912.* Chapel Hill: University of North Carolina Press, 1991.

Manheim, James. "Austin, Junius C., Rev. 1887-1968." In *Contemporary Black Biography.* 2004. Encyclopedia.com. Accessed February 8, 2016. http://www.encyclopedia.com/doc/1G2-3431000009.html.

Marks, Carol. *Farewell–We're Good and Gone: The Great Migration.* Bloomington: Indiana University Press, 1989.

Martin, Tony. *Race First: The Ideological and Organizational Struggles of Marcus Garvey and the Universal Negro Improvement Association.* Dover, Mass.: Majority, 1986.

Mays, Benjamin E. *Born to Rebel: An Autobiography.* 1971. Reprint, Athens: University of Georgia Press, 2003.

———. "The Faith of the Church." *Intercollegian* 72, no. 4 (1954).

———. "Why Dives Went to Hell." August 17, 1980, Mays Collection, Moorland-Spingarn Research Center, Howard University, Washington, D.C.

McKim, Donald. *The Bible in Theology and Preaching.* Nashville: Abingdon, 1985.

McMickle, Marvin A. "How Much of Leviticus Do You Really Want?" Garnett-Nabrit Lecture, Nashville, Tennessee, April 2012.

———. *Preaching to the Black Middle Class.* Valley Forge, Pa.: Judson Press, 2000.

———. *Where Have All the Prophets Gone? Reclaiming Prophetic Preaching in America.* Cleveland: Pilgrim, 2006.

McNeil, Genna Rae, Houston Bryan Roberson, Quinton Hosford Dixie, and Kevin McGruder. *Witness: Two Hundred Years of African-American Faith and Practice at the Abyssinian Baptist Church of Harlem, New York.* Grand Rapids: Eerdmans, 2014.

Meier, August, and Elliot M. Rudwick. *From Plantation to Ghetto.* 3rd ed. New York: Hill & Wang, 1976.

"Memphis Sanitation Workers Strike (1968)." *King Encyclopedia* (online). The Martin Luther King, Jr. Research and Education Institute, Stanford University. Accessed February 8, 2016. http://kingencyclopedia.stanford.edu/encyclopedia/encyclopedia/enc_memphis_sanitation_workers_strike_1968/.

Miller, Patrick D. *The Religion of Ancient Israel.* Louisville, Ky.: Westminster John Knox, 2000.

Mitchem, Stephanie Y. *Name It and Claim It? Prosperity Preaching in the Black Church.* Cleveland: Pilgrim, 2007.

Moldovan, Russell. *Martin Luther King, Jr.: An Oral History of His Religious Witness and His Life.* Lanham, Md.: International Scholars, 1999.

Moses, Wilson Jeremiah. *The Golden Age of Black Nationalism, 1850–1925.* Oxford: Oxford University Press, 1978.

———, ed. *Texts That Linger, Words That Explode: Listening to Prophetic Voices.* Minneapolis: Augsburg Fortress, 2000.

Moss, Otis, Jr. "A Prophetic Witness in an Anti-Prophetic Age." *The African American Pulpit* 7, no. 4 (2004). Reprinted in Simmons and Thomas, *Preaching with Sacred Fire,* 777–82.

Mumford, Debra. *Exploring Prosperity Preaching.* Valley Forge, Pa.: Judson Press, 2012.

Osmer, Richard. *Practical Theology: An Introduction.* Louisville, Ky.: Westminster John Knox, 2008.

Osofsky, Gilbert. *Harlem: The Making of the Ghetto.* 2nd ed. New York: Harper & Row, 1971.

Padilla, Elaine, and Peter C. Phan. *Contemporary Issues of Migration and Theology.* New York: Palgrave Macmillan, 2013.

Painter, Nell Irvin. *Exodusters: Black Migration to Kansas after Reconstruction.* New York: Alfred A. Knopf, 1977.

Paris, Peter J. *The Social Teaching of the Black Churches.* Philadelphia: Fortress, 1985.

Patterson, Orlando. *Rituals of Blood: Consequences of Slavery in Two American Centuries*. Washington, D.C.: Civitas Counterpoint, 1998.

Phillips, Kimberly L. *AlabamaNorth: African-American Migrants, Community, and Working Class Activism in Cleveland, 1915–45*. Urbana: University of Illinois Press, 1999.

Pinn, Anne H., and Anthony B. Pinn. *Fortress Introduction to Black Church History*. Minneapolis: Fortress, 2002.

Pinn, Anthony B., ed. *Making the Gospel Plain: The Writings of Bishop Reverdy C. Ransom*. Harrisburg: Trinity International, 1999.

Powell, Adam Clayton, Sr. *Against the Tide*. 1938. Reprint, New York: Arno Press, 1980.

———. "The Colored Man's Contribution to Christianity and When It Will Be Made, 1919." Schomburg Center for Research in Black Culture, New York.

———. "A Graceless Church." *New York Age*, September 21, 1911.

———. *Palestine and Saints in Caesar's Household*. New York: Richard R. Smith, 1939.

Powery, Luke A. *Dem Dry Bones: Preaching, Death, and Hope*. Minneapolis: Fortress, 2012.

Preuss, Horst Dietrich. *Old Testament Theology*. Vol. 2. Louisville, Ky.: Westminster John Knox, 1996.

"Proctor, Henry Hugh (1868–1933)." *BlackPast.org*. Accessed July 8, 2015. http://www.blackpast.org/aah/proctor-henry-hugh-1868-1933.

Proctor, Samuel D. "The Bottom Line." In *Sermons from the Black Pulpit*, edited by Samuel D. Proctor and William D. Watley, 87–97. Valley Forge, Pa.: Judson Press, 1984.

Proctor, Samuel D., and Gardner C. Taylor. *We Have This Ministry: The Heart of the Pastor's Vocation*. Valley Forge, Pa.: Judson Press, 1996.

Raboteau, Albert J. "The Black Experience in American Evangelicalism: The Meaning of Slavery." In *The Evangelical Tradition in America*, edited by Leonard Sweet, 181–97. Macon, Ga.: Mercer University Press, 1984.

———. *Canaan Land: A Religious History of African Americans*. New York: Oxford University Press, 2001.

"Randolph, Florence Spearing, Biographical Note." New Jersey Historical Society. Accessed July 8, 2015. http://www.jerseyhistory.org/findingaid .php?aid=1321.

Randolph, Florence Spearing. "Hope." Sermon preached before the National Association of Colored Women in 1898. In Collier-Thomas, *Daughters of Thunder*.

Ransom, Reverdy C. *The Disadvantages and Opportunities of the Colored Youth*. Cleveland: Thomas & Mattill, 1894.

———. *First Quadrennial Report of the Pastor and Warden of the Institutional Church and Social Settlement to the Twenty-Second Session of the General Conference and to the Connectional Trustees of the African Methodist Episcopal Church.* Chicago: Quinn Chapel, 1904.

———. "Heralds and Prophets of a Changed Order and New Day." *A.M.E. Church Review,* n.d. Quotations correspond to pages 215–22 in appendix C of Gilbert, "A Time to Preach, a Time to Cry."

———. "The Industrial and Social Conditions of the Negro: A Thanksgiving Sermon." Sermon preached at Bethel AME Church in Chicago, November 26, 1896. Box 15, folder 12, Reverdy C. Ransom Collection, Payne Theological Seminary, Wilberforce, Ohio.

———. *The Pilgrimage of Harriet Ransom's Son.* Nashville: A.M.E. Sunday School, 1949.

———. "Quadrennial Sermon: The Church That Shall Survive." In Singleton, *Romance of African Methodism,* 142–56.

———. "Thanksgiving Sermon: The American Tower of Babel; or, The Confusion of Tongues." Sermon delivered at Bethel AME Church, New York, November 25, 1909. In Reverdy C. Ransom, *The Spirit of Freedom and Justice: Orations and Speeches.* Philadelphia: A.M.E. Sunday School Union, 1926. Reprinted in Pinn, *Making the Gospel Plain,* 102–11.

Ray, Sandy F. *Journeying through a Jungle.* Nashville: Broadman, 1979.

"Ray, Sandy F. (1898–1979)." *King Encyclopedia* (online). The Martin Luther King, Jr. Research and Education Institute. Accessed July 8, 2015. http://mlk -kpp01.stanford.edu/index.php/encyclopedia/encyclopedia/enc_ray_sandy _frederick_1898_1979/.

Richardson, Ben. *Great American Negroes,* rev. ed. New York: Thomas Crowell, 1945.

Richardson, W. Franklin. Introduction to Ray, *Journeying through a Jungle,* 18–21.

Ricoeur, Paul. *Lectures on Ideology and Utopia.* Edited by George H. Taylor. New York: Columbia University Press, 1981.

Roberts, Ric. "Old Man Eloquent: Bishop Ransom, 95, Last of First Generation," *Pittsburgh Courier,* February 18, 1956, city edition.

Robinson, Betty. "Florence Spearing Randolph." *Charisma Magazine,* January 31, 2004. Accessed August 8, 2013. http://www.charismamag.com/ site-archives/24-uncategorised/9848-florence-spearing-randolph.

Sanders, Cheryl J. "What Does God Require of Us?" Lecture, Third Street Church of God, Washington, D.C., January 19, 2014.

Schipani, Daniel S. *Conscientization and Creativity: Paulo Freire and Christian Education.* Lanham, Md.: University Press of America, 1984.

Sernett, Milton C. *Bound for the Promised Land: African American Religion and the Great Migration.* Durham, N.C.: Duke University Press, 1997.

Simmons, Martha, and Frank Thomas, eds. *Preaching with Sacred Fire: An Anthology of African American Sermons, 1750 to the Present.* New York: W. W. Norton, 2010.

Singleton, George. *Romance of African Methodism: A Study of the African Methodist Episcopal Church.* New York: Exposition, 1952.

Smiley, Tavis, ed. *The Covenant with Black America.* Chicago: Third World, 2006.

Spear, Allan H. *Black Chicago: The Making of a Negro Ghetto, 1890–1920.* Chicago: University of Chicago Press, 1967.

Stiver, Dan R. *Theology after Ricoeur: New Directions in Hermeneutical Theology.* Louisville, Ky.: Westminster John Knox, 2001.

Taylor, Gardner C. "Parting Words." In *The Words of Gardner Taylor.* Vol. 4, *Special Occasion and Expository Sermons,* 109-13. Valley Forge, Pa.: Judson Press, 2001.

Theising, Andrew J. *Made in the USA: East St. Louis, The Rise and Fall of an Industrial River Town.* St. Louis: Virginia Publishing, 2003.

Thiong'o, Ngugi wa. *Something Torn and New: An African Renaissance.* New York: Basic Civitas Books, 2009.

Thomas, Rhondda Robinson. *Claiming Exodus: A Cultural History of Afro-Atlantic Identity, 1774–1903.* Waco, Tex.: Baylor University Press, 2013.

Thurman, Howard. *Meditations of the Heart.* 1953. Reprint, Boston: Beacon, 1981.

Tinder, Glen. *The Political Meaning of Christianity: An Interpretation.* Baton Rouge: Louisiana State Press, 1989.

Tisdale, Lenora Tubbs. *Preaching as Local Theology and Folk Art.* Minneapolis: Augsburg Fortress, 1997.

———. *Prophetic Preaching: A Pastoral Approach.* Louisville, Ky.: Westminster John Knox, 2010.

Towner, W. Sibley. "On Calling People 'Prophets' in 1970." *Interpretation* 24, no. 4 (1970): 495.

Trimiew, Darryl. "The Social Gospel and the Question of Race." In *The Social Gospel Today,* edited by Christopher H. Evans, 27-37. Louisville, Ky.: Westminster John Knox, 2001.

Trotter, Joe William, Jr. *Coal, Class and Color: Blacks in Southern West Virginia, 1915–32.* Urbana: University of Illinois Press, 1990.

Tucker, Gene. "Prophetic Speech." In *Interpreting the Prophets,* edited by James L. Mays and Paul Achtemeier, 27-40. Philadelphia: Fortress, 1987.

Tucker-Worgs, Tamelyn. *The Black Megachurch: Theology, Gender, and the Politics of Public Engagement.* Waco, Tex.: Baylor University Press, 2011.

Umoja, Akinyele. "Searching for a Place: Nationalism, Separatism, and Pan-Africanism." In Hornsby, *Companion to African American History,* 529-30.

Van Gelder, Craig. "Defining the Center—Finding the Boundaries: The Challenge of Re-visioning the Church in North America for the Twenty-First Century."

In *The Church between Gospel and Culture: The Emerging Mission in North America*, edited by George R. Hunsberger and Craig Van Gelder, 26–51. Grand Rapids: Eerdmans, 1996.

Walters, Ronald, and Robert C. Smith. *African American Leadership*. New York: SUNY Press, 1999.

Walton, Jonathan L. *Watch This! The Ethics and Aesthetics of Black Televangelism*. New York: New York University Press, 2009.

Walzer, Michael. *In God's Shadow: Politics in the Hebrew Bible*. New Haven: Yale University Press, 2012.

Warnock, Raphael. *The Divided Mind of the Black Church: Theology, Piety, and Public Witness*. New York: New York University Press, 2014.

Westfield, Nancy Lynn, ed. *Being Black, Teaching Black*. Nashville: Abingdon, 2008.

White, Ronald C., Jr. *Liberty and Justice for All: Racial Reform and the Social Gospel, 1877–1925*. San Francisco: Harper & Row, 1990.

Wilkerson, Isabel. *The Warmth of Other Suns: The Epic Story of America's Great Migration*. New York: Vintage Books, 2010.

Williams, Reggie. *Bonhoeffer's Black Jesus: Harlem Renaissance Theology and an Ethic of Resistance*. Waco, Tex.: Baylor University Press, 2014.

Willimon, William, and Richard Lischer, eds. *Concise Encyclopedia of Preaching*. Louisville, Ky.: Westminster John Knox, 1995.

Wills, David. "Reverdy C. Ransom: The Making of an A.M.E. Bishop." In *Black Apostles: Afro-American Clergy Confront the Twentieth Century*, edited by Richard Newman and Randall K. Burkett. Boston: G. K. Hall, 1978. Reprinted in Pinn, *Making the Gospel Plain*, 9–43.

Wilmore, Gayraud S. *Black Religion and Black Radicalism: An Interpretation of the Religious History of African Americans*. 3rd ed. Maryknoll, N.Y.: Orbis Books, 1998.

Wilson, Paul Scott. "Imagination." In Willimon and Lischer, *Concise Encyclopedia of Preaching*, 266–69.

———. *Imagination of the Heart: New Understandings in Preaching*. Nashville: Abingdon, 1988.

———. *Setting Words on Fire: Putting God at the Center of the Sermon*. Nashville, Abingdon, 2008.

Wilson, William Julius. *More Than Race: Being Black and Poor in the Inner City*. New York: W. W. Norton, 2007.

———. *The Truly Disadvantaged: The Inner City, the Underclass, and Public Policy*. Chicago: University of Chicago Press, 1987.

———. *When Work Disappears: The World of the New Urban Poor*. New York: Vintage, 1996.

Wogaman, J. Philip. *Speaking the Truth in Love: Prophetic Preaching in a Broken World*. Louisville, Ky.: Westminster John Knox, 1998.

Woodson, Carter G. *A Century of Negro Migration*. Washington, D.C.: Association of Negro Life and History. 1918. Reprint, Mineola, N.Y.: Dover, 2002.

Woodward, C. Vann. *The Strange Career of Jim Crow*. 1955. New York: Oxford University Press, 2002.

Woofter, Thomas T. *Southern Race Progress: The Wavering Color Line*. Washington, D.C.: Public Affairs Press, 1957.

INDEX

Abernathy, Ralph, 106, 158
Abyssinian Baptist Church (Harlem), 5, 21, 22, 31–32, 45, 92, 95, 124, 145
Addams, Jane, 26, 43
aesthetics, cultural/homiletic, 8, 66–68, 72, 98, 115
African Americans/Blacks: myth/sense of inferiority among, 85, 87, 90, 118; social dislocation of, 50, 53, 65, 74; social/ moral progress of, 12, 14, 17, 32, 47, 72, 75, 77, 80, 81, 95, 100, 138, 141, 150; southern/migrant, 1–2, 4, 7, 15, 16, 18, 21, 26, 28, 33, 36, 62, 65, 134, 170n2; urban/northern, 22–24, 36, 45, 50, 72, 74, 91, 98, 133, 172n10
African Methodist Episcopal Church (AME), 27, 37–38, 42–43, 81–82, 102
African Methodist Episcopal Zion Church (AMEZ), 27, 28, 29, 38, 88, 102, 176n60
Albrecht, Gloria, 65, 182n38
Alexander, Michelle, 134
Allen, Richard, 3, 41, 81, 84, 138, 142
American Christianity, 74, 83, 86, 99, 142, 143
American National Baptist Convention, 38

"The American Tower of Babel; or, The Confusion of Tongues, 1909" (Ransom), 74–76
Amos, 54, 160, 187n3
Anderson, Mother Leafy, 13, 48
Andrews, Dale, 171n8
androcentrism: see discrimination, gender
"Antipathy to Women Preachers, 1909" (Randolph), 87–89, 90, 100
assimilation, 22, 36, 40, 182n48
Austin, Junius Caesar, 20, 22, 66

Baptist churches: Black/African American, 32, 37, 38, 180n43; schism of 1915, 38–39, 106; see also the entries for individual Baptist denominations
Baptist Foreign Mission Convention of the United States of America, 38
"beloved community," 65, 169n1
Bitzer, Lloyd F., 170n7
Black Nationalism, 47–48
Bond, Adam, 117–18
Bonhoeffer, Dietrich, 31, 176n73
"The Bottom Line, 1984" (Proctor), 117–20
Boyd, Henry H., 39
brotherhood of man/humanity, 47, 74, 76, 85, 102

Brueggemann, Walter, 59, 62, 66, 136, 181n15

Burroughs, Nannie Helen, 40, 177n14

Cannon, Katie Geneva, 120–22, 155–57, 189n52, 189n53

church(es)/congregations, 36, 114; Black/African American, ix, 4, 19–20, 40, 62, 77, 85, 101, 103, 115, 125, 131, 133–34; Black institutional, 20, 23, 30–32, 40–45, 53, 78, 81, 100, 102, 122; "model," 92–94; Black traditionalist, 20, 37, 48; northern/urban Black, 1, 2, 4, 5, 7, 19–20, 23, 26, 31, 33–34, 36, 39–41, 45, 48, 53, 64–66, 69–70, 71, 91, 98; perspectives on, 20–23; southern Black, 19, 21; Spiritualist, 13, 48, 179n42; White, 28, 36, 38, 39; see also instrumentalist churches/pastors

Church of God in Christ (COGIC), 39, 105

"The Church That Shall Survive, 1936" (Ransom), 79–83

Civil Rights era/movement, 70, 102, 104, 122, 129, 134, 166; post-, 8, 102, 122, 129

clergy/minister(s)/pastor(s)/preacher(s): Black/African American, 42, 46, 61, 66, 72, 125, 129, 134–35; female, 87–89; as hope of the race, 21, 23; northern Black/urban, 3, 4, 20, 23, 26, 43, 55, 72, 100; southern Black, 12, 46, 72; Spiritualist, 13, 48; White, 91, 95, 117; see also instrumentalist churches/pastors

Collier-Thomas, Bettye, 30, 88

"The Colored Man's Contribution to Christianity and When It Will Be Made, 1919" (Powell), 94–101, 145–54

Colored Methodist Episcopal Church (CME), 37, 38, 39

conscience, 71, 105, 116, 147; coalitions of, 129; freedom of, 96, 148

conscientization, 63–64

consciousness, 45, 59–60, 63, 71, 82, 100, 107, 117, 134, 183n48; prophetic, 2, 5, 7, 59, 85, 90

context(s)/contextualization, xi, 6–7, 42, 49, 62, 63, 80, 84, 86, 100, 133, 136, 174n31; African American, 63, 66, 77, 103, 170n8; agrarian, 14, 15; homiletic, 6, 7, 62, 68, 126; northern, 7, 15, 33, 38; prophetic, 55, 56

culture, 59, 68, 112; in Black prophetic preaching, 6, 68, 89, 135–36; Christian, 40

cultures of silence, 2, 63, 65, 85

dehumanization, Black, 2, 7, 24, 34, 41, 63–65, 82, 98, 102, 135–36

democracy, American, 7, 86, 87, 90, 99, 141–43

denominations: Black/African American, 4, 19, 21–24, 29, 33, 37–40, 76, 128, 173n28, 174n39, 180n43; White, 36

dialogue, 63–64

dignity, 7, 14–16, 18–19, 24, 34, 55, 61, 76, 83, 84, 98, 102, 139, 141, 143, 159

discourse/speech, 6, 59, 60, 66, 68, 72, 100, 170n7, 170n8; Black religious, 7, 45–50, 101; contextual, 6, 69; conversionist-renewalist, 48–50; nationalistic-jeremiadic, 47–48; oral-based, 45; preaching/homiletic, 6–7, 13, 50, 54, 65–67, 69–70, 95, 98, 102, 133, 135; priestly-evangelistic, 45–46; prophetic, 5–8, 24, 42, 55, 56, 59, 61–63, 66, 69–70, 79, 87, 98–99, 102, 105, 109, 121, 129, 131, 133, 135–36; see also oral expression/culture; speech-act(s)

discrimination: gender, 2, 18, 30, 65, 88–89, 100; racial, 2, 18, 30, 33, 36, 65, 74, 91, 101, 176n60

Du Bois, W. E. B., 2, 21, 37, 43, 47, 75

education, Black, 25, 32, 34, 37, 43, 47, 67, 81–85, 96, 99, 102, 120–21, 123, 133–34, 138–39, 150, 161 emotion, and religion, 96–98, 101, 140–42, 148–49

empowerment, 4, 7, 55, 82, 100, 102, 167

evangelicals/evangelicalism: Black, 117; White, 23, 40, 42, 54

evangelism, 36, 92, 94, 102

Exodus story, 1–4, 35, 80, 108, 113, 170n3, 187n3

fasting, 97–98, 129, 153, 167

Father Divine (George Baker Jr.), 47, 49

Fosdick, Harry Emerson, 117–18

Franklin, Robert Michael, 114, 134, 179n42

Frazier, E. Franklin, 180n47

Freire, Paulo, 8, 62–65, 136

Garvey, Marcus Mosiah, 47

Gladden, Washington, 39, 41–42

God: Fatherhood of God, 47, 74, 76, 85, 102; will/intention/purpose of, 2–3, 6, 14, 34, 40, 53, 62, 65, 66, 72, 77, 81, 83, 88, 100, 102, 120, 121, 135, 156, 157, 167

Grace, Charles "Sweet Daddy," 48–49

"A Graceless Church, 1911" (Powell), 78–79

Great Migration/Exodus, ix–xi, 1–5, 7–8, 12–13, 17, 19–20, 23–24, 27, 30–31, 33–34, 35, 37, 39–40, 45, 49, 53–54, 60, 64–66, 68–70, 71, 79, 88, 98–102, 104, 135, 169n2; reasons for, 15–16; role of clergy in, 2–4, 101; roots of, 14; routes of, 14–15

Harvey, Thomas Watson, 11–13, 19, 46

"Heralds and Prophets of a Changed Order and a New Day, 1920s" (Ransom), 79, 83–87, 137–44

HIV/AIDS, 125–27, 134, 161–62, 164

holiness, 30, 69, 90, 102, 132; codes, 126

Holiness churches/tradition, 13, 28, 48, 49, 129, 140, 166, 179

Holy Spirit, 13, 27, 84, 92–93, 119, 123, 157, 159–60, 179n42

home mission movement, 38, 41

hope, 2, 4, 6, 8, 18, 24, 25, 30, 53, 55–57, 60–66, 68–70, 72, 76–77, 80, 82–83, 86, 89, 91, 94, 98–100, 102, 103, 108, 109, 112–13, 115, 120–22, 124, 129, 132, 134–36, 138, 141, 144, 149, 166–67

"Hope, 1898" (Randolph), 76–78

"How Much of Leviticus Do You Really Want? 2012" (McMickle), 124–27, 162–65

humanization/dehumanization, 6, 24, 63, 87, 96, 98, 136

Hurston, Zora Neale, 8, 66–68, 120, 182n48

"If I Were White, 1941" (Randolph), 89–92, 100

imagination, 3, 4, 59, 62, 63, 67, 91, 129, 134; hopeful, 15, 47

"The Industrial and Social Conditions of the Negro, 1896" (Ransom), 73–74

injustice, 6, 8, 30, 46, 58, 62, 66, 82, 84, 90, 91, 97, 100, 103–5, 109, 120, 123, 126, 128, 132, 142–43, 149–50, 153, 166, 183n53; economic, 99, 108, 142

Institutional Church and Social Settlement (ICSS), 27, 34, 42–43, 175n55

instrumentalist churches/pastors, 20–21, 174n30

intentionality, divine, 5, 6, 7, 24, 53, 70, 96, 102, 108, 131, 136

Isaiah/Deutero-Isaiah, 54, 73–74, 85, 119, 138, 157

"I've Been to the Mountaintop, 1968" (King), 105–110, 113

Jackson, Thomas H., 24, 174n44, 174n45

Jennings, Willie James, 67

Jeremiah, 54–58, 88, 187n3

Jesus, 13, 33, 59–61, 74, 78–80, 86–87, 89, 90, 92–94, 100, 112–14, 116–18, 122–23, 129, 135–36, 143–44, 149, 157–58, 164–66, 174n39, 187n3; ethics of, 75–76

Jim Crow laws/South, 1, 8, 17–18, 37, 45, 62, 73

Jones, Absalom, 3, 5, 41

"Journeying through a Jungle, 1979" (Ray), 110–13

judgment, 45, 53–55, 57, 60, 62, 67, 69–70, 98, 118

justice, ix, 6, 24, 27, 34, 47, 50, 53, 55, 59, 61, 63, 65, 68, 70, 71, 82, 86, 87, 99, 102, 104, 105, 114–15, 119, 123, 126–29, 132–34, 136, 142, 156, 165–67, 169n1, 171n8, 181n21, 187n3, 190n3; divine, 55, 82, 87, 96; economic, 99, 105, 115; racial, 1, 85, 105; social, 8, 13, 20, 23, 32, 40, 122, 128, 166, 170n8, 177n14, 182n38

Kansas, as migrant destination, 16–17

Kidd, Benjamin, 79, 149

King, Martin Luther Jr., 1–2, 5, 8, 47, 102, 103–11, 113, 114, 117, 122–24, 126–29, 134–35, 158–59, 165–66, 187n3, 187n11

kingdom/reign of God/heaven, 20, 25, 39, 40, 50, 86, 144, 152

Kozol, Jonathan, 122, 156

LaRue, Cleo, 170n8

Lewis, David Levering, 42, 108

liberation, 3, 50, 63, 83, 87, 170n3, 181n15, 182n38; theology of, 63, 117, 123, 160, 181n15

liberty, 82, 142, 157; religious, 96, 138, 148

Lischer, Richard, 134, 189n35

Luker, Ralph, 41, 178n22

Luther, Martin, 84, 97, 138, 151

lynching, 8, 15, 16, 73, 82–83, 87, 98, 99, 173n13

Marks, Carol, 172n10, 173n17

Mays, Benjamin Elijah, 53, 114–16

McMickle, Marvin A., 124–27, 131, 162–65, 171n8

metaphor, 17, 56, 59, 67–68, 72, 109, 112, 121, 134; migration as, x–xi; Philadelphia as, 13

Methodism, Black/African American, 5, 13, 25, 27, 37–38, 43–44, 82, 99, 175n55, 180n43; see also the entries for individual Methodist denominations

Micah, 128–29, 160, 165

migrant(s)/exodus participants, 1–2, 4, 7, 11, 13–16, 18–23, 26, 33, 36–37, 47, 62–63, 65, 69, 72, 134, 172n10; as carriers of culture, 19, 36

ministry, 6, 88, 113, 114, 118, 123, 128, 166–67; of hospitality, 93–94; prophetic, 82, 99, 101, 108, 123–24, 190n3; urban, 23, 43

missiology, 21–23

mission(s), 40, 41; congregational, 7, 19, 20, 22, 27, 44, 74, 92, 174n31, 179n42, 184n34; foreign, 38, 81–82; home/local, 38–39, 41, 92, 99, 128, 131, 146, 166

"The Model Church, 1911" (Powell), 92–94, 95, 101

Moses, 1, 4, 54, 58, 59, 80, 85, 106–7, 110, 112, 113, 138, 187n6; Black/figurative, 2, 3

Moss, Otis, Jr., 122–24, 129, 157–62

Mumford, Debra, 171n8

mutual aid societies, 40–41

NAACP, 37, 47

National Baptist Convention, 22, 38, 39, 123

National Baptist Convention of America, 39

National Baptist Educational Convention of the U.S.A., 38

nonviolence, 104–6, 109, 166

oppression, 8, 19, 47, 58, 62, 63, 65, 69, 82, 86–88, 91, 97, 103, 109, 112, 123, 132, 142–44, 153, 160; economic, 15, 17, 99; racial, 15, 90

oral expression/culture: Black, 8, 45, 48, 49, 68

Payne, Daniel Alexander, 25, 81, 138
peace, 55, 75, 80, 86, 89, 99–100, 105, 142, 144, 156; prophets of, 160–61
pedagogy, 8, 62–63, 65, 87
personhood, 16, 64, 85, 133
Philadelphia, as migrant city, 12–13, 48
piety, personal, 24, 25, 43, 46, 128, 141, 166–67
poetic speech/language, 5, 59, 62, 66, 68, 82–83, 86–87, 92, 98, 108, 123, 139, 142
poverty, 33, 74, 92, 104, 105, 108, 112, 128, 141, 166
Powell, Adam Clayton, Jr., 5, 32
Powell, Adam Clayton, Sr., 1, 4, 5, 7–8, 22, 24, 42, 50, 53, 62–63, 65, 67, 70, 71–72, 103, 112; biography/background of, 30–34; sermons by, 78–79, 92–102, 145–53
power, 59–60, 65, 67, 68, 79, 86, 96, 97, 104, 108, 138–39, 141, 143, 148–49, 181n15, 183n53; Black religious, 8, 22, 45, 49, 66, 68, 84, 102, 142; God's, 60, 64, 85, 93, 157; speaking truth to, 1, 34, 59, 124, 135; White/established, 25, 55, 59, 66, 72, 83, 85, 87, 89, 94, 98, 147, 151, 182n38
Powery, Luke, 171n8
praxis/orthopraxis, 6, 8, 25, 40, 62–65, 68, 71, 91, 99–101, 109, 119, 170n8, 183n2
prayer(s), 6, 46, 97–98, 107, 128–29, 153, 166–67
preaching: African American/Black, x, 7, 13, 23, 25, 50, 60, 62, 66–67, 69, 89, 102, 105, 122, 131, 133, 136; defined, 6–7; Exodus, 61, 68–70, 79; prophetic Black, ix, xi–xii, 1–2, 4–8, 24, 34, 41–42, 45–46, 50, 55, 60–70, 72, 79, 82, 86, 91, 93, 97–98, 101–2, 103–4, 108, 120, 122, 124, 131–32, 135–36; spiritualistic, 13; traditional, 1–2, 12, 67; trivocal, ix–x, 6; see also proclamation; sermon(s)

prejudice, racial, 5, 36, 90, 91, 100, 149, 163; see also discrimination, racial; oppression
proclamation, 4, 6, 50, 60, 65, 79, 89, 91, 93, 120, 124, 133, 136; see also preaching; sermon(s)
Proctor, Henry Hugh, 45–46
Proctor, Samuel Dewitt, 5, 66, 117–20, 124
Progressive National Baptist Convention, 123, 158–59
Promised Land, American, 4, 13, 15, 18, 47, 69, 106, 110, 113
prophetic discourse/speech, 8, 24, 42, 55, 59–60, 62, 66, 70, 79, 121, 129, 135
prophetic tradition, 5, 8, 157
"A Prophetic Witness in an Anti-Prophetic Age, 2004" (Moss), 122–24, 157–62
prophetic Word, 34, 57, 60–62, 69, 103, 105, 131–33
prophet(s): agenda of, 58–59, 131; Black/African American, 62, 70, 84, 103, 121–22; call of, 55–58; classical, 54; false, 54; Hebrew/biblical, 5, 8, 53–60, 62, 68, 79, 105, 119, 121, 128, 135; postexilic, 54; preclassical, 54; preexilic, 53–54; role of, 56–57; "writing," 54; see also Amos; Isaiah/Deutero-Isaiah; Jeremiah; Micah; Moses
"Prophets for a New Day, 1998" (Cannon), 120–22, 155–57
prosperity theology, 132, 151, 171n8, 179n42, 190n3
providence, divine, 96, 113, 148

quietism, vocational, 133

racism, 16, 40–42, 104, 108, 172n10, 183n53; non-, 101
Randolph, Florence Spearing, 1, 4, 5, 7–8, 24, 32–34, 42, 50, 53, 62–63, 65, 67, 70, 71–72, 95, 98–102, 103; biography/background of, 27–30; sermons by, 76–79, 87–92

Ransom, Reverdy Cassius, 1, 4, 5, 7–8, 31, 32–34, 38, 40, 42–44, 50, 53, 62–63, 65, 67, 70, 71–72, 79, 90, 95, 98–99, 101–2, 103, 112, 174n45, 175n47, 175n55, 178n31; biography/background of, 24–27; sermons by, 73–76, 80–87, 137–44
Rauschenbusch, Walter, 39, 41–42, 124
Ray, Sandy Frederick, 66, 110–13, 187n11
Reconstruction, 1, 16–18, 136
resettlement, 3, 4, 18, 19, 21
resistance, 59, 61, 65, 106
rhetoric/rhetorical methods, 4–5, 45, 62, 68, 72, 132
Ricoeur, Paul, 25, 175n46, 181n15

Sanders, Cheryl J., 127–29, 165–67
Scripture, 2, 7, 25, 59, 69, 74, 88, 90, 91, 93, 98, 121, 125, 135–36; authority of, 25, 89; contextual view of, 4; Hebrew, 55, 60; revelation of God in, 6, 55, 70
segregation, 18, 35–37, 107–8, 135, 143, 174n39
sermon(s), 2, 4, 98–99; Civil Rights era, 104–20; Great Exodus, 6, 7, 33, 54–55, 79–100; post-Civil Rights, 120–29; pre-Exodus, 7, 45–46, 73–79; prophetic, 4–5, 24, 30, 55, 60, 63–66, 68, 70, 71, 98–99, 101–2, 129, 133, 135; salvation-centered, 23; see also preaching; proclamation
Sernett, Milton, 173n28, 174n30
sexism: see discrimination, gender
slavery, 17, 18, 41, 62, 63, 138, 170n3, 174n39, 180n47
Social Gospel/Social Gospel Movement, 26, 39–43, 119, 124, 177n14, 178n22; Black, 31, 77, 117–18, 177n14
Southern Baptist Convention, 39
Southern Christian Leadership Conference (SCLC), 105, 111, 122, 158
speech-act(s), 6, 65, 67–68, 89, 99, 101, 109, 119, 126, 183n53; see also discourse/speech
spirituality, Black, 18, 94, 98, 99

stewardship, 92–93, 101, 116
suffering, 32, 44, 61, 65, 72, 79, 83, 87, 89, 92, 94, 97, 98, 100, 108, 109, 112, 121, 125–26, 128, 132, 134–36, 141, 143, 166–67, 169n1

Thanksgiving sermons (Ransom), 73–76
Thomas, Rhondda Robinson, 170n3
Thurman, Howard, 66, 71, 114, 117
Tinder, Glen, 181n21
Tisdale, Leonora Tubbs, 171n8
Turner, Henry McNeal, 44, 47, 81

unity/unification, 108; Christian, 38, 79, 82, 99

Van Gelder, Craig, 174n31
Vietnam War, 107, 123, 158–59
voice(s): Black religious, 3, 4, 8, 84, 87, 104, 135, 183n53; priestly, ix–x; prophetic, ix–x, 7, 32, 65, 70, 72, 82, 84, 101, 120, 124, 137, 181n15; sagely, ix–x
voting rights, 17, 83, 99

Walker, Charles Thomas, 12, 20, 46, 172n4
Warnock, Raphael G., 174n39
Washington, Booker T., 17, 37, 75, 81
"What Does God Require of Us? 2014" (Sanders), 127–29, 165–67
"Why Dives Went to Hell, 1980" (Mays), 114–16
White supremacy, 16–18, 90, 91, 99, 108, 117–18, 170n3, 178n22
Whites, 4, 12, 35–37, 40–42, 48, 54, 84, 90–92, 96–97, 100, 173n13
women, Black/African American, 27–30, 46, 48, 76–78, 87–89, 100, 102, 120
Woodson, Carter G., 11, 16, 21
worship, Black, 3, 20, 23, 25, 26, 41, 43, 66, 171n8

youth/young people, Black/African American, 11, 26, 34, 84–86, 106, 120–22, 138–39, 141, 143, 156–57